BARBARA GRAY

The Twilight Economy

How Coronavirus is Accelerating Disruption

BRADY CAPITAL RESEARCH Inc.
BRADYCAP

Contents

Welcome to Future Shock

"Imagine an entire society...suddenly transported into this new world. The result is mass disorientation, future shock on a grand scale." – Alvin Toffler, *Future Shock*, 1970

We are experiencing future shock on a global scale. When I started researching structural disruption developments over three years ago, I never imagined I would end up publishing such a dystopian research report as the one I did on April 1. As I explored in *The Survival Guide to the New Ghost Town Economy*, we are witnessing what Toffler deems as the *"premature arrival of the future"* and structural disruption is no longer just accelerating — it is now arriving in the form of quantum leaps. Most importantly, this shift into the future tense will not be temporary, but permanent.

If you look at the cover of my last book, which I submitted to the publisher on February 28, 2020, you will see that it is ironically titled, *The New Cyber Decade: Are You Driving Towards Utopia or Dystopia?*. And you will see I used an image of Elon Musk's new Tesla Cybertruck to foreshadow the radical transformation of the corporate landscape. However, the start of our new decade quickly turned into dystopia...

I just wanted to let you know that Brady will not be participating in tomorrow's spring concert and I sincerely wish the school would consider postponing the event in light of the escalating risk of the coronavirus — it does not seem prudent to bring together students and parents (many of whom travel for business and pleasure) in a crowded gym. We are up to 27 cases in B.C. (which is most likely Vancouver) — for context, in Iran, they had 61 cases just two weeks ago, and now they are up 7,161. And Italy, which is up to 9,172 cases, just extended the quarantine to the entire country.

Before March this year, I wouldn't have thought twice about attending a school concert but as you can see from this e-mail that I just sent to my son's elementary school on March 9, this was no longer the case. When I shared my e-mail with my husband, he told me my 9-year-old was fine with not going and had told him, *"I don't care, I can go global on my YouTube channel"*.

A week later, I found myself gazing panic-struck out the window of my makeshift office in my bedroom with my mind racing with anxiety as I try to process the escalating discussions I had with my snowbird parents over the past five days, which went from pleading with them to stop shaking hands with people, to stop socializing with their friends, to coming home from their vacation home in Palm Springs.

We're keeping the boys home from school... I'm cancelling my WeWork membership, putting my Equinox membership on hold and pulling the boys out of spring camp...they just discovered three coronavirus cases at the seniors' home two blocks from us...they've closed the West Vancouver Rec Centre...you need to stop socializing with your friends...Trump just closed down the U.S. border to Europeans...they've closed down Science World, Whistler and Cypress Mountain...you should think about coming home...the number of coronavirus cases in B.C. has risen to 73... ...Trudeau just closed Canada's borders to foreigners and is urging all Canadians to come home...San Francisco just put the city on lockdown and France is forcing people to stay inside their homes.

These events seemed eerily similar to the scenario that unfolded nearly a century ago as detailed by British science journalist, Laura Spinney, in her book, *Pale Rider: The Spanish Flu of 1918 and How It Changed the World:*

> *Schools, theatres and places of worship were closed, the use of public transport systems was restricted and mass gatherings were banned. Quarantines were imposed at ports and railway stations, and patients were removed to hospitals, which set up isolation wards in order to separate them from non-infected patients. Public information campaigns advised people to use handkerchiefs when they sneezed and to wash their hands regularly; to avoid crowds...*

I was shocked to discover that the Spanish Flu, which I had never heard mention of, killed a staggering 50–100-million people in the two years between March 1918 and March 1920. When I asked my Mom if my Grandma, who was born in Victoria, B.C. in 1902, had ever spoken about it, she said she hadn't, which was surprising because the Spanish Flu led to the deaths of 55,000 Canadians and 675,000 Americans.

As Spinney writes, the Spanish Flu of 1918 was *"an example of what today we would call, with appropriate avian overtones, a black-swan event"*. The coronavirus, which I started tracking back on January 27 when there were only 2,886 global confirmed cases, with only 5 case in the U.S. and 1 case in Canada, has definitely also turned out to be a black swan. The concept of the black swan, which Nassim Nicholas Taleb popularized in his best-selling 2007 book, *The Black Swan: The Impact of the Highly Improbable*, refers to an event, positive or negative, that is highly improbable yet causes massive consequences.

The next week, the coronavirus pandemic reached panic stage here at home, with the number of cases exploding by 10 times in the U.S. to over 43,000 cases and by 5 times in Canada to over 2,000 cases. The U.S. invoked the Defense Production Act and we saw more and more companies taking war-time measures, with auto and auto parts makers looking to re-tool their factories to produce ventilators, apparel manufacturers making masks and gowns, and brewers and distillers making hand sanitizers. We also witnessed vacant hotels, dorms, sports arenas and convention centres being turned into makeshift hospitals. Meanwhile, essential retailers, facing an unprecedented surge in demand, called in the troops, hoping to recruit hundreds of thousands of recently unemployed service workers.

Tech companies were also called to duty, launching research and development initiatives to combat coronavirus and voice assistants and chatbots to consult with us on if we have come down with coronavirus. We also saw an online cultural renaissance as educators, fitness instructors, musicians, comedians and performers migrated to livestreaming platforms. And Zoom became our saviour.

As our days got darker and the reality of our new dystopian ghost town world set in, I advised my clients to keep this quote (which went viral on Twitter) in mind: *"Your grandparents were called to war. You are being called to sit on your couch and watch Netflix. You can do this."*

Welcome to Future Shock.

Survival Guide to the Ghost Town Economy

"Lacking a systematic framework for understanding the clash of forces in today's world, we are like a ship's crew, trapped in a storm and trying to navigate between dangerous reefs without compass or chart." – Alvin Toffler, *The Third Wave, 1980*

As I was sat at my desk at WeWork on March 9, composing the email to my boys' school to try to convince them to cancel the concert, I had the revelation that the coronavirus pandemic could quickly turn our world into a dystopian ghost town. And to survive, we would need to leave behind the physical world and embrace the digital world, creating an acute shift in both societal behaviour and corporate behaviour. To understand the clash of these new forces and navigate between the dangerous waves of disruption, I turned to my Value Pyramid – the product of my nearly decade-long intellectual journey into researching the convergence of emerging societal, technological and economic forces.

The Value Pyramid illustrates how the value equation is changing for companies. The three sides of the Value Pyramid are:

- **Customer Capital (*value origination through customer value proposition*):** In the age of Amazon, companies can no longer compete on a functional customer value proposition basis (i.e., price, convenience, variety of choice), so they need to create emotional connections and psychological attachments with their customers.

- **Structural Capital** (*value capture through capital investments*): Companies that operate on only the physical layer need to invest in moving up to the digital and AI (artificial intelligent) layers while companies operating on just the digital layer might find it of value to invest in the physical layer.
- **Economic Capital** (*value extraction through economic system*): Companies operating in the traditional corporate economy might want to explore how they can move up to the platform economy.

And my Value Pyramid would prove itself invaluable in terms of gaining insight into how the coronavirus pandemic was changing the value equation for companies — first as we entered the Ghost Town Economy and later as we entered the Twilight Zone Economy.

Customer Capital

The customer capital side of the value pyramid corresponds to Maslow's hierarchy of needs as the functional level is about meeting physiological and safety needs, which is all we cared about back in March and April. Forget the emotional level — the experience economy was totally dead. And totally forget the psychological level — self-actualization didn't matter back then — safety was more important than sustainability and people were avoiding community, but accessibility was good if it didn't involve contact. But what we needed to keep in mind is that once the fear was gone, we would zoom back up the customer capital side to the experience economy and re-embrace sustainability and community.

Psychological

Social Mission

Emotional

Experience, Relationship

Functional

Price, Convenience, Variety of Choice

Originate Value (temporary)

Source: Brady Capital Research Inc.

Structural Capital

We were experiencing future shock on a global scale as we were now at war against the coronavirus, and to survive both individuals and companies needed to go on lockdown and embrace the digital world as we left behind the physical world. This necessitated the fast adoption of digital technologies on a massive scale, resulting in what Toffler deems as the *"premature arrival of the future"*. Structural disruption was no longer just accelerating, but arriving in the form of quantum leaps. And, most importantly, this shift into the future tense would not be temporary — but permanent.

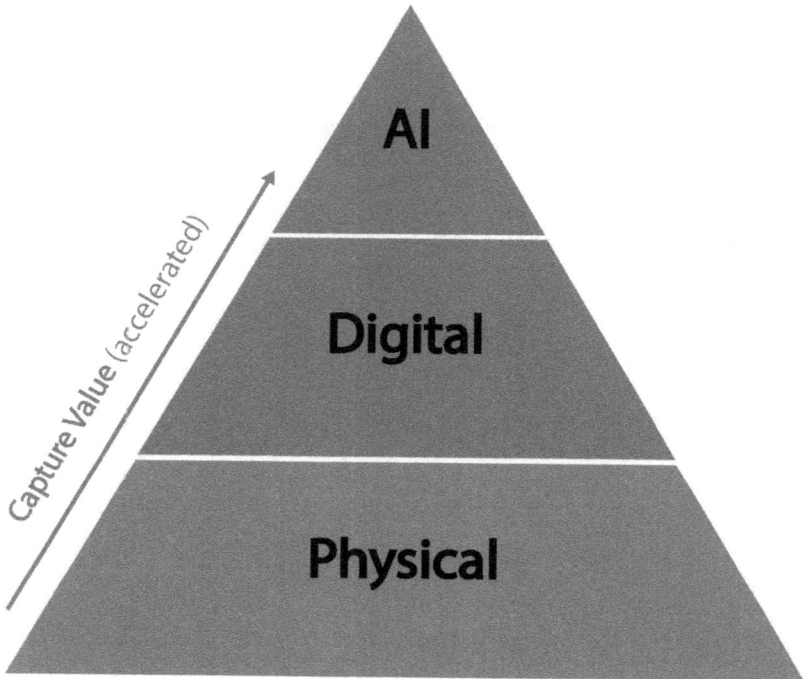

Source: *Brady Capital Research Inc.*

Economic Capital

The coronavirus pandemic was bifurcating the platform economy layer:

- **Digital Economy**: We would see a big increase in the time people spend online and on social networks as privacy concerns abated as we just wanted to keep in touch with friends and family, keep up-to-date on the latest developments and escape reality. We would also see a spike in the long tail of digital content as artists and trainers migrated to livestreaming to monetize their talents.

- **Sharing Economy**: The sharing economy was totally dead as anything that involved travel or personal contact was now taboo. The exception was gig economy companies that could offer contactless service, like freelancing sites or delivery platforms.

The migration to digital and delivery platforms would be long-lasting. Although the current highly variable cost structure of sharing economy platforms would help them survive, I did see an existential threat to their underlying platform economy business model.

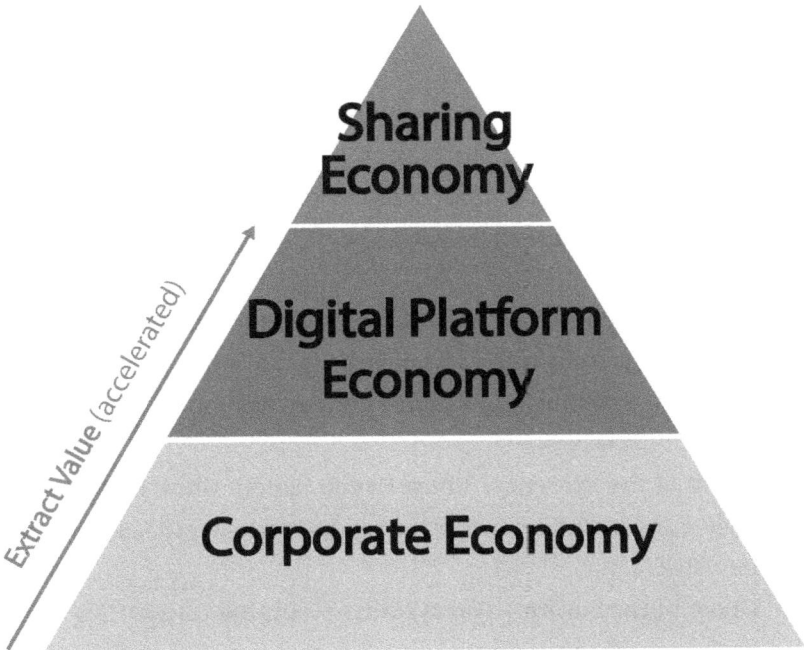

Source: Brady Capital Research Inc.

As Spinney concluded: *"What isn't arguable is that the 1918 pandemic accelerated the pace of change in the first half of the twentieth century, and helped shape our modern world."*

Welcome to the Twilight Economy

With the physical world re-opening at the beginning of June, we started to exit the "Ghost Town Economy" and entered a new way of life that I called the "Twilight Zone Economy" — the area where society's physical and digital states of existence meet.

Although the dark months of the ghost town economy were behind us, dawn had not yet broken as in the twilight, lurked the three ghosts arising from the coronavirus pandemic. As illustrated in the cover image (which was adapted from the cover of my July 2019 book, *Secrets of the Amazon III*), these three ghosts are:

- **Ghost of the Past − Ghost Ship (Economic Ghost):** The Great Recession is back as the coronavirus is capsizing companies, big and small, and causing economic ruin for many who have lost their jobs or businesses.
- **Ghost of the Present − Ghost Castle (Safety Ghost):** Home has been our safe haven and as we re-enter the world, safety is the new risk factor.
- **Ghost of the Future − Ghost Unicorn (Digital Ghost):** The coronavirus pandemic is acting as a catalyst to fast-forward structural disruption to the inflection point.

As these new societal, technological and economic ghosts come together, we are seeing radical shifts in both societal and corporate behaviour. Although we were still trapped in the storm of the coronavirus, I had a systematic framework that I could use to understand the clash of these new forces and navigate between the dangerous waves of disruption — the Value Pyramid.

Customer Capital

As we exited the ghost town economy, value origination was starting to rebound from scarcity to abundance. As we moved beyond our survival mindset of meeting Maslow's base functional physiological needs, we were now looking to fulfill our emotional desires for love/belonging and esteem. But as we tried to cross this threshold, we confronted the safety abyss.

Source: Brady Capital Research Inc.

Safety was emerging as the new risk factor, impacting all three levels of the customer capital side of the value pyramid:

Functional Level: We are seeing a bifurcation on the pricing side between the:

- **Haves**: Those that haven't lost their jobs or businesses are willing to pay a safety premium for convenience and variety of choice as the trauma of living in lockdown has lowered their price elasticity of demand.
- **Have Nots**: Those that lost their jobs or businesses are much more cost conscious as their price elasticity of demand has increased.

Emotional Level: Although people are craving emotional connections more than ever, safety is the new risk factor and constraint for physical experiences.

Psychological Level: Safety is trumping self-actualization when it comes to accessibility, community and sustainability. Accessibility is good if it minimizes physical contact, community is constrained as many people are still avoiding crowds and safety is still taking precedence over sustainability concerns.

Structural Capital

A new civilization is emerging in our lives...Millions are already attuning their lives to the rhythms of tomorrow. Others, terrified of the future, are engaged in a desperate futile flight into the past...The dawn of this new civilization is the single most explosive fact in our lifetimes.

— Alvin Toffler, *The Third Wave,* 1980

The coronavirus pandemic was acting as a catalyst to catapult us into the new civilization I call the New Cyber Age. I was no longer talking about *The New Cyber Decade* — in the past three months, the digital divide had deepened into a digital abyss. And we started to see the reckoning as coronavirus attacked those stranded on the wrong side of the abyss while the digital world thrived.

Value capture had taken a quantum leap from scarcity to abundance as we rapidly adopted the digital world to survive lockdown. With the physical world re-opening, we were in an omnichannel state with safety emerging as the new risk factor, revenue constraint and cost driver.

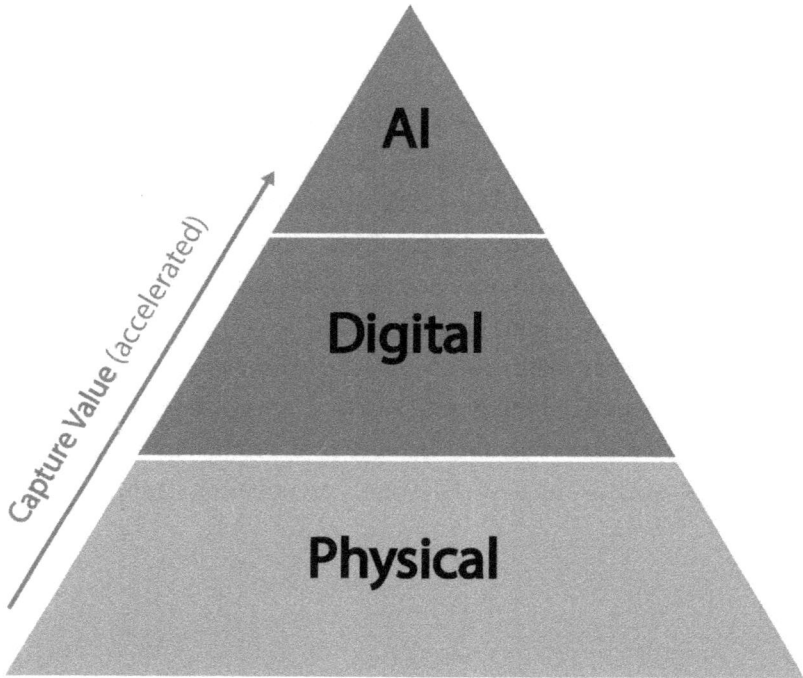

Source: Brady Capital Research Inc.

- **Physical Layer:** Although the physical world was starting to re-open, social distancing and capacity constraints would negatively impact companies' profit equation, especially those with a high fixed cost structure that rely on a high level of physical traffic.
- **Digital Layer:** The digital world was thriving as people have rapidly adopted new ways to socialize, learn, work, shop and meet their healthcare needs. Although I expected to see a reduction from the exponential growth we saw at the peak of lockdown in April, I believed the acceleration in growth would continue.
- **AI Layer:** I expected the coronavirus pandemic would speed up companies' adoption of AI and the cloud.

Economic Capital

Value extraction was still bifurcating on the platform economy layer, with digital platforms continuing to accelerate. However, the sharing economy was slowly starting to come back to life as the world re-opened.

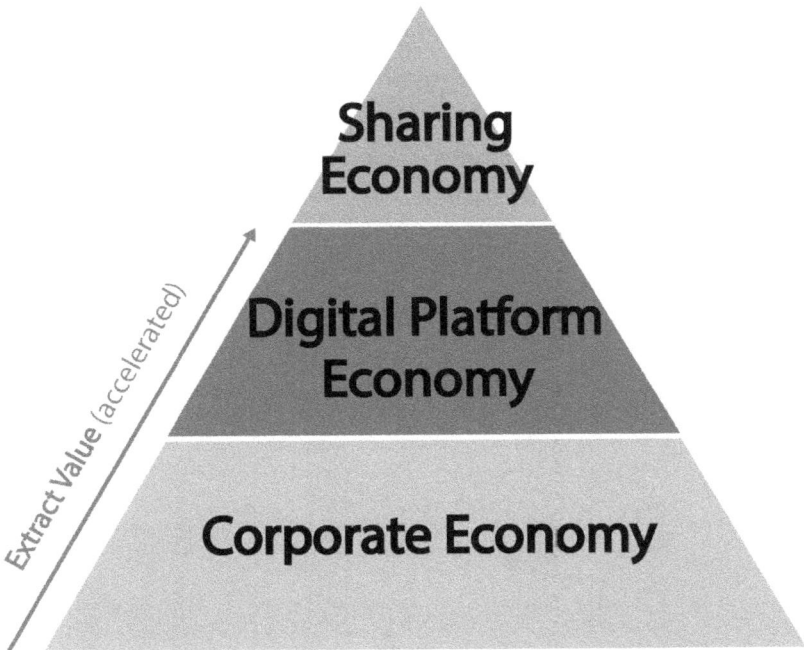

Source: Brady Capital Research Inc.

Digital Platform Economy: Digital platforms would continue to accelerate as the lockdown brought forth rapid tech adoption and an online cultural renaissance.

Sharing Economy: The survival weapon for those that made deep job cuts would be their highly variable cost structure. As the physical world re-opened, I expected to see the following play out:

- **Demand Side**: Would see bifurcation in demand as it returned for domestic and personal travel, not international and corporate travel. But individual shared assets could emerge as an attractive safer alternative to traditional assets (e.g., Uber versus subway, single family home Airbnb versus hotel).
- **Supply Side**: Would see a huge increase in the supply of human capital from newly unemployed looking for work once government benefits end. But, at the same time, independent contractors could be reclassified as employees as the coronavirus pandemic exposed their lack of a social safety net.

We Have Arrived at the Inflection Point...

Today it takes an act of courage to suggest that our biggest factories and offices may, within our lifetimes, stand half empty, reduced to use as ghostly warehouses or converted into living space. A return to the cottage industry – a new emphasis on the home as the center of society.

– Alvin Toffler, *The Third Wave*, 1980

Home has emerged as the centre of society — the place from which we go online to socialize, learn, work, shop and even meet our healthcare needs. And guess who is positioned to help us digitally meet our basic needs and desires? The tech giants. In my June 16 in-depth research report, *The Three Ghosts Haunting the New Twilight Zone Economy,* I actually used Maslow's Hierarchy of Needs Pyramid as a framework to gain insight into how the tech giants are positioned to expand their market and gain wallet share by fulfilling our:

- **Physiological Needs**: Health, Live, Eat
- **Safety Needs**: Work
- **Love/Belonging Needs**: Shop, Socialize, Travel

As evidenced by these statements from CEOs of the world's biggest tech companies during the last week of April, the coronavirus pandemic was acting as a catalyst to accelerate the digital transformation of society.

"It's now clear that once the emergency is past, the world will not look the same... Ultimately, we'll see a long-term acceleration of movement from businesses to digital services, including increased online work, education, medicine, shopping and entertainment. These changes will be significant and lasting." – Sunar Pichai, CEO, Alphabet

"At this time of social distance, of shuttered school and gathering places, of delayed plans and new ways of socializing, we have seen significant evidence that our products have taken a renewed importance for customers." – Tim Cook, CEO, Apple

"We have seen 2 years' worth of digital transformation in two months." – Satya Nadella, CEO, Microsoft

Three months later, at the end of July, Satya Nadella, Microsoft's CEO, provided further insight into how critical it had become for companies to advance up to the digital layer of the structural capital side of the value pyramid:

"the last five months have made it very clear that digital tech intensity is key to business resilience"

But companies shouldn't just look to be resilient, they should look to become antifragile. As Nassim Nicholas Taleb writes in his book, *Antifragile: Things that Gain from Disorder:* *"Antifragility is beyond resilience or robustness. The resilient resists shocks and stays the same; the antifragile gets better."* As Taleb illustrates in his book, the Phoenix bird from Greek mythology is resilient as it is reborn from its own ashes when it is destroyed. However, the serpent-like Hydra monster is antifragile as each time one of its heads is cut off, two grow back. The digital platforms of the tech giants are positioning them to not just rise from the ashes of the pandemic like the Phoenix, but to grow new heads like the Hydra by expanding their market through fulfilling more and more of our basic needs and desires. The market is recognizing their magical power as the combined weight of Apple, Microsoft, Amazon, Alphabet and Facebook in the S&P 500 Index had risen from 17% at the beginning of this year to 22% near the end of July. And this is double their 11% weighting from when I first started researching structural disruption in 2017.

As background, one of my favourite paintings is A Sunday Afternoon on the Island of La Grande Jatte by Georges Seurat, a French post-impressionist painter and the father of pointillism. If you think about it, pointillism, a technique in which small dots of colour are applied to a canvas to form an image, is analogous to the mosaic theory. And like Georges Seurat, I start each week with a blank canvas and piece together emerging structural disruption trends in order to come up with investment ideas. Each week, as I hang a new completed canvas on the wall, the image of structural disruption comes sharper into focus.

But I didn't recognize the true richness of this collection until I was invited in October 2017 to present to the advisory board of a major corporation in Toronto. As I started going through the 40-plus research notes I had written for my institutional investment clients since I published my first *Ubernomics Fault Lines Update* research note in January that year, I discovered they equated to over 60,000 words. Ironically, this was longer than the book I had published the year prior — *Ubernomics: How to Create Economic Abundance and Rise Above the Competition* — a radical business book about my six-year intellectual journey into the new breed of "rebel with a cause" companies, such as lululemon, Starbucks, Whole Foods, Chipotle Mexican Grill, LinkedIn,

Zillow, Uber and Airbnb, whose founders relish disruption of the status quo.

Thus, the idea for Secrets of the Amazon was born... and 45 days later I hit publish on Amazon. But I faced a major dilemma — I didn't want anyone to actually buy my book as I had written it to exclusively give as a Christmas gift to my institutional investment clients. So for fun, I decided to price my book at Amazon's closing stock price on the date of publication, November 30, 2017: $1,167.27.

As I share in the Introduction chapter titled *The Return to My Tribe* in my *Secrets of the Amazon* book:

> *It had been a decade since I had set foot in a boardroom and my Ubernomics presentation was quite a radical departure from most sell-side equity research, so I was quite nervous when Ed and I embarked on our first marketing trip in Toronto in September 2016. But it was fun and, more importantly, the portfolio managers from the dozen investment firms we met with gave us valuable feedback and I realized there was real demand to figure out how to capitalize on the emerging disruption and when this disruption would reach the Inflection Point. As one portfolio manager observed: "...the key for us will be figuring out how to make money from it — and maybe even more importantly how not to lose money as companies/perception gets shifted through these trends."*

We have arrived at the Inflection Point...

Chapter 1: The Triad

January 28, 2020

*"an unveiling or unfolding of things not previously known and which could
not be known apart from the unveiling"*

This is the definition for "apocalypse" which comes from the Greek word
"revelation". As you will recall, I started the New Year with my January 7
research note "The Next Apocalypse?" in which I asked whether the raging
forest fires in Australia foreshadows the next apocalypse — the climate
apocalypse, which was the central theme at Davos last week. Now, with the
sudden onset of the Wuhan coronavirus, I can't help but wonder whether
we are the brink of another apocalypse — a heath apocalypse.

Whereas the retail apocalypse and climate apocalypse are each a "gray
rhino" (e.g., a term coined by Michele Wucker at Davos in 2013 to represent
a highly probable, high impact yet neglected threat that occurs after a
series of warnings and visible evidence), I'm thinking the emerging health
apocalypse is more of a "black swan". The concept of the black swan, which
Nassim Nicholas Taleb popularized in his best-selling 2007 book, The Black
Swan: The Impact of the Highly Improbable, refers to an event, positive or
negative, that is highly improbable yet causes massive consequences.

In the short term, black swans are scarier for investors as the market is
quick to start discounting the potential risk despite uncertainty over the

1

impact level and time horizon. For example, yesterday the Dow tumbled by over 450 points as investor fears escalated over the spreading Wuhan coronavirus, with U.S. consumer stocks with Chinese exposure declining the most.

But in the long run, gray rhinos like the retail and climate apocalypse are a greater threat as they represent a real structural shift that will require investors to change the way they look at and value stocks. For example, investors that were just looking at the numbers would have fallen into the value trap of Intu Properties, the U.K. retail REIT that has declined 80% in the past year and is now seeking emergency cash. The new climate apocalypse is changing the rules of the game for investors in terms of their actual research process as MSCI just warned that those who ignore ESG factors will dramatically underperform, just a week after Blackrock's CEO asserted the climate change will fundamentally reshape finance.

CLIMATE APOCALYPSE: MSCI sounds alarm bell for investors ignoring ESG factors as Bloomberg Green debuts

"...portfolios are going to underperform dramatically because there's a common repricing and common reallocation of assets around the world according to the ESG criteria". This warning came from Henry Fernandez, Chairman & CEO of MSCI, on January 21 as he sounded the alarm bell for investors ignoring ESG factors (cnbc.com). In its new 6-page publication, *Principles of Sustainable Investing*, MSCI concludes: *"MSCI urges all investors globally to integrate ESG considerations into their investment processes. There should not be specialized 'ESG Investing' on one side and 'Non-ESG Investing' everywhere else."* As further evidence that climate change is going mainstream, Bloomberg just launched Bloomberg Green, a multi-platform editorial brand focused on climate change news, analysis and solutions that leverages its 2,700 journalists and analysts. And if you're interested in digging into real-time climate data on hot topics such as the global temperature, air pollution and

electricity mix by country, you can now check out Bloomberg Green's global interactive climate data dashboard (bloomberg.com).

To tackle climate change, Marc Benioff, **Salesforce**'s founder & CEO, launched 1t.org in partnership with the World Economic Forum at Davos and the support of President Trump and over 300 companies. 1T.org has a sustainability driven mission to plant one trillion trees over the coming decade to efficiently sequester carbon, which could provide up to one-third of the needed climate solutions by 2030 to meet the 1.5 degree goal. Notably, during an interview at Davos, Benioff shared his controversial view that "capitalism is dead" and will be replaced by stakeholder capitalism which marries shareholder with stakeholder returns. The shift is being accelerated by the planetary emergency which is requiring everyone to make changes.

RETAIL APOCALYPSE: Intu looks to raise emergency cash while store closures hit Canada

Intu Properties, the U.K. retail REIT, is seeking to raise emergency cash of up to £1 billion by the end of February to shore up its balance sheet, which is weighed down by nearly £5 billion of debt (theguardian.com). We note that Intu Properties' stock price has tumbled 80% in the past 12 months. The retail apocalypse is hitting Canada as Schurman Retail Group is closing all its North American greetings cards stores, including 59 Carlton Cards and 17 Papyrus stores in Canada (ctvnews.ca). And Bench, is closing all its 24 streetwear apparel stores across Canada. Bench, which was founded in the U.K. in 1989, was acquired by restructuring and liquidation firm Gordon Brothers in July 2018. But its Canadian operations are managed by Montreal-based Freemark Apparel Brands Group (bnnbloomberg.com). In addition, **Express** is closing 100 stores by 2022. This represents 17% of Express' current base of over 600 stores and is part of its strategy to cut its annual costs by $80 million over the next three years (cnbc.com).

On January 23, Fairway Market filed for Chapter 11 bankruptcy protection for the second time. Fairway Market will be selling its five Manhattan stores (including its flagship location on the UWS that started out as a fruit and vegetable stand in the 1930s) to Village Super Market for $70 million and plans to keep its remaining nine stores in New York, New Jersey and Connecticut open as it tries to sell them in a court-supervised process (businessinsider.com). We note that Fairway Market first filed for bankruptcy in May 2016 after expanding too aggressively following its IPO in 2013.

HEALTH APOCALYPSE: Dow drops over 450 points as investor fears escalate over spreading coronavirus

On January 27, the Dow dropped over 450 points, or 1.6%, as investor fears escalated over the spreading Wuhan coronavirus. U.S. consumer stocks with Chinese exposure were the worst hit: Cruise Lines (**Royal Caribbean** down 8%), Casinos & Gaming (**Wynn Resorts** down 8%, **Las Vegas Sands** down 7%), Airlines (**American Airlines** down 6%, **United Airlines** 5%), Restaurants (**Luckin Coffee** down 9%, **Yum China** down 5%, **Starbucks** down 4%), Consumer Brands (**Estee Lauder** and **Tapestry** down 4%, **Apple** down 3%) and Hotels (**Hilton** down 3%) (cnbc.com). If you've become obsessed with following the coronavirus, you might want to check out John Hopkins, which was developed a real-time dashboard with map that tracks the spread of the Wuhan coronavirus. As of the time of writing (1:30pm ET on January 27), there were 2,886 global confirmed cases and 81 deaths, with nearly 80% of the confirmed cases in Mainland China (2,285) and only 5 in the U.S. and 1 in Canada.

Amazon files to trademark "Amazon Pharmacy" in Canada, U.K. & Australia

As a foreshadowing of **Amazon**'s international expansion into healthcare, it filed to trademark "Amazon Pharmacy" in Canada, the U.K. and Australia on January 9 (cnbc.com). We note that two months ago Amazon rebranded PillPack to "Amazon Pharmacy" in the U.S.

Meanwhile, Apple is adding a digital layer to gyms with the launch of its Apple Watch Connected program. Apple is partnering with Basecamp, Crunch Fitness, Orange Theory and YMCA in the U.S. to increase membership retention and engagement by enabling those with an Apple Watch to buy goods using Apple Pay, track their workouts on cardio machines equipped with GymKit and earn rewards for working out. For example, to incentivize you to work out, Crunch Fitness will let you earn $3–$4 in weekly credits, Orange Theory will give gift cards to Apple and **Nike**, Basecamp will give you an Apple Watch 5 GPS model that you can earn back by participating in three weekly classes for a year, and YMCA will offer free classes for children (cnbc.com).

GM spending $3.1 billion to retool Detroit plant for production of electric & autonomous vehicles

On January 22, **GM**'s autonomous vehicle unit, Cruise, unveiled The Origin — a toaster-shaped robot taxi with no steering wheel and doors that slide open like an elevator. The Origin is not a concept car, but a fully engineered vehicle that is on its way to production. As a passenger vehicle, it seats six with the seats facing each other but it can also be configured for commercial deliveries (wsj.com). Five days later, GM announced it will be investing $3.1 billion to retool its Detroit/Hamtramck Assembly Plant for the production of electric vehicles and The Origin. GM will spend $2.2 billion to upgrade its plant and more than double its workforce from 900 to over 2,200 and invest another $800 million in equipment for auto parts suppliers. GM expects the first electric vehicle will roll off the production line in 2021 and soon after it will begin manufacturing The Origin (siliconangle.com).

Boeing has signed an exploratory agreement with Israel-based Tactical Robotics to work together to develop, produce and market a VTOL aircraft (techcrunch.com). Meanwhile, it was just made public that Apple filed a U.S. patent back in August for the *"Guidance of Autonomous*

Vehicles in Destination Vicinities Using Intent Signals". Basically, you could tell your car where to go using gestures, touchscreens, or voice commands via Siri (digitaltrends.com).

Starbucks & Pernod Ricard announce sustainability initiatives as Lundin Petroleum pledges to become carbon neutral

On January 21, Spain declared a national climate emergency (apnews.com) while **Starbucks** committed to cut in half the carbon emissions from its direct operations, the water it uses and the waste it sends to landfills by 2030. In addition, Starbucks plans to serve more coffee in reusable cups and offer more plant-based options (wsj.com). That same day, **Pernod Ricard**, the world's second-largest alcohol producer, declared it will shift to 100% renewable energy by 2025 and reduce absolute carbon emissions at its production sites by 30% by 2030. A few months ago, Pernod Ricard joined RE100, a group of influential companies committed to 100% renewable electricity (forbes.com).

On January 27, **Lundin Petroleum**, one of Europe's largest independent oil producers, pledged to become carbon neutral by the end of the decade as it announced it will be changing its name to Lundin Energy. Lundin plans to achieve carbon neutrality by reducing emissions from its operations, increasing its energy efficiency and developing carbon capture mechanisms. However, Isadora Wronski, head of Greenpeace Sweden, accused Lundin of hypocrisy: *"There is an inherent paradox in Lundin Petroleum setting a goal of 'carbon neutrality' while their ambition is being a 'leading provider of oil and gas in the future'"*.

Coca-Cola has no plans to ditch its single-use plastic bottles

Coca-Cola has pledged to use at least 50% recycled material in its plastic bottles and to recycle as many as it produces by 2030. But according to Bea Perez, Coca Cola's Head of Sustainability, the company has no plans to ditch its single-use plastic bottles as consumers like them because they are lightweight and reseal. This is not good news from an environmental sustainability perspective as Coca-Cola produces 3 million tonnes of plastic packaging a year and was ranked last year by Break Free from Plastic as the world's top plastic-polluting company, followed by **Nestle** and **PepsiCo** (theverge.com).

Uber sells Uber Eats to Zomato for 10% stake as Grubhub shifts focus to pick-up

In India, Uber is selling Uber Eats to Zomato in exchange for a 9.99% equity stake in Zomato. This makes strategic sense as Uber is looking to cut its global losses in areas where it is not the #1 or #2 player — and in India, Uber is the #3 food delivery player and India accounts for over 25% of Uber Eats' losses but just 3% of its revenue (wsj.com). We note Zomato just raised a $150 million private equity round from Ant Financial (**Alibaba**), valuing it at $3 billion (indiatimes.com). This implies that Uber's equity stake in Zomato is worth $300 million, less than the $400 million expected last month when Uber was in advanced talks with Zomato.

Belgium's labour authority has launched a court case against Deliveroo for failing to respect Belgium labour law for its 3,500 riders in Brussels. As Deliveroo's riders are considered self-employed rather than employees, they do not receive access to healthcare, overtime pay or holidays (reuters.com).

Grubhub just unveiled Ultimate — a digital workflow solution for restaurants to offer an easy pick-up experience. According to NDP Group, pick-up currently accounts for 58% of all digital restaurant orders and is growing at twice the rate of delivery, at 32% versus 16%. Ultimate provides customers with the real-time ETA of their order and comprises a combination of proprietary hardware and software, including POS with direct integration to the Grubhub app and website, kitchen display system, in-store self-ordering kiosks to complement the app. Grubhub is testing Ultimate at three Chick-fil-A locations, Ohio State University, and over 100 restaurants in

Chicago and NYC (cnbc.com). Most importantly, Ultimate could enable Grubhub to capitalize on its customer relationships to shift away from the increasingly competitive gig economy food delivery business to pick-up, which currently only comprises less than 10% of its orders.

Amazon files motion to halt Microsoft's work on JEDI contract, Amazon Music reaches 55 million customers

On January 22, Amazon filed a motion to halt **Microsoft**'s work on the JEDI (Joint Enterprise Defense Infrastructure) cloud services contract until a court rules on its protest of the award (cnbc.com). We note that two months ago, AWS filed a protest with the U.S. Court of Federal Claims on the Pentagon's award to Microsoft of the highly sought-after JEDI contract, which could be worth as much as $10 billion over the next decade. In the protest, Amazon alleges: *"Numerous aspects of the JEDI evaluation process contained clear deficiencies, errors, and unmistakable bias, and it's important that these matters be examined and rectified"*.

On the customer capital front, Amazon announced Amazon Music has reached over 55 million customers globally. Amazon's customer base grew over 50% in the U.S., U.K., Germany and Japan while more than doubling in newer countries like France, Italy, Spain and Mexico. In addition, paid subscriptions for Amazon Music Unlimited, which offers a catalog of 50 million songs for $7.99 per month, grew more than 50% last year (blog.aboutamazon.com). On the delivery front, Amazon was just granted a U.S. patent it filed back in June 14, 2017 for *"storage compartment vehicles"*. Notably, Amazon filed the patent two days before it announced the acquisition of Whole Foods. The storage compartment vehicle is designed to roam the sidewalk and make deliveries to multiple customers, as well as pick up items for return (geekwire.com).

Sonos faces huge customer backlash after warning it will cut off support for legacy devices

Sonos experienced a massive customer backlash and the threat of customer attrition after sending an e-mail to customers on January 21 warning them that any legacy Sonos smart speakers (i.e., those introduced between 2005 and 2011) they own will stop receiving security and software updates as of May (cnbc.com). To the company's credit, two days later its CEO, Patrick Spence, issued an apology letter and pledged to keep legacy devices updated with bug fixes and security patches for as long as possible and promised the company is working on a way to split systems so legacy and new devices can work together (blog.sonos.com). Although the initial e-mail likely destroyed some trust and customer goodwill, we believe the company's quick response to reassure customers will prevent mass-scale customer attrition. We note that on November 6, **Best Buy** quietly shut down its Insignia Connect platform, so all its Insignia smart home appliances and devices are no longer smart, but dumb.

Ralph Lauren praises closet sharing economy as Louis Vuitton opens first ever restaurant

"Consumers today are not necessarily excited about owning, particularly the younger population". This comment comes from Patrice Louvet, CEO of **Ralph Lauren**, as he shared his views during a panel discussion at Davos on how the wardrobe of a typical consumer will transform over the next 5–10 years to embrace the closet sharing economy having three distinct sections: 1) rented clothes (e.g. Rent the Runway); 2) pre-owned (e.g., **The RealReal**); and 3) new (fastcompany.com). To attract customers to come to its store and enhance the emotional experience, Louis Vuitton (**LVMH**) is opening its first-ever restaurant at its new Osaka flagship store in Japan. Le Café V, which will be located on the top floor of its four-level store, will feature a menu designed by an acclaimed Japanese chef (standard.co.uk).

Uber & Lyft launch in Vancouver, Uber tests letting drivers set own fares in California

On January 24, **Uber** and **Lyft** made their long-awaited debut in Vancouver. It's interesting as at 11:20am, I checked to see how much it would cost to Uber or Lyft from my WeWork in downtown Vancouver to the airport, an 11-km drive. Lyft was actually cheaper than Uber, quoting me $23.88 versus $27.17, but the wait time for Lyft was two minutes longer, seven minutes versus five minutes. Interestingly, when I looked it up on the Google (**Alphabet**) Maps app, the only ridesharing option shown was Uber, not Lyft. And when I checked to see how much it would cost to catch a ride to my home in West Vancouver, Lyft said it was not available for that location.

In California, in response to AB5, Uber is testing a new feature to enable its drivers to be more like independent contractors – the ability to set their own fares. Uber is testing this new feature at three airports in California and starting next week, drivers will be able to set fares lower than the base rate (marketwatch.com). Although this will empower Uber drivers, it is more likely to result in a dangerous race to the bottom as the service they offer is a pure commodity.

In the U.K., Uber has entered into an agreement with **Nissan** to offer a fleet of 2,000 electric Leaf hatchbacks to its drivers at a discount (cnbc.com). This is part of Uber's environmental sustainability strategy to ensure all its vehicles will be fully electric in London by 2025. What makes this move interesting is that Uber was stripped of its license two months ago by Transport London over passenger safety concerns and is only operating on a provisional basis – it seems like Uber is trying to win over regulators through promoting environmental sustainability.

Walmart tests a higher-paying "team associate" position

As part of its shift to a new workflow model, **Walmart** is creating a new "team associate" position which will offer a slight higher starting hourly pay ($12 versus $11) as workers will be trained with a broader range of retail skills. Walmart is testing this new position in 500 of its stores (cnbc.com).

Is Casper getting desperate as it looks to price its IPO at 30% below $1.1 billion private valuation last March?

On January 27, Casper announced it is looking to raise up to $182 million by selling 9.6 million shares at between $17 and $19 per share. This would yield a valuation of up to $768 million, which is 30% below its valuation of $1.1 billion reached last March when it raised $100 million in a Series D round (cnbc.com). However, as we expressed in our January 14 research note, *Déjà Vu?*, like with WeWork, our concerns with Casper are less about valuation than the sustainability of its business model given the number of glaring red flags in its S-1 filing, including: 1) unprofitable (losing $0.21 for every $1 it generates); 2) slowing growth (DTC revenue growth has plummeted to 13%); 3) high customer acquisition costs despite low retention rate ($248 per customer but only 16% repeat purchase rate); and 4) TAM is limited (not a tech platform and faces intensifying competition).

WeWork continues to divest portfolio, selling TEEM and equity stake in The Wing

WeWork continues to divest its portfolio to focus on its core WeWork co-working operations, selling Teem to iOFFICE and its equity stake in The Wing (cnbc.com). We note that WeWork acquired Teem, a cloud-based software and analytics platforms for meeting management and analysis, for $100 million in September 2018. WeWork had planned to use Teem internally to help it better utilize the space of its co-working locations, such as conference room scheduling and desk reservations and offer the software itself as part of a broader package to enterprises and its Powered By We clients. WeWork led The Wing's $32 million Series B round in December 2017 and participated as a strategic investor in its $75 million Series C round, alongside Airbnb, in January 2019. WeWork is selling its 23% equity stake in The Wing, valued at $59 million as of last August, to a consortium of new and existing investors, including Google Ventures.

Chapter 2: The Rockstar

February 4, 2020

"Don't doubt ur vibe... Be ... cause ... it's ... you"

These are the lyrics to *"Don't Doubt ur Vibe"*, the uplifting electric dance music song composed by Elon Musk that he shared with his cult of 31 million followers on Twitter the evening of January 30. The next day he published his song on Spotify under his new artist name, *"Elon 'EDM' Musk"*, cleverly subtly marketing the Cybertruck through the image of a Cybertruck flying in outer space. And if you were a Tesla shareholder, you were definitely in a mood to party as Tesla beat earnings and Musk defied skeptics, sharing that he expects positive cash flow going forward, deliveries to exceed 500,000 units this year and that Model Y only took 10 months to go from prototype to production. Tesla's stock price itself seems to be defying gravity as yesterday it reached an all-time high of $780, rocketing over 130% in just the past two months. The other tech rockstar CEO that crushed earnings is Jeff Bezos who shared that Amazon now has over 150 million global Prime members and AWS has secured $30 billion in future commitments, up 54% year-over-year.

On a more somber note, the Wuhan coronavirus is unfolding as a "black swan" event as it was designated as a public health emergency by the World Health Organization on January 30. As of the time of writing (6:15pm ET on

February 3), there were 19,853 confirmed cases and 426 deaths, with 99% of the confirmed cases in Mainland China (19,665) and still only 11 in the U.S. and 4 in Canada. In comparison, a week ago, there were 2,886 global confirmed cases and 81 deaths, with nearly 80% of the confirmed cases in Mainland China (2,285) and only five in the U.S. and one in Canada.

Amazon's stock soars 7% after reporting stellar Q419 results

On January 31, **Amazon**'s stock price soared 7% after reporting stellar Q419 results. Amazon's net sales rose 21% in Q419 to $87.4 billion, owing to a strong holiday performance as a result of One Day and growth in Prime which has reached over 150 million members globally. Amazon also beat on the bottom line, reporting a record quarterly EPS of $6.47 versus expectations of $4.03.

Amazon's profit driver continues to be its high-margin AWS division, where net sales rose 34% to $10.0 billion, but its operating margin declined 310 bp to 26.1% as it continued to invest in expanding its sales & marketing team and capital leases. On the positive side, it now has $30 billion in future commitments for AWS, up 54% year-over-year, and it expects to be able to leverage sales & marketing costs as it scales. The company's overall operating margin fell 80 bp to 4.4% as its operating margin in North America, which accounts for 61% of its net sales, declined 160 bp to 3.5%, more than offsetting the 50 bp improvement in its International operating margin to -2.6%. Amazon's "Other" revenue, which is mainly advertising revenue, rose 41% to $4.8 billion, totalling over $14 billion for the year. As Amazon is still in the process of materially changing its whole network topology, it expects to spend an extra $1.0 billion in shipping costs in Q1 for One Day. Amazon's negative shipping delta widened by $2.6 billion in Q4 to $7.6 billion as the 43% increase in its shipping costs to $12.9 billion more than offset the 32% increase in its subscription services revenue to $5.2 billion.

Amazon is expanding its warehouse footprint in Staten Island as it looks to increase its speed of delivery to its customers in NYC. Amazon is leasing 450,000 square feet of warehouse space at the Matrix Global Logistics Park where it already has an 855,000-square-foot fulfillment centre (wsj.com). Amazon continues to expand its physical retail footprint as it has opened five mall-based pop-up stores which will rotate new themes and brands. For example, it is starting with four Food Network-themed pop-ups and one camera-themed pop-up (amazon.com). On the banking front, **Goldman Sachs** is in talks with Amazon to offer small business loans to its merchants (cnbc.com). We note that Amazon launched its Amazon Lending program for its third-party suppliers in 2011 and partnered two years ago with **Bank of America** Merrill Lynch for the program.

Tesla's stock soars 12% after beating Q419 earnings

On January 30, **Tesla**'s stock price soared 12% after beating Q419 earnings and Musk defying skeptics by announcing he expects positive cash flow and net income going forward (with the exception of when Tesla launches and ramps up new products) and deliveries in 2020 will exceed 500,000 units. But what I love is how Musk is changing the rules of the game for the auto industry, as evidenced by his statement during Tesla's Q419 conference call: *"It's hard to think of a similar product with such strong demand that it can generate more than $20 billion in revenue with zero advertising spend...Regarding Model Y, it was only 10 months ago that we revealed a Model Y prototype."*

He also alluded to his intent to use Tesla Insurance, which is currently just available in California, to enable car-sharing before the robo-taxi fleet is enabled and Tesla's competitive advantage of being able to leverage real-time data on how cars are being driven to price insurance.

True to my thesis that we are entering the New Cyber Decade, Musk's Cybertruck has inspired the Cyberphone. Caviar, a Russian luxury electronics studio, just debuted the Cyberphone an iPhone 11 Pro that comes in a protective titanium case. Caviar is going for exclusivity as it is pricing the Cyberphone starting at $5,256 and only making a limited run of 99 units (fastcompany.com).

CNBC's Jim Cramer boldly proclaims "I'm done with fossil fuels"

"Over the longer term it is possible there is a financial stability risk from climate change." This comment made on January 29 by Fed Reserve Chair, Jerome Powell, indicates that even the U.S. government is now joining the climate change movement (fxstreet.com). The climate change movement is also spreading to media companies. The Guardian is no longer accepting money from companies that extract fossil fuels, becoming the first major global news organization to ban advertising for fossil fuel companies (theguardian.com). And Big Oil is facing the threat of legal risk as it comes under increasing pressure from citizens, government and activist groups. For example, **Total**, the French oil giant which accounts for 1% of the world's CO_2 emissions, is being sued for "climate inaction" by 14 French cities and 4 NGOs (fortune.com). On January 31, Jim Cramer shared his view on CNBC that fossil stocks are now in the death knell phase, comparing them to tobacco stocks (cnbc.com) as he boldly proclaimed: *"I'm done with fossil fuels ... they're just done."*

WeWork sobers up as it takes away the free beer & appoints real estate veteran as its new CEO

No more free beer? It looks like WeWork is starting to cut location operating costs as it will no longer have beer on tap for its members in the U.S. and Canada as of the end of February (mediapost.com). *"The sum of the parts is far greater than GGP's current stock price."* And WeWork will likely be cutting out more than free beer as I'm thinking this comment made back on May 1, 2017 by GGP's CEO, Sandeep Mathrani, during its Q117 conference call, could be a foreshadowing of the fate of WeWork which just appointed Mathrani as its new CEO.

Mathrani joins WeWork from **Brookfield Property Partners**, where he served as CEO of retail since August 2018 following its acquisition of GGP. Prior to this, Mathrani spent nearly eight years as the CEO of GGP, joining GGP in 2010 to help it emerge from bankruptcy (wsj.com).

Simon Property Group partners with Accor to enter ghost kitchen space

Kitopia, a ghost kitchen platform launched in Dubai in 2018, has raised a $60 million Series B round. Kitopa currently operates 30 kitchens across Dubai, Abu Dhabi, London, Kuwait, Riyadh, and New York in partnership with over 100 restaurants. Kitopia plans to use the capital to add 50 ghost kitchens in the U.S. and 100 globally by the end of this year (investing.com). Meanwhile, **Simon Property Group** and **Accor** have formed a consortium with SBE Entertainment Group (50%-owned by Accor) to repurpose obsolete real estate assets into ghost kitchens. The C3 (Creating Culinary Communities) consortium plans to open 85 ghost kitchens this year, starting with big U.S. cities like NYC, Chicago, LA and Miami, and then open at least 100 by the end of 2021. Interestingly, C3 has partnered with Travis Kalanick's CloudKitchens to open four ghost kitchens at SBE properties in LA. Ghost kitchens seem to have attractive economics relative to restaurants as they require 1/15 the space (230 square feet versus 3,500 square feet), take 1/8 the time to build (2 weeks versus 16 weeks) and can be built for 1/33 of the cost ($30,000 versus $1 million) (wsj.com). As Travis Kalanick ominously tweeted in March 2018 as he announced he was starting a company focused on the redevelopment of distressed real estate in parking, retail and industrial: *"over $10 trillion in real estate assets will need to be repurposed for the digital era in the coming years"*.

Instacart shoppers in Chicago unionize, Instacart partners with Publix to launch digital deli counter

On February 1, Instacart grocery shoppers in Chicago voted to unionize with the United Food and Commercial Workers to improve their working conditions, despite efforts from Instacart to deter them. Although the shoppers are employees, they only receive $13 per hour, work under a timer to meet a strict quota run by Instacart's algorithm, and are not eligible for health benefits as they are capped at working 29 hours per week to keep them as part-time employees (vice.com). The boundaries are blurring between food and grocery delivery as Instacart partners with the U.S. supermarket chain Publix to launch Instacart Meals. Instacart Meals offers Publix's customers a "digital deli counter" as it will enable them to build their own sub to be delivered with their grocery order. Publix plans to roll out Instacart Meals across Florida in the coming weeks and then expand to the Southeast (techcrunch.com).

Lucky's Market files for bankruptcy as Earth Fare shuts all its 50 stores

On January 27, Lucky's Market filed for bankruptcy. The natural and organic grocery chain with 39 stores across the U.S. will be selling 6 stores to Aldi and 5 to Publix (cnn.com). We note **Kroger** made a meaningful strategic investment in Lucky's Market in April 2016 but decided to divest its ownership position in December 2019 and took a non-cash impairment charge of $283 million in Q319. Less than a week later, on February 2, Earth Fare announced it will close all of its 50 stores and commence liquidation of its inventory and store fixtures as it seeks to find a buyer. The natural and organic goods merchant, which was founded in 1975, operates stores in 10 states in the Southeast, Atlantic and Midwest. Earth Fare's landlords include retail REITs, **Kite Realty Group Trust** and **Regency Centers Corp.** (wsj.com).

The greeting card market also seems to be heading toward obsolescence as people are increasingly sending wishes through texts or free social channels like **Facebook** and Instagram. Hallmark Cards will be closing at least 16 stores across the U.S. as it restructures its operations (wsj.com). This comes only a week after the bankruptcy of Schurman Fine Papers who is closing all of its 254 greeting card and stationery stores, notably Papyrus, American Greetings and Carlton Cards.

The Vitamin Shoppe seeks alternative distribution channel to malls – fitness clubs

The Vitamin Shoppe is testing adding a staffed 300-square-foot shop into nine LA Fitness gyms, enabling it to leverage both LA Fitness' customer capital and structural capital. In return, The Vitamin Shoppe will provide LA Fitness with supplier capital in terms of a curated assortment of 900 different health food products (e.g., vitamins, minerals, sports nutrition products, supplements, to-go healthy snack and beverages) (chainstoreage.com). We note that Vitamin Shoppe was bailed out last August by The Franchise Group for $208 million.

Nordstrom launches second-hand shop in its new NYC flagship department store

Nordstrom is embracing the closet-sharing economy with the launch of a resale platform on its website as well as a second-hand shop in its new flagship store in NYC. It is a strong strategic move — in addition to appealing to the rising number of socially and cost-conscious consumers, it will enable it to capitalize on its supplier capital (i.e., its inventory of returned and damaged pieces) (footwearnews.com). We note that in November, Nordstrom started to rent its apparel through Rent the Runway.

Pinterest launches virtual lipstick try-on feature

Pinterest is leveraging the AI layer with the launch of a feature which enables you to virtually try on lipstick. You just need to open Pinterest's smart Lens camera in Search and click on "Try It". This will help Pinterest increase user engagement with brands that advertise on Pinterest and enable it to capitalize on the over 52 million U.S. monthly visits to its app from people searching and engaging with its beauty content (techcrunch.com). While this is a positive move, we note that

Amazon launched its virtual "try on" feature for lipstick back in June 2018.

Did you ever dream of staying in an Atari hotel?

Atari is capitalizing on its brand name legacy to license its name and brand to True North Studio, a U.S. real estate developer, which plans to build eight Atari-branded hotels across the U.S. The first hotel will break ground in Phoenix this summer and include video game-themed attractions like an e-sports studio and an Atari gaming playground which will include AR and VR games (theverge.com).

Apple preparing to launch AirTags

Apple is apparently preparing to launch a new product called AirTags in the first half of this year, a smart tag which can attach to any object and be tracked on an iPhone through a Find My app (businessinsider.com).

Starbucks adding 4,000 AI-enabled espresso machines this year

Starbucks plans to bring its AI-enabled Mastrena II espresso machine to all its stores in the U.S. and Canada by 2022. Starbucks will add 4,000 machines this year, on top of the 1,900 it added last year. In addition to being able to collect data through sensors built into the machine, the AI can be used for preventative maintenance (finance.yahoo.com).

UPS purchases 10,000 electric delivery vans from Arrival

UPS is purchasing 10,000 electric delivery vans and taking a minority stake in Arrival, a U.K.-based technology company that develops electric vehicles. The delivery vans, which will be deployed in North America and Europe, will be customized for UPS with a modular design to allow for standardized parts that will reduce the cost of maintenance. Last year, UPS partnered with Arrival on a trial of 35 EVs in London and Paris (cnbc.com). We note that in January, Arrival raised a £100 million corporate round from **Hyundai Motor** and **Kia Motors**. Although UPS is trying to catch up with Amazon, it is only purchasing one-tenth of the number of electric delivery vehicles as Amazon, which announced back in September that it was ordering 100,000 electric delivery vehicles from Rivian, which it made a $440 million strategic investment in back in February.

Ola launching soon in London

Ola will begin operations in London on February 10. Ola has signed up over 20,000 drivers in London since late November and is looking to eventually board 50,000 drivers through incentives like not charging them any commission for six weeks. On the customer side, Ola is looking to attract passengers by giving them £25 of ride credit if they sign up in the first week after launch (techcrunch.com). We note Ola announced that it would be coming to London in late November, the day after **Uber**'s license was revoked.

Architects looking to develop sustainable neighbourhood in the Netherlands

Architects in the Netherlands are looking to develop a new sustainable neighbourhood in the city of Utrecht. The new proposed Merwede neighbourhood will look to house 12,000 people on a 60-acre site where residents can walk to everything they need with a focus on pedestrians, cyclists and public transport with one shared car for every three households. The neighbourhood will also be almost energy-neutral; in addition to installing solar panels on building roofs, it will use water from a nearby canal to build the largest underground heat and storage facility in the Netherlands to heat and cool the district (fastcompany.com).

Chapter 3: Back to Reality

February 19, 2020

I took a sip of my pina colada and smiled as I watched my boys playing in the sand while the sun set over the Pacific Ocean. But our week of fun and sun at Club Med Ixtapa is now a distant memory. Likewise, as evidenced by this admission by Dara Khosrowshahi on Uber's Q419 conference call: "We recognize that the era of growth at all costs is over", it is now back to reality for many high-flying unicorns that have been enjoying the all-inclusive lifestyle as they chased rainbows in the bountiful flower-filled meadows of Silicon Valley.

For example, Casper ended up pricing its IPO at nearly 60% below its pre-IPO valuation of $1.1 billion while Walmart has shut down Jetblack after it was unable to find a buyer or investor for its NYC-based yummy mummy text-driven personal shopping service. And the Softbank-backed Brandless, which was heralded as the "Procter & Gamble for Millennials", is completely shutting down. This makes me wonder what will happen to Airbnb's planned IPO for this year as this once high-flying unicorn is not only facing slowing growth, combined with escalating regulatory risks and costs, but it just turned unprofitable. As I cautioned last summer in the intro of my "Secrets of the Amazon III" book:

Although the Amazon castle is illuminated by a rainbow that stretches across the pink-coloured sky over its kingdom, the hard truth is that not every unicorn deserves a rainbow valuation, especially those that are not yet self-sufficient (i.e., profitable).

Softbank-backed Brandless shuts down while Kroger's marketing arm offers CPGs access to transaction data

Brandless, known as the **"Procter & Gamble** for Millennials", is shutting down. It turns out Brandless' DTC business model of selling highly-quality unbranded household staples for a low price was unsustainable in the fiercely competitive retail environment (cnbc.com). San Francisco-based Brandless launched its online store in July 2017 when it raised a $35 million Series B round. This was followed a year later by a massive $240 million Series C round led by **Softbank** Vision Fund. Interestingly, this marks the first failed start-up backed by the Softbank Vision Fund. The other good news for CPGs is that **Kroger** is enabling CPG brands to gain insights into the effectiveness of their media campaigns through **Microsoft's** commerce marketing platform. Microsoft Promote IQ gives CPGs access to transaction data (in-store and online sales) so they can optimize their media investment with Kroger's self-service advertising platform (mediapost.com). Although this improved transparency is positive for CPGs, they still don't control the customer relationship or have access to customer data through other food retailers.

Simon Property Group acquires Taubman Group for $3.6 billion & Forever 21 for $81 million

We are seeing consolidation in retail REITs. On February 10, **Simon Property Group** announced it was acquiring **Taubman Group** for $3.6 billion in cash (cnbc.com). Although the $52.50 share price represents a 51% premium, we note that Taubman, which operates 26 super-regional shopping malls across the U.S. and Asia, has seen its stock price decline in half the past year and was trading at this price just last April. And Simon Property Group (SPG) along with **Brookfield Property Partners** (BPP) and Authentic Brands Group LLC are paying $81 million for Forever 21, the teen apparel retailer that filed for bankruptcy on September 29 (wsj.com). We note that Forever 21 started restructuring talks with SPG and BPP back in June 2019.

Stage Stores & Modell's Sporting Goods face bankruptcy as Pier 1 Imports files for Chapter 11

The retail apocalypse continues... **Stage Stores** is preparing for a financial restructuring which could include a Chapter 11 bankruptcy. Stage Stores is facing a liquidity squeeze after its holiday sales failed to meet its expectations and it has recently been late in paying its vendors (wsj.com). We note that Stage Stores has been making a number of recent desperate moves, including its decision in September to abandon the department store model and go all-in on the off-price model as well as follow **Kohl's** lead and partner with **Amazon** in October on a return service. Modell's Sporting Goods, which was founded in NYC in 1889, is exploring restructuring options as it also hopes to avoid bankruptcy following weak holiday sales. To preserve cash, the sporting goods retailer with 140 stores across the Northeastern U.S. has stopped paying some landlords and vendors (wsj.com). And on February 17, Pier 1 Imports filed for Chapter 11 bankruptcy protection. The company will use the bankruptcy process to complete the closure of the 450 stores it announced last month, which includes all its stores in Canada (wsj.com).

Introducing the new IOT: Intelligence of Things

"The last decade was about connectivity, and we describe that dynamic with the Internet of Things... This decade is really about adding intelligence to different devices, services, etc. We're confronted with a new IoT: the intelligence of things." According to Steve Koenig, VP of Research at the Consumer Technology Association, the new Cyber Decade will be about a new kind of IOT — the Intelligence of Things — where networked

23

devices leverage AI to work together to solve problems. For example, a smart smoke alarm that detects smoke could turn off the oven, furnace and power, and call the fire department (digitaltrends.com).

Walmart reports weaker-than-expected Q420 results & shuts down Jetblack

On February 18, **Walmart** reported weaker-than-expected Q420 results, with net sales up 2.1% to $141.7 billion and EPS of $1.38. Walmart U.S. achieved only 1.9% comparable sales growth, with ticket up 0.9% and transaction up 1.0%, owing to softness in sales in toys, apparel and video games in the weeks leading up to Christmas. Walmart continues to leverage its structural capital to achieve cost-effective e-commerce growth — in the past quarter it added 200 new pick-up locations (now at nearly 2,300 stores) and 200 new delivery locations (now at over 1,600 stores). But its e-commerce sales growth slowed to 33%, down from 41% in Q320. For 2021, Walmart is forecasting sales to rise 3% (versus 2.7% in 2020) and EPS to rise by 1.5%-4.5% to $5.00-$5.15. However, it is expecting a slowdown in sales growth for both its U.S. stores (up 2.5% versus 2.8% in 2020) and e-commerce (up 30% versus 37%) (walmart.com). Just days earlier, Walmart announced it was shutting down Jetblack after being unable to find a buyer or investor (cnbc.com). Walmart launched its text-driven personal shopping service in NYC in May 2018, targeting affluent moms by offering services such as gift recommendations, free wrapping, fast delivery and easy returns for a $50 monthly subscription fee. But the problem was Jetblack failed to scale (was only able to attract 600 active members as of this summer) and was unprofitable (lost an estimated $15,000 per member).

Target could come under pressure as delivery workers complain of changes to Shipt's pay algorithm

Although Shipt has been a positive catalyst for **Target** with same-day delivery shipments up over 100% in Q3, the platform is coming under criticism from its delivery workers. Shipt seems to be abandoning its traditional pay scale of a $5 flat rate plus 7.5% of the order value as it starts rolling out a new algorithm pay model. But the problem is the algorithm is opaque and some workers are complaining that it has led to a 30–50% drop in their pay (gizmodo.com). Although Instacart, DoorDash and Postmates have been come under criticism for similar opaque algorithms, the difference is that Target owns Shipt so it could be directly impacted by any negative press.

U.K. banning sale of fossil fuel cars by 2035; Couche-Tard exploring future without gas stations

The U.K. government plans to end the sale of gasoline, diesel and hybrid cars by the end of 2035, five years ahead of its previously announced target date of 2040. This would create a dramatic shift in the landscape as 94% of cars are still powered by fossil fuels (65% petrol, 25% diesel, 4% hybrid EVs). Although this is a progressive move, the U.K. would still lag Ireland and Denmark who plan to ban the sale of fossil fuel cars by 2030 (cnbc.com). Norway is ahead of all those countries as 20% of its cars are already fully electric and the government is ending sales of fossil fuel-powered cars in five years. Because of this, **Alimentation Couche-Tard** is using Norway as a laboratory as it tries to figure out how to add value in a future without gas stations. Couche-Tard is replacing fuel pumps with EV chargers in some of its Circle K gas stations but the problem is most EV charging takes place at home and work, so most of the demand will just be at highway locations. As a result, it is also testing home and workplace charging services (electrek.co).

BP ending oil-centric organizational style; Delta will be first airline to go carbon neutral

On February 12, Bernard Looney, CEO of **BP**, announced it is breaking up its traditional oil-centric upstream-downstream organizational style as it targets to slash greenhouse gas emissions to net zero by 2050.

Specifically, in addition to cutting the 55 million tons of CO2 emissions directly produced by its operations, BP is looking to cut the 415 million tons of CO2 emissions from the oil and gas it takes out of the ground. From an organizational standpoint, BP plans to re-invent itself as 11 teams, including "gas and low carbon emissions" and "innovation and engineering", and reveal its specific strategies in September (forbes.com). Two days later, on February 14, Ed Bastion, CEO of **Delta Air Lines**, announced that starting on March 1 it will be the first airline to go carbon neutral on a global basis. Delta is committing to spend at least $1 billion over the next decade to reduce its environmental impact, focusing on clean technology investments for engine and carbon removal. However, Delta has no plans to eliminate jet fuel (cnbc.com).

Bezos pledges $10 billion of personal wealth to fight climate change

On February 17, Jeff Bezos pledged $10 billion of his personal wealth to start the Bezos Earth Fund to fight climate change. The fund will issue grants to scientists, activists and organizations to assist them in their efforts to *"preserve and protect the natural world"* (cnbc.com). We note that less than six months ago, on September 19, Bezos unveiled Amazon's Climate Pledge, declaring that Amazon is committed to achieving net zero carbon commissions by 2040.

Amazon gets temporary block on Microsoft's work on JEDI contract

On February 13, a federal court ordered a temporary block on **Microsoft's** work on the JEDI (Joint Enterprise Defense Infrastructure) cloud services contract which could be worth as much as $10 billion over the next decade (cnbc.com). And three days earlier, AWS filed court documents seeking to depose President Donald Trump about his involvement in the bidding process as well as six other individuals that played pivotal roles in the Pentagon's awarding of the contract (cnbc.com). Amazon continues to innovate as it was just granted a patent it filed back in 2017 for an *"Energy-efficient launch system for aerial vehicles"*. According to the filing, the system *"uses principles of whip dynamics to launch payloads at high speeds"* (geekwire.com). Amazon continues to invest in structural capital as it has purchased the historic 119-acre site of the former Old Chicago amusement park and mega mall for $50 million from Cox Automotive. Amazon is expected to use the land to build either a new fulfillment centre or customer service centre (businessinsider.com).

Starbucks re-imagining airport experience as 7-Eleven tests Amazon Go-like concept

Can you imagine the magical convenience of having your online **Starbucks** order delivered to you as you board the plane or land at the airport? Starbucks is non-exclusively partnering with OTG to re-imagine the customer experience just a week after HMSHost ended its U.S. airport exclusivity agreement with Starbucks, which has been in place since 1991. OTG, which operates over 350 restaurants and retail locations at 10 U.S. airports, is already tech savvy as customers can place orders via **Apple** iPads in their restaurants (skift.com). 7-Eleven (**Seven & I Holdings**) is also pushing the edge of the convenience frontier as it looks to create a frictionless shopping experience similar to Amazon Go. 7-Eleven is testing a 700-square-foot cashierless concept store, featuring in-house, custom-built technology, with employees at its headquarters in Irving, Texas (techcrunch.com). We note that in November 2018, 7-Eleven piloted a new mobile check-out process called "Scan & Go" in which customers scanned a product's QR code with their 7-Eleven rewards mobile app and then pay using Apple Pay, Google Pay, credit card or debit card. In addition, in January 2019, Seven & I Holdings collaborated with NEC to open a trial 7-Eleven store in Tokyo that utilized facial recognition technology to enable NEC employees to pay using their face.

Casper goes public at nearly 60% below pre-IPO valuation of $1.1 billion

On February 6, **Casper** went public at $12 a share, which is one-third below its expected price of $17–$19 per share when it announced its IPO on January 27. Even more significantly, its IPO valuation of under $500 million is nearly 60% below the pre-IPO valuation of $1.1 billion reached last March when it raised $100 million in a Series D round (cnbc.com). Although shares started trading optimistically at $14.50, the stock has since traded down to $10.12, 16% below its IPO price. As we expressed in our January 14 research note, *Déjà Vu?*, like with WeWork, our concerns with Casper are less about valuation than the sustainability of its business model given the number of glaring red flags in its S-1 filing, including: 1) unprofitable (losing $0.21 for every $1 it generates); 2) slowing growth (DTC revenue growth has plummeted to 13%); 3) high customer acquisition costs despite low retention rate ($248 per customer but only 16% repeat purchase rate); and 4) TAM is limited (not a tech platform and faces intensifying competition).

Google Health grows to over 500 employees

As evidence of Google's (**Alphabet**) intent to focus on healthcare, its newly created Google Health division has now grown to over 500 employees (cnbc.com). We note that in December, David Feinberg, the head of Google Health and former President of Geisinger and UCLA Health, revealed he would be focusing his efforts on Google's core expertise in search.

Facebook quietly launches Pinterest competitor

Facebook has quietly launched a competitor to **Pinterest** called Hobbi. The photo and video-sharing app lets you organize and document your personal projects and hobbies into themed collections. Hobbi was developed by Facebook's NPE (New Product Experimentation) team and was launched in July to develop consumer-focused apps. Hobbi is currently available on iOS in the U.S., Columbia, Belgium, Spain and the Ukraine (techcrunch.com).

Staples thinks outside the big box with launch of Staples Connect concept store

It seems like Staples may be looking to shift its business model away from just selling office supplies to providing experiences and services as it has just redesigned six of its stores in Boston into Staples Connect stores. The Staples Connect concept stores feature community events, coworking, and even a podcast studio, as well as technology, print, marketing and professional services (chainstorage.com).

Airbnb's IPO could be challenged as it turns unprofitable and faces rising safety costs

Although Airbnb has stated its intent to go public this year, it may face challenges as its growth is slowing and it has become unprofitable. For the first nine months of the year, Airbnb has turned from a profit of $200 million in 2018 to a loss of $322 million in 2019. In Q319, Airbnb's revenue rose by only 30% to $1.65 billion, but even worse, its net profit declined 21% to $266 million. In addition to further pressure on its revenue growth rate from the combination of a loss of customer trust and rising competition, Airbnb is apparently also seeing an 80% hit to its China business as a result of the spreading coronavirus (wsj.com). We expect Airbnb's margins will also continue to come under pressure as it has committed to spend $150 million on safety initiatives as a result of its promise to verify all 7 million homes listed on its platform by December following the Vice expose and Halloween party shooting.

Uber now expects to achieve positive EBITDA in Q420, up from 2021

"We recognize that the era of growth at all costs is over." This statement by Dara Khosrowshahi, CEO of **Uber**, underlines how reality is returning to once upon-a-time high-flying unicorns. Investors seem to appreciate this new mindset as on February 7 Uber's stock

price rallied 10% after the company beat Q4 earnings expectations and management stated that is expects Uber to now be EBITDA positive in Q420, ahead of its forecast last quarter of 2021 (seekingalpha.com). However, Uber still lost $1.1 billion (including $243 million in stock-based compensation), or $0.64 per share. Uber grew its platform bookings 28% to $18.1 billion as gross bookings increased for Ridesharing by 18% to $13.5 billion and Uber Eats by 71% to $4.4 billion. On a customer basis, this was driven by a 22% increase to 111 million monthly active users, which, combined with the 5% increase to 17.2 quarterly trips per user, led to a 28% increase in the total number of trips to 1.91 billion. The average booking cost per trip was flat at $9.51.

- Uber's adjusted revenue rose 41% to $3.7 billion. Its cut of bookings for Ridesharing increased 210 bp to 22.5%, resulting in its adjusted revenue increasing 30% to $3.0 billion. Uber Eats' cut of bookings improved 310 bp to 9.5%, resulting in its adjusted revenue increasing 152% to $415 million. On the conference call, management disclosed that Uber Eats' margin would have been 10.1% excluding its recently sold Uber Eats India operations.
- Uber is still unprofitable but it is gaining operating leverage as its operating cost per ride (excluding stock-based compensation) declined 6% to $2.52 with all its line expense items declining except sales and marketing and R&D. This, combined with its average revenue per ride increasing 7% to $2.13, resulted in its operating loss per ride narrowing by 45% to $0.38.
- On the conference call, management disclosed that Uber Eats has expanded its inventory of restaurants in the U.S. by 78% to nearly 400,000 and has 25 million global loyalty members.

Now you can call an Uber just like a taxi. To make its ridesharing platform more available to elderly people that don't have a smartphone or feel comfortable using apps, Uber is piloting a dial-an-Uber service in Arizona with plans to expand into more states. You just need to call 1-833-USE-UBER and you will be able to speak to a real person who will book an Uber for you, and if you don't have an Uber account they will set one up for you (techcrunch.com). Although this service may expand Uber's TAM, it will also increase its fixed cost structure, making the incremental rides less profitable.

Lyft's revenue growth rate is decelerating and it is still not gaining operating leverage

Although **Lyft** beat Q419 estimates, its stock price declined 10% after management maintained its prior guidance that it will achieve EBITDA profitability by Q421. The company's growth rate is also decelerating and it still does not seem to be gaining operating leverage.

- Lyft's revenue in Q419 rose 52% to $1.017 billion, driven by a 23% increase in active riders to 22.9 million and a 23% increase in revenue per active rider to $44.40 (seekingalpha.com). We note Lyft's revenue growth rate has declined significantly from its 94% level a year ago and its forecast 28% growth rate for this year is down over half from its revenue growth rate of 68% in 2019.
- We estimate Lyft's number of rides increased 26% to 225 million, based on its 23% active rider growth and our assumption of a 2% increase in average rides per rider. This implies its revenue per ride rose 23% to $4.52.
- Lyft still does not seem to be gaining operating leverage as we estimate its total cost per ride was $6.22, up 18% from $5.27 in Q418 with all its line expense items rising on a per-ride basis, with the exception of sales & marketing and operations & support. This resulted in its operating loss per ride widening by 12% to $1.70.

Investors are discovering that Uber is a different species of unicorn than Lyft after Uber moved up its expectation of achieving positive EBITDA from 2021 to Q420 and Lyft maintained its expectation of Q421. However, the problem is they both seem to still be willfully ignoring the potential existential threat that the rising gig economy labour rights movement poses to their underlying platform business model. For example, on February 10, a U.S. District court judge rejected Uber and Postmates' request for a preliminary injunction against AB-5 (techcrunch.com). We note that Uber and Postmates filed their suit against the state of California on December 30 alleging that AB-5 is unconstitutional.

Coronavirus update: 75,198 confirmed cases and 2,009 deaths

As of the time of writing (10:15pm ET on February 18), there were 75,198 confirmed cases of the Wuhan coronavirus and 2,009 resulting deaths, with 99% of the confirmed cases in Mainland China (74,185) and still only 29 in the U.S. and 8 in Canada. In comparison, two weeks ago, there were 19,853 confirmed cases and 426 deaths, with 99% of the confirmed cases in Mainland China (19,665) and 11 in the U.S. and 4 in Canada.

Chapter 4: The Future

February 25, 2020

"more wealth could be created over the next ten years than was over the previous century"

I watched in despair yesterday as the Dow plunged by over 1,000 points on investor fears of a dystopian future as the black swan coronavirus spread outside Mainland China, with cases spiking in South Korea, Italy and Iran. But in this time of uncertainty, we should keep in mind these inspiring words from Peter H. Diamandis and Steven Kotler. In their newly published book, "The Future is Faster than You Think: How Converging Technologies Are Transforming Business, Industries and Our Lives" they discuss how structural disruption is accelerating as they write: "convergences are happening at an ever-increasing rate. This has turbo-boosted both the rate of change in the world and the scale of that change" and share their belief that "every major industry on our planet is about to be completely reimagined."

As we enter the New Cyber Decade, sustainability is emerging as a driving force behind the re-invention of industries as JetBlue just became the first airline to receive a sustainability-linked loan, Procter & Gamble has designed stainless steel Tide re-usable containers for Loop's expanding circular economy shopping platform and Gap has embraced the closet sharing economy. The corporate landscape is also being radically trans-formed through the complete decimation of industry boundaries as Amazon prepares to debut a new shoppable fashion design competition on Amazon Prime Video called "Making the Cut". The magic is you'll be able to buy the winning designs immediately after each episode on Amazon. And while you're being seduced by Amazon as you watch Prime Video, your kids can play with Alexa in their own kitchen as they're unknowingly trained for the future of commerce — v-commerce.

Amazon Prime Video debuting a shoppable fashion design competition show

On March 27, Amazon Prime Video is debuting a new shoppable fashion design competition called *Making the Cut*, hosted by fashion icons Heidi Klum and Tim Gunn. The 10-episode series will feature a dozen designers from around the world competing to win $1 million. The real magic is the power of Amazon's flywheel as all the winning designs will be available to buy at an affordable price of under $100 immediately after each episode on Amazon's new "Making the Cut" store (marketwatch.com). Meanwhile, **Farfetch**, the luxury fashion marketplace, will be introducing a new online product drop strategy in April called Farfetch Beat. Farfetch seems to be following a scarcity strategy with Beats to create a feeling of exclusivity by limiting the variety of choice (it will control the distribution by curating products from its 650 boutique partners and own brand portfolios) and convenience (it will online be available every Wednesday). In addition, this will enable Farfetch to move up the customer capital side of the value pyramid to the emotional level by creating a weekly buzz which will serve as a valuable customer acquisition tool (highsnobiety.com).

JetBlue receives sustainability-linked loan, CPGs shift toward new sustainability-driven subscription model

On February 24, **JetBlue Airways** became the first airline to receive a sustainability-linked loan. JetBlue is amending its existing $550 million credit facility with **BNP Parabis** to include a "sustainability-linked" provision to align its strategic initiatives with its ESG goals and initiatives (globalnewswire.com). CPGs are also starting to embrace sustainability. Loop, which launched last May in Paris and NYC, will soon be bringing its circular economy shopping platform to physical stores, partnering with **Walgreens** and **Kroger** in the U.S., **Loblaw** in Canada, **Carrefour** in France and **Tesco** in the U.K. Loop's online store currently features over 150 products in re-usable packaging from a wide coalition of CPG companies. The exciting part is that by shifting the ownership of the package back to the CPG company it incentivizes CPG companies to design innovative re-usable containers and introduces a new subscription model. For example, **Procter & Gamble** has designed stainless steel containers for its Tide detergent and Pantene shampoo, **General Mills** has created metal containers to keep Haagen Daaz ice cream frozen while Nature's Path granola comes in glass jars. This improves the customer value proposition by adding functional and aesthetic features on the physical layer, as evidenced by this observation from Tom Szaky, CEO of Loop, *"People actually are attracted to Loop first for design, second for reuse"* (fastcompany.com).

Spread of coronavirus slows in Mainland China but spikes in South Korea, Italy and Iran

In the past six days, the number of deaths related to the coronavirus has risen by 31% to 2,628, resulting in the death rate rising from 2.7% to 3.3%. The good news is the spread of the coronavirus in Mainland China has started to slow down, with the number of reported cases rising by only 4.0% in the past six days, from 74,185 to 77,150. However, the scary thing is the coronavirus has spread outside Mainland China, with the number of confirmed cases more than doubling in the past six days from 1,103 to 2,403, raising concerns about a coming slowdown in the global economy. For example, South

Korea has declared a "red alert" as the number of coronavirus cases has exploded from 31 to 833. Likewise, as the number of cases in Italy has spiked to 230, towns in Northern Italy are under lockdown and cultural events like the Venice Carnival have been cut short. And Iran is closing public spaces such as schools, universities and cultural centers after the number of cases has reached 61. At home, everything still seems calm, as the number of cases has risen slightly from 29 to 35 in the U.S. and from 8 to 10 in Canada.

Victoria's Secret is sold for only $1.1 billion, Gap partners with thredUP as act of desperation

Victoria's Secret, which has become increasing irrelevant for maintaining its sexy image in the wake of the #metoo movement and has been disrupted by new DTC entrants such as Third Love, has just been sold for only $1.1 billion. **L Brands** is selling a 55% majority stake in Victoria's Secret to Sycamore Partners for $525 million. As part of the deal, Leslie Wexner, who ran the retail empire for over 50 years and has come under recent scrutiny for his ties with Jeffrey Epstein, will step down from his roles as CEO and Chairman of L Brands. With this divestment, L Brands will focus on running its only remaining brand — Bath & Body Works (wsj.com). To avoid the fate of Victoria's Secret, **Gap** is joining thredUP's "Resale-As-A-Service" platform. Starting in April, you will be able to clean out your closet and put your second-hand apparel items in a "clean-out kit" in exchange for credits redeemable at any Gap, Banana Republic, Athleta or Janie & Jack stores in the U.S. (chainstorage.com). Although this seems like a positive move toward sustainability, we view it as a red flag as thredUP is capitalizing on the desperation of retailers needing to attract the new generation of cost conscious and socially conscious consumers. For example, thredUP first partnered in November 2018 with **Stage Stores**, which is now on the brink of bankruptcy, and more recently in August with **Macy's** and **JC Penney**, two struggling department stores. As we cautioned back in August, we expect these partnerships to only accelerate the awareness and adoption of apparel resale online platforms, leading to a rising rival threat of substitutes for department stores and apparel retailers. The shift to online continues as according to the Census Bureau of the U.S. Department of Commerce, traditional U.S. retail sales rose 2.3% in Q4 19. E-commerce retail sales growth was much stronger, up 16.7% to $158.1 billion, capturing 11.4% of total sales, up from 11.2% in Q3 and 10.1% a year ago (www.census.gov).

Montreal kicks out Lime and Bird as it bans e-scooters

Montreal is kicking out the fleets of Lime and Bird e-scooters, which landed on its streets in August, following mass non-compliance by users (cbc.ca). This move isn't surprising given the high safety and liability risks of e-scooters. However, we're wondering whether this will make the CDPQ re-think its decision to lead the $275 million Series D round in Bird back in October at a pre-IPO valuation of $2.5 billion.

Now your kids can play with Alexa in their own kitchen

At the New York Toy Fair, KidKraft debuted the Alexa 2-in-1 Kitchen & Market, a $300 deluxe wooden playset that comes with 100 play pieces integrated with RFID and sensors. The playset features over 700 different voice commands and responses from Alexa. For example, if your child places a pot on the stove Alexa might say *"now that the water is boiling, can you open up the fridge and grab the vegetables"* (engadget.com). In addition to training the next generation on v-commerce, it's interesting as this represents an opportunity to merge the bottom and top layers of the structural capital side of the value pyramid (physical play and AI via voice technology) instead of just the middle layer (digital screens).

Cushman & Wakefield enters office flex space market as Soho House opens Soho Works

Cushman & Wakefield is launching Indego, a new flexible workplace service in the U.K. for its landlord clients. Unlike WeWork, which leases office space from landlords and then sub-leases it to individuals and enterprises, Cushman & Wakefield plans to partner directly with landlords under a management agreement to help it meet the demand from its enterprise tenants for flex space by offering design and build, marketing, sales and on-site operations service (cityam.com). We note that back on October 31, **CBRE Group** announced the launch of a similar service called Hana. Soho House is opening its first co-working space in the U.S. in Brooklyn. Interestingly, you don't need to be a member of the exclusive Soho House to join Soho Works. Soho House, which operates 26 member-only clubs, plans to open Soho Works locations in NYC, London and Hong Kong, with Berlin and Barcelona also on the horizon (vogue.com).

Domino's Pizza sees carryout as a huge opportunity

On February 20, **Domino's Pizza**'s stock price soared 25% to reach an all-time high after beating Q419 sales and profit expectations. Domino's sees carryout, which currently accounts for nearly half of its orders, as a huge opportunity as the carryout market has stronger margins with 2.5 times as many transactions as the delivery market. Domino's grew its U.S. carryout business 8.1% (3.9% on a same-store basis) in Q4 and sees the opportunity to take friction out of the experience by making it more digital and adding more carry-out windows (it currently has them in 600 of its stores). On the delivery side, although it remained a tough competitive environment, it sequentially improved over Q3 (seekingalpha.com). Looking forward, as we wrote in our October 16 research note, *The Power Shift:* "*with the rising gig economy labour rights movement resulting from the passage of AB5 in California, combined with the expected fallout in unicorn funding, we are thinking the rules of the game may start to change further in the favour of companies like Domino's Pizza who treats its delivery drivers as actual employees.*"

NBCUniversal in talks with Walmart to acquire Vudu

NBCUniversal (**Comcast**) is in advanced talks with **Walmart** to acquire Vudu. With its installed base of 100 milion devices, Walmart's on-demand movie streaming service would complement NBCUniversal's Fandago movie ticketing and rental business, which has 30 million monthly visitors. It would also complement Peacock, the new streaming service that NBCUniversal will be debuting in April to Comcast and Cox Communications customers and in July to all customers (wsj.com).

Ford partners with Nationwide to offer usage-based auto insurance

Ford is partnering with Nationwide to offer usage-based auto insurance on its new connected vehicles. By using built-in modems on select 2020 Ford and Lincoln models to track car and driver data such as distance, idle time, night driving and even how hard you push the pedals, Ford is able to adjust insurance rates to driving habits and offer discounts up to 40% (automotiveworld.com).

Chapter 5: The Next 10 Years

March 3, 2020

I'm excited to share with you that on Friday afternoon I submitted my new book to Amazon. But between the new dystopian reality of the black swan coronavirus and plunging rollercoaster markets, I haven't felt much like celebrating. However, I do look forward to giving many of you a personal calligraphy-signed copy of my book when we meet in early April. As my book is titled "The New Cyber Decade", I've been thinking lately about how the next 10 years will be different than the last 10 years. The big thing is that we are leaving behind the "growth at all costs" decade of high-flying unprofitable unicorns, exploitive sharing/gig economy platforms and the Milton Friedman shareholder-centric business doctrine. On this note, sustainability will take centre stage as CEOs follow the lead of Jeff Bezos and Satya Nadella and ring the alarm bell on climate change. As illustrated by my Value Pyramid, the value equation will be not only be shaped by the Fourth Industrial Revolution, but also by the merging of technology with humanity.

Amazon is disrupting food retail with the opening of first Amazon Go Grocery

On February 25, **Amazon** opened its first Amazon Go Grocery store in Capitol Hill in Seattle. At 10,400 square feet, the store is five times the size of Amazon Go but it is more of a neighbourhood market at only one-quarter the size of a typical grocery store. The store stocks 5,000 items, including fresh produce, dairy, bakery treats, packaged seafood, household goods, meal kits, and beer and wine. To remove complexities such as weighing of items from the buying process, each item is priced individually (cnbc.com). In addition to Amazon Go Grocery, Amazon is opening a new chain of grocery stores in the U.S., targeting middle-income consumers living outside urban cores. Amazon is looking to directly fulfill online orders from these stores as it is partnering with automation specialist Dematic (**Kion Group**) to add a micro-fulfillment section to its first grocery store in Woodland Hills, California. The 7,200-square-foot micro-fulfillment section will comprise just over 20% of the new 33,500-square-foot grocery store and store packaged food and alcoholic beverages (chainstoreage.com).

Dow plunges over 3,500 points last week as coronavirus explodes in South Korea, Italy & Iran

In the past week, the number of total cases of the coronavirus has risen 13% to 90,284, while the number of related deaths has risen 17% to 3,085, resulting in the death rate rising slightly from 3.3% to 3.4%. The good news is the spread of the coronavirus in Mainland China continues to slow, with the number of reported cases rising only 3.7% in the past week, from 77,150 to 80.026. However, it is absolutely frightening how fast the coronavirus is spreading outside Mainland China as the number of confirmed cases more than quadrupled in the past week from 2,403 to 10,258 with three countries accounting for over three quarters of the new cases: South Korea, Italy and Iran.

In South Korea, the number of coronavirus cases has exploded the past week from 833 to 4,335, with nearly 60% of the infected being members of the cult-like Shincheonji Church of Jesus. The situation is so dire that the mayor of Seoul is suing the leaders of the church *"for murder, injury and violation of prevention and management of infectious*

41

diseases" (reuters.com). In Northern Italy, the number of cases has exploded nearly ten-fold the past week, from 230 to 2,036, and the number of people under lockdown has doubled from 50,000 to 100,000. The situation has worsened in Iran, where the number of cases in the past week has skyrocketed by 24-fold, from 61 to 1,501, although it is expected the actual number could be much higher. Iran is deploying drones to disinfect the streets and is mobilizing 300,000 teams to conduct door-to-door coronavirus checks (wsj.com). Although there has not been a major outbreak yet here at home, the number of cases the past week has nearly tripled in the U.S. (from 35 to 100) and Canada (from 10 to 27).

Walmart looking to add 5G to improve in-store digital health services as it opens second Walmart Health store

Walmart is in discussions with **Verizon Communications** to install rooftop antennas to test 5G services in some of its stores. Specifically, Walmart is looking to improve its digital health services, as 5G offers lower latency, enables real-time communications and improves network security. For example, customers in the store could stream video communications with doctors over their smartphones (wsj.com). This comes as Walmart opens a second Walmart Health following higher-than-expected patient volume at its first supercentre for basic healthcare services that it opened in Georgia in September. Walmart Health is a stand-alone concept store that offers primary care, dental, optometry, auditory and behavioural health services, as well as laboratory tests and X-rays and wellness education. Walmart seems to be focusing on the state of Georgia for Walmart Health as it opened its second in Calhoun and its third will open in Loganville this summer (beckershospitalreview.com).

Walmart developing Amazon Prime competitor as it integrates online/offline buying process

Walmart is developing a competitor to Amazon Prime called Walmart+ that it will begin testing publicly this month (cnbc.com). It's interesting as it was only back in September that Walmart rolled out Delivery Unlimited, its grocery delivery membership program for $98 per year. And now it seems like Walmart is looking to expand the selection beyond groceries. The problem though is that Walmart will have to price it below Amazon Prime, which is only $119 a year and includes Amazon Prime Video and ad-supported Amazon Music. This comes as Walmart starts to integrate the buying process between its physical and e-commerce distribution channels as it combines its offline and online product buying teams. As part of the restructuring, Walmart will be creating six category teams, with the consumable and food group immediately beginning joint buying (wsj.com). We note this follows Walmart's move back in June to integrate Jet.com into its e-commerce layer.

CPGs re-embrace glass packaging with Loop as Just Eat develops recyclable takeout box

With the introduction of new circular economy shopping platforms like Loop, CPG companies are starting to re-embrace glass as they look to design containers that are refillable, fully recyclable, and provide a longer shelf life for food and drinks. It's interesting as according to the Beverage Marketing Corporation, back in 1975, the use of glass in soda bottles was 58% but has since fallen to 1% as the beverage industry has embraced plastic, which doesn't break and is lighter to transport (wsj.com). Delivery platforms are also looking for sustainability solutions as **Just Eat** has developed a fully recyclable takeout box. The takeout box, which is made from tree and grass pulp and lined with seaweed with no synthetic additives, will decompose in four weeks in a home compost. Just Eat is testing the recyclable takeout box with its three restaurant partners in London (cnbc.com).

Apple Watch overtakes Swiss watch industry, RenalytixAI develops lab-based AI tools for Americans with kidney disease

The wristwatch is moving up to the digital and AI layers. Sales of the **Apple** Watch overtook those of all Swiss watch brands for the first time last year. According to Strategy Analytics, sales of the Apple Watch rose 36% last year to 31 million units while sales of Swiss watch brands like **The Swatch Group**'s Swatch and Tissot and **LVMH**'s TAG Heuer declined 13% to 21 million units (theverge.com). As Apple crowdsources health data collected by its Apple Watches, RenaltytixAI has developed an AI clinical diagnostic tool that predicts a person's chance of developing kidney disease as well as a lab-based AI tool that predicts the risk of adverse transplant incomes, including early kidney rejection. This is a major breakthrough as the U.S. spends $100 billion annually to treat the nearly 40 million Americans with chronic kidney disease. In addition, 23% of people on kidney dialysis die each year owing to the shortage of donor organs as 100,000 are added to the transplant list each year while there are only 21,000 donor organs available (cnbc.com).

Amazon in talks with WeWork to acquire iconic Lord & Taylor flagship in NYC

Amazon is rumoured to be in talks with WeWork to acquire the iconic Lord & Taylor century-old flagship luxury department store on Fifth Avenue in Manhattan for as much as $1 billion (therealdeal.com). We note that back in July, Amazon was in talks to lease the entire 12-storey building from WeWork, which WeWork bought from **Hudson's Bay Company** in October 2017 for $850 million.

JPMorgan Chase announces sustainability initiatives as Alphabet looks to save the ocean

On February 25, at **JPMorgan Chase**'s Investor Day, CEO Jamie Dimon announced his firm's sustainability initiatives. In addition to pledging to facilitate $200 billion in environmental and economic development deals this year, JPMorgan will impose restrictions on financing new coal-fired power plants and phase out credit exposure to the industry by 2024 and stop funding oil & gas drilling projects in the Arctic (cnbc.com). Although these initiatives are a positive step, the reality is that JPMorgan is currently the world's largest investor in the fossil-fuel industry, having lent out $196 billion in the past three years (rollingstone.com). We note that back on December 15, **Goldman Sachs** made a similar sustainability pledge. Speaking of sustainability, **Alphabet**'s moonshot division just unveiled Tidal, its new ocean sustainability initiative. For the past three years, Tidal has been logging the behaviour and environment of thousands of fish by tracking and monitoring them using underwater cameras and machine perception tools (cnbc.com).

Westfield's expanded mall in Silicon Valley adds small section for DTC brands

Westfield Valley Fair (**Unibail-Rodamco-Westfield**) in Silicon Valley is devoting a new The Digital District section in its expanded mall to feature eight DTC brands. However, at 10,000 square feet, The Digital District only accounts for 2% of the mall's 500,000-square-foot expansion. In addition, it seems like more of an incubator for DTC brands to graduate to a real store as the landlord is offering leases on a percentage basis for only a 12-month duration and is supporting build-outs with the inclusion of RetailNext technology and assistance with music and licensing systems (bisnow.com). We note the fifth floor of **Nordstrom**'s newly opened seven-floor Manhattan flagship store is called Pop in @Nordstrom and features a rotating selection of DTC brands every few weeks.

Uber makes it easier to message your driver with launch of in-app language translation tool

Uber just launched an in-app messaging language translation tool to enable international travelers to communicate with drivers. The tool integrates with Google Translate and is available in over 100 languages (venturebeat.com).

The hammer starts to come down on gig economy companies for misclassifying workers

A San Diego judge just issued a preliminary injunction against Instacart for misclassifying its shoppers as independent contractors. This could be a critical step in enforcing AB5 against Instacart and other gig economy platform companies (theverge.com). The hammer is also coming down on gig economy companies in Canada as the Ontario Labour Relations Board has ruled that Foodora delivery workers are not independent contractors, but dependent contractors. This is precedent setting for the gig economy as this ruling gives Foodora delivery workers the right to now unionize with the Canadian Union of Postal Workers, as they attempted to do last August (cbc.ca). We note that in September, Foodora delivery workers in Norway reached a collective bargaining agreement following a five-week strike that will guarantee compensation for equipment used on the job (e.g., bikes, clothes, smartphones) and an annual wage increase for full-time workers of $1,647. Meanwhile, in NYC, the City Council is looking to introduce legislation to regulate food delivery platforms like **Grubhub** and Uber Eats whose business practices are hurting local restaurants. They are looking at a number of measures, including limiting the commission to 10%, disclosing to consumers the fees/commissions they charge restaurants and requiring them to be licensed through the city's Department of Consumer Affairs (nytimes.com).

Just Eat offering ice cream delivery via drone in Dublin as Grubhub launches delivery subscription program

Students at University College Dublin will soon be able to receive Ben & Jerry's (**Unilever**) ice cream via drone delivery. Just Eat is partnering with Manna Drone Delivery on the commercial pilot which will launch next month and promises delivery in under three minutes (silliconrepublic.com). We note Manna Drone Delivery has raised $5 million in seed capital since launching its "Drone Delivery as a Service" in 2018 to restaurant chains, dark kitchens and online food delivery platforms like Just Eat. On the demand side, to increase customer retention, Grubhub is launching a delivery subscription program. For a cost of $9.99 per month for Grubhub+, customers will receive free unlimited delivery from participating restaurants and 10% cash back on orders. College students at 150 campuses will receive Grubhub+ for free. The problem with this idea is that Grubhub is just copying its competitors like Postmates and DoorDash, who have not had much success with their subscription programs with less than 20% adoption rate (forbes.com).

Panera Bread launches coffee subscription program

Panera Bread is launching a coffee subscription program for members of its loyalty program. For a monthly cost of $8.99, you will receive a free cup of coffee, iced coffee or hot tea a day. This seems like win-win for customers — if you order a large cup of coffee, which retails for $2.25, the payback is only four visits. And it looks like it will be a win-win for Panera — during its test, the number of monthly visits rose from 4 to 10 with food sales increasing 70% and nearly one-quarter of subscribers becoming new members of its loyalty program (cnbc.com). This seems like better value than the BK Café subscription program launched last March by Burger King (**Restaurant Brands International**) which offered a $1 small cup of coffee per day for $5 per month.

Toyota invests $400 million in autonomous driving start-up

Toyota Motor just made a $400 million strategic investment in Pony.ai, a start-up that builds full-stack autonomous driving solutions. Toyota is the lead investor in the $462 million Series B round for Pony.ai, which has raised $726 million since launching in Freemont, California in 2016. Toyota is also partnering with Pony.ai on a pilot program in Fremont, offering shared, on-demand autonomous last-mile service for the city's employees (mediapost.com).

Chapter 6: The Ghost Town Economy

March 10, 2020

I just wanted to let you know that Brady will not be participating in tomorrow's spring concert and I sincerely wish the school would consider postponing the event in light of the escalating risk of the coronavirus — it does not seem prudent to bring together students and parents (many of whom travel for business and pleasure) in a crowded gym. We are up to 27 cases in B.C. (which is most likely Vancouver) — for context, in Iran, they had 61 cases just two weeks ago, and now they are up 7,161. And Italy, which is up to 9,172 cases, just extended the quarantine to the entire country.

A week ago, I wouldn't have thought twice about attending a school concert but as you can see from this e-mail that I just sent to my son's elementary school, this is no longer the case. When I shared my e-mail with my husband, he told me my 9-year-old was fine with not going and had told him, "I don't care, I can go global on my YouTube channel".

As fear escalates over the coronavirus, this is causing an acute shift in societal behaviour, which is leading to a rapid transformation of the corporate landscape as it starts to distort all three sides of the value pyramid:

Customer Capital: Originating value through customer value proposi-

tion

The customer capital side of the value pyramid corresponds to Maslow's pyramid as the functional level is about meeting physiological and safety needs, which is all we care about now. Forget the emotional level — the experience economy is totally dead for now. And totally forget the psychological level — self-actualization doesn't matter right now — safety is more important than sustainability and people are avoiding community, but accessibility is good if it doesn't involve contact.

Structural Capital: Capturing value through capital investments

Our physical world is starting to turn into a ghost town, accelerating the shift to online shopping and necessitating the fast adoption of digital technologies. For example, we are starting to see the emergence of ghost schools (students are receiving instruction online), ghost colleges (Stanford, University of Washington and Princeton have announced they will be closing their classrooms and conducting all classes online) and ghost churches (Pope Francis delivered his Sunday sermon online). We are also seeing the widespread cancellation of conference and events like SXSW in Austin (which I was supposed to attend this week!), TED 2020 in Vancouver (which will either be postponed or be held online) and the BNP Parabis Open tennis tournament in Palm Springs. Business travel has also come to an abrupt halt with many companies cancelling all non-essential travel and requesting employees work from home, increasing the demand for video-conferencing platforms like Skype and Zoom. AI is starting to be used to fight the spread of the coronavirus, with the deployment in China of disinfecting robots and drones and fever detection technology.

Economic Capital: Extracting value through economic systems

We are starting to see a bifurcation on the platform economy layer. I'm guessing we will see a big increase in the time people spend online and on social networks as privacy concerns abate and they just care about keeping in touch with friends and family, keeping up-to-date on the latest developments and escaping reality, especially those in quarantine. In terms of the sharing economy, we are starting to see a rise in demand for at-home delivery of groceries, especially as people start to stock up on pantry foods and household goods like toilet paper, disinfecting spray and hand wipes. We could also see a rise in demand for food delivery, especially for those that are quarantined. Ridesharing will also become an attractive option versus public transit for those that can afford it but this could be offset by the disappearance of demand from business and leisure travelers, which will also severely impact Airbnb. I'm thinking that Airbnb could be the hardest hit of all the sharing economy companies as it is likely being hit by a tsunami of cancellations and will see a sharp drop-off in future bookings. On a personal note, I was happy to receive a full refund from my Airbnb host in Austin after I had to cancel my trip to SXSW.

Although it is unknown how long the coronavirus will last, once the fear is gone, I think we will zoom back up the customer capital side to the experience economy and re-embrace sustainability and community. On the positive side, I think the coronavirus will bring to light the lack of safety nets for gig economy workers as well as the strict cancellation policies of Airbnb versus hotels. And at the end of the day, I think it will accelerate the digital transformation of society and permanently shift our behaviour as we discover the time and cost-saving efficiencies of doing things online.

Coronavirus reaches home as cases rise six-fold to over 600 in U.S. and triple to over 70 in Canada

In the past week, the number of total cases of the coronavirus has risen 26% to 113,579, while the number of related deaths has risen 29% to 3,995, resulting in the death rate rising slightly from 3.4% to 3.5%. The spread of the coronavirus in Mainland China continues to slow, with the number of reported cases rising only 0.9% in the past week, from 80,026 to 80,735. However, it is absolutely terrifying how fast the coronavirus is spreading outside Mainland China as the number of confirmed cases more than tripled in the past week from 10,258 to

32,844 with three countries accounting for over 70% of the new cases: South Korea, Italy and Iran.

In South Korea, the number of coronavirus cases rose 73% in the past week, from 4,335 to 7,478, but the country is hopeful its aggressive actions (which includes drive-up testing booths) have led to a peak in the virus as the rate of new infections is starting to finally decline. In Italy, the number of coronavirus cases has completely exploded over the past week, more than quadrupling from 2,036 to 9,172. In response, the government just expanded its lockdown to the entire country. In Iran, the number of cases has also more than quadrupled, from 1,501 to 7,161, although it is still expected the actual number could be much higher. Iran has closed all its schools and universities and is deploying drones to disinfect the streets and public places.

In the past week, the coronavirus has reached home as the number of cases has risen six-fold in the U.S. (from 100 to 607) and more than tripled in Canada (from 27 to 71). Looking forward, the really scary thing is that two weeks ago there were only 61 cases in Iran and 230 cases in Italy.

Amazon raises delivery bar for retailers with opening of mini-fulfillment centres

Amazon is opening mini-fulfillment centres in cities to bring faster same-day delivery of up to 3 million items to Prime members. The mini-fulfillment centres are 100,000 square feet, one-tenth the size of a 1 million-square-foot traditional fulfillment centre. Prime members in cities with the new mini-fulfillment centres, like Philadelphia, Phoenix, Orlando and Dallas, will be able to shop during the day as they can now view on Amazon how quickly an item will arrive on their doorstep. In addition to enhancing the convenience value proposition for members, this is a sustainability initiative as it shrinks the carbon footprint by decreasing the need for air transport and reducing the delivery distance (techcrunch.com).

The end of cashiers is near as Amazon starts selling its Amazon Go technology

Amazon is selling its Amazon Go cashierless technology to other retailers. The company has apparently signed deals with retail customers for its "Just Walk Out" technology. Under the deal, Amazon will install the technology, which includes cameras and shelf weight sensors. Instead of scanning the Amazon app to enter the gated turnstile like you do with Amazon Go, you will just need to insert your credit card to enter the store (reuters.com).

Amazon is working on a cure for the common cold

As part of Amazon's healthcare initiatives, it has been secretly working on "Project Gesundheit" the past few years, seeking to find a cure for the common cold (cnbc.com). I just wish Amazon was working on finding a cure for the coronavirus.

Online panic buying leads to delivery delays for Amazon and Walmart

We are seeing an online panic buying spree as households stock up on pantry food and household products like toilet paper, hand wipes and disinfecting spray. This is leading to delays for both Amazon Prime Now's same-day delivery service and **Walmart**'s next-day grocery delivery service (cnbc.com). Interestingly, Walmart is integrating grocery services (which was a separate app) into its Walmart app (businessinsider.com). This follows just a week after Walmart disclosed it will soon begin testing a competitor to Amazon Prime called Walmart+.

Target looks to open smaller-format convenience-like stores

Target's Q419 sales rose 3.7% to $23.0 billion and EPS 11% to $1.69. It achieved a 1.5% same-store-sales (SSS) growth, with digital sales rising 20%. Target's sales for its same-day fulfillment options drove 80% of its e-commerce sales growth through its pick-up, drive-up and Shipt distribution channels. On the conference call, the company disclosed how sales through Shipt have increased 2.5 times over the past year. In addition, over the past year, Target has reduced its average online fulfillment cost per unit by 25%. The company is also looking to sign a lease this year for a 6,000-square-foot space to open a convenience-like store offering products like beauty, home and grab-and-go food next year. If it is successful, Target sees the potential to open hundreds of these convenience stores which will provide the added benefit of offering more convenient pick-up spots for online orders (seekingalpha.com).

Waymo raises $2.25 billion to fund expansion of autonomous driving operations

Alphabet's Waymo just raised $2.25 billion in a venture round from its first set of outside investors to fund the expansion of its autonomous driving operations. Alphabet itself invested in the round and remains the majority owner and brought in strategic investors such as **Magna International**, **AutoNation** and even the Canadian Pension Plan Investment Board. Waymo also announced the launch of Waymo Via, its new trucking goods delivery service (cnbc.com).

Cities in China using AI to fight coronavirus

Cities in China are ascending up to the AI layer of the structural capital side of the value pyramid to fight against the coronavirus. For example, the city of Guangahou is deploying robots and drones to disinfect areas potentially contaminated with virus and bacteria. Meanwhile, the city of Beijing is starting to screen citizens at one of its railway stations by using fever detection technology from **Baidu** that uses infrared sensors and AI to predict temperatures (venturebeat.com).

Brooklinen, a rare profitable DTC start-up, raises $50 million

Brooklinen, a DTC bed linen company, just raised $50 million. But unlike many DTC start-ups, Brooklinen has not pursued a "growth at all costs" strategy as it has only raised $10 million since it launched in

NYC in 2014 and is actually profitable. In January, Brooklinen opened its first physical store in Brooklyn and it plans to use the funds to open more physical stores and expand internationally (techcrunch.com). Ironically, the theme of Amazon's new pop-up store in Seattle is "Everything Sleep. From A to Zzz" and it features a selection of AmazonBasics-branded bed linen, as well as mattresses and Echo devices (geekwire.com). Amazon is using pop-up stores to enhance its emotional connection with customers as instead of just offering a selection of goods, it is curating items from its private-label brands and third-party sellers to tell a story and create an experience. For example, the themes at its other five stores have included **Mattel's** Barbie's 50th Anniversary and Fisher Price's "Let's Be Kids" and an Audible reading room.

Quibi raises $750 million ahead of debut of new video streaming service

Quibi just raised $750 million as it prepares to launch its new video streaming service on April 6, following its $1 billion seed round in July. Quibi is looking to differentiate itself from the crowded streaming space as it offers short-form content (under 10 minutes per episode) designed for watching on smartphones. It was founded in LA in 2018 by Jeffrey Katzenberg, the co-founder of DreamWorks and former Chairman of **Walt Disney** Studios, and Meg Whitman, the former CEO of **HP**. Quibi has lined up a strong base of advertising partners, including **Procter & Gamble, T-Mobile, PepsiCo, Anheuser-Busch InBev, Walmart, Progressive**, Google, Taco Bell (**Yum! Brands** and **General Mills** (deadline.com).

Uber & Lyft will compensate workers infected with coronavirus

Gig economy workers are highly vulnerable in the face of the coronavirus as they come into contact with strangers as part of their job yet lack the safety net of having health benefits and being covered by workers' compensation and unemployment insurance. To provide them with some protection, **Uber** has committed to compensate both Uber and Uber Eats drivers worldwide if they are infected with the coronavirus or quarantined by a public health agency for a period of up to 14 days. **Lyft** has also made a similar commitment (engadget.com). In addition, Uber and Lyft are in talks with DoorDash, Postmates and Instacart about joining forces to set up a fund to compensate workers in the U.S. that are infected or quarantined (wsj.com). To enable for non-contact delivery, Postmates has introduced Dropoff Options (theverge.com). Likewise, Instacart has introduced a new feature called "Leave at My Door Delivery" (cnn.com).

France rules Uber drivers have right to be recognized as employees

"When connecting to the Uber digital platform, a relationship of sub-ordination is established between the driver and the company. Hence, the driver does not provide services as a self-employed person, but as an employee." This statement came from France's top court as it ruled that Uber drivers have the right to be recognized as employees (reuters.com). This ruling could have direct ramifications for gig economy platforms in France such as Uber Eats, Deliveroo and **Just Eats** and, more importantly, add fire to the rising gig economy labour rights movement.

UBS pledges to stop funding new oil & gas projects in Arctic

On March 7, **UBS** announced it would no longer provide financing for new offshore oil & gas drilling projects in the Arctic. According to a recent study by Rainforest Action Network, UBS invested $300 million between 2016 and 2018 on Arctic oil & gas projects (adn.com). We note UBS follows similar sustainability pledges recently made by **Goldman Sachs** and **JPMorgan Chase**.

WeWork sells recently acquired Managed by Q for rock-bottom price of $25 million

WeWork has sold Managed by Q for apparently only $25 million,

55

a small fraction of the $220 million it paid for the office services management platform last April. Managed by Q, which offers office services ranging from cleaning and maintenance to supply replenishment and wellness, is being acquired by Eden, a competing workplace management platform. Eden raised a $25 million Series B round in November and recently raised a new $29 million round led by JLL (techcrunch.com).

Chapter 7: LOCKDOWN

March 17, 2020

We're keeping the boys home from school... I'm cancelling my WeWork membership, putting my Equinox membership on hold and pulling the boys out of spring camp...they just discovered three coronavirus cases at the seniors' home two blocks from us...they've closed the West Vancouver Rec Centre...you need to stop socializing with your friends...Trump just closed down the U.S. border to Europeans...they've closed down Science World, Whistler and Cypress Mountain...you should think about coming home...the number of coronavirus cases in B.C. has risen to 73... ...Trudeau just closed Canada's borders to foreigners and is urging all Canadians to come home...San Francisco just put the city on lockdown and France is forcing people to stay inside their homes.

As I look out the window of my makeshift office in my bedroom, my mind races with anxiety and panic. For over the past five days, the discussions I have had with my snowbird parents have escalated from pleading with them to stop shaking hands with people, to stop socializing with their friends, to book a flight home from Palm Springs now. Everyone needs to start self-isolating — and soon, the government will do that for us like they just did in San Francisco.

On March 16, San Francisco issued a Public Health order lockdown for the next three weeks, requiring all non-essential businesses to close and legally prohibiting people from leaving their homes, except to meet basic needs, including visiting the doctor and buying groceries or medicine. However, people will still be allowed to go outdoors to take a walk, exercise or take a pet out as long as they remain at least 6-feet away from any non-household member. Restaurants are allowed to remain open for takeout and delivery only. As part of the lockdown, all non-essential travel out of San Francisco is also prohibited (sfexaminer.com). Although this is severe, it isn't as bad as in France which just imposed an even stricter 15-day lockdown that forces people to stay inside their homes and not even go for a walk (thelocalfr.com).

As I discussed in last week's research note, "The Ghost Town Economy", the coronavirus pandemic is quickly turning our world into a dystopian ghost town. As we've witnessed in the past week, and notably the past few days, this is creating an acute shift in not just societal behaviour, but now corporate behaviour. This will act as a catalyst to disrupt even faster all three sides of the value pyramid and quickly accelerate the digital transformation of society. For we are now at war against the coronavirus and to survive, both individuals and companies will need to go on lockdown and embrace the digital world as we leave behind the physical world.

Coronavirus pandemic hits home as cases skyrocket to 4,237 in the U.S. and 415 in Canada

In the past week, the coronavirus pandemic hit home with the number of coronavirus cases skyrocketing in the U.S. by seven-fold (from 607 to 4,287) and in Canada by nearly six-fold (from 71 to 415). As of the time of writing (2:08 Pacific Time on March 16), the number of total cases of coronavirus has exploded in the past week by 59% to 181,127, while the number of related deaths has risen 78% to 7,114, resulting in the death rate rising from 3.5% to 3.9%. The spread of the coronavirus in Mainland China continues to slow, with the number of reported cases rising only 1.0% in the past week, from 80,735 to 81,032.

However, it is scary how fast the coronavirus is spreading outside Mainland China as the number of confirmed cases once again more than tripled this week from 32,844 to 100,095. More importantly, the coronavirus is starting to explode beyond the initial outbreak zones of South Korea, Italy and Iran, which now account for just over half of cases, down from over 70% just last week. Europe became the epicentre of new outbreaks, with the number of coronavirus cases surging to 9,942 in Spain, 7,272 in Germany and 6,650 in France.

It is absolutely terrifying what is happening in Italy as the number of cases has tripled in the past week from 9,172 to 27,980, despite the government imposing a draconian lockdown on the entire country a week ago. What is even more frightening is that because of its more elderly population, it is experiencing a much higher related death rate of 7.7%. In Iran, the number of cases has doubled from 7,161 to 14,991, although it is still expected the actual number could be much higher. South Korea's aggressive actions (which includes drive-up testing booths) have led to a peak in the virus as the number of coronavirus cases in the past week rose by only 10%, from 7,478 to 8,236.

Panic buying of consumer staples leads to stock outs at grocery stores and on Amazon

As cities start to shut down, we are seeing panic buying of consumer staples in grocery stores, both physical and online. **Amazon** is not able to keep up with demand caused by online panic buying of households stocking up. In addition to running out of stock on household staple items, its logistics network is being overwhelmed and same-day and next-day deliveries are being delayed by several days (cnbc.com). To meet the unprecedented surge in e-commerce demand, Amazon is hiring an additional 100,000 employees and is temporarily raising wages by $2 per hour through April (wsj.com).

Amazon debuts "Just Walk Out" technology at Newark airport as traffic plummets

Amazon's timing for launching its "Just Walk Out" technology at OTG's CIBO Express store at Newark airport is off as airport traffic is set to plummet with airlines reducing capacity and borders shutting down (cnbc.com). It's interesting as back in October we shared how Amazon was looking to bring its Amazon Go cashierless technology to airports, movie theatres and concession stands at baseball stadiums and was in talks with OTG. OTG operates over 300 in-terminal dining locations in 10 airports and with Regal Theatres (**Cineworld Group**). But this is likely to be delayed as movie theatres and baseball stadiums go dark.

A tsunami of retail bankruptcies is starting to build

We expect to see a tsunami of retailer bankruptcies as the physical world shuts down. A good way to determine the survivors though is to make note of which retailers were the most proactive to shut down, which means they are confident in the loyalty of their community and their ability to shift their sales online. Patagonia stands out as the most proactive retailer — on March 13, it announced that it would be suspending its business operations, closing all its stores and online operations: *"Dear Patagonia community, As COVID-19 spreads — and is now officially a pandemic — we are taking additional safety measures to protect our employees and customers. The scale of impact is still unknown, and we want to do our part to protect our community especially while testing availability is unknown."* (cnbc.com).

lululemon was also among the first retailers to proactively respond with its CEO, Calvin McDonald, tweeting on March 13: *"As we navigate this rapidly changing situation, the health and safety of our employees and the @lululemon community continues to be our highest priority. Today,* *we announced to limit store hours in NA and established a Global Relief Pay plan for our people.*" Then on March 16, he tweeted "*In light of the rapidly changing COVID-19 developments, @lululemon has decided today to close all stores in North America & Europe from March 16-March 27*".

On March 14, **Apple** announced it would be closing all its stores outside Greater China. On Sunday, a wave of retailers announced they would also be proactively closing their stores. This list includes privately held retailers (Columbia Sportswear, Lush, REI), publicly traded retailers (**Abercrombie & Fitch, Aritzia, Levi Strauss & Co., Under Armour, VF Corp., Urban Outfitters**) and DTC retailers (Allbirds, Away, Everlane, Glossier, Outdoor Voices, Peloton, Rent the Runway, Warby Parker). As a red flag, **Gap** is not closing its store, only cutting hours of operation. To allow for overnight cleaning of its stores, **Walmart** is reducing the hours of its stores open 24 hours to 6am–11pm (cnbc.com).

Retail REITs are in danger as store closures create dystopian ghost malls

On March 12, **Intu Properties**, the U.K. retail REIT, warned it could go bankrupt (bbc.com). We note Intu warned in late January that it was seeking to raise emergency cash of up to £1 billion by the end of February to shore up its balance sheet, which is weighed down by nearly £5 billion of debt. As a red flag of things to come for retail REITs, on March 16, **Macerich** cut its dividend by one-third, from $0.75 to $0.50, and shifted the form of payment from cash to 80% stock/20% cash (marketwatch.com).

Theme parks are becoming ghost towns as Disneyland shuts down

On March 12, **Disney** announced that it would be shutting down Disneyland, Disney World, Disneyland Paris and its Disney Cruise line (wsj.com). The American Dream Mall, a mega theme park mall, which started operations in late October, is also shutting down and postponing its grand opening that was scheduled for this week (cnbc.com). This is not surprising given 55% of the 90-acre mall in New Jersey is focused on experiences, featuring a professional-sized ice rink, Nickelodeon Universe (**Viacom**) theme park and a DreamWorks WaterPark, with plans to open a Legoland Discovery Centre and Sea Life Aquarium this spring, as well as a luxury movie theatre, performing arts theatre and ferris wheel. The problem is that the Ghermezian family's Triple Five has mortgaged nearly half its stake in West Edmonton Mall and the Mall of America to spend $5.7 billion on the new American Dream mall.

As traffic plummets 47%, restaurants will need to shift to a "to go" model for survival

According to data shared by OpenTable (**Bookings Holdings**), restaurant traffic (including phone, online and walk-in diners) on a global basis turned negative starting March 2, went down double digits on March 9 and was down 47% year-over-year on March 15. Interestingly, traffic is down equally in the U.S. and Canada (down 48% and 47%, respectively), although there are regional differences as traffic is down only 38% in B.C. versus 53% in Ontario, and on a city-level basis traffic is down the most in San Francisco at 72% (docs.google.com). We expect the numbers will plummet as more and more restaurants are forced to close their doors as the lockdown intensifies. To survive, restaurants will need to shift now to a "to go" model. For example, **Starbucks** is shifting to a "to go" model, offering only pick-up and delivery as it proactively removes seating. Starbucks is also closing stores in high-traffic areas like malls and reducing operating hours and closing select stores in areas of cities like Seattle and NYC with clusters of coronavirus cases (cnbc.com). Tim Hortons (**Restaurant Brands International**) is also shifting to a "to go" model as it closes its dining rooms, offering only take-out and drive-thru service (financialpost.com). **The Second Cup** has also moved to a "to go" model and is taking additional steps such as shutting down its self-serve stations and no longer accepting cash (secondcup.com).

Companies are taking war-like measures to produce needed medical supplies

LVMH has quickly re-purposed its factories that make perfume and makeup for its Christian Dior and Givenchy luxury brands to instead make hand sanitizer. And LVMH is not looking to make a profit as it will be giving the hand sanitizer for free to French authorities and Europe's largest hospital system, the Assistance Publique-Hôpitaux de Paris (cnbc.com). U.K. Health Secretary, Matt Hancock, has called on British manufacturers to switch parts of their production to make medical ventilators. The U.K. needs to ramp up its production of ventilators as it currently only has 5,000 in stock. The government is looking for help from automobile manufacturers like **Rolls-Royce**, **Ford**, **Honda**, Vauxhall (**Peugeot**), as well as industrial equipment manufacturer JCB and logistics and manufacturing consultancy firm Unipart (theguardian.com). As industrial medical supply chains struggle to keep pace, 3D printing is now being used to save lives in Italy. In Brescia, Issonova, a local 3D-printer start-up, came to the rescue of a hospital with 250 coronavirus patients that had run out of respirator valves and whose supply had also run out. In 24 hours, Issonova was able to design and print 100 respirator valves (bbc.com).

Google and Amazon are leading the digital health rescue mission

Verily, **Alphabet**'s healthcare unit, just launched its pilot COVID-19 screening and testing website in the San Francisco Bay Area. High-risk individuals that meet eligibility and requirements for testing will be directed to mobile testing sites in San Mateo and Santa Clara countries. Verily stated that it will scale capacity as more testing kits become available. Verily is working in partnership with the U.S. federal government, the state of California and local public health authorities (cnbc.com). In Seattle, Amazon is in talks with the Bill &

Melinda Gates Foundation and local public health organizations about delivering at-home coronavirus testing kits to people in the Seattle area. The goal is to process thousands of tests per day and deliver kits in just a few hours (cnbc.com). We believe this could provide Amazon with the opportunity to expand Amazon Care, its private healthcare clinic offering that it started piloting with its employees in Seattle in September. We note that in October, Amazon acquired Health Navigator, a digital healthcare start-up that routes patients to the right place by using online symptom checking and triage tools. It has been integrating Health Navigator into the digital layers (i.e., care chat, video care) of Amazon Care. **Uber** is also doing its part, offering to deliver free meals to healthcare workers and first responders. It will also waive delivery fees for over 100,000 independent restaurants (cnbc.com).

Zoom is emerging as a saviour as offices and schools close

On March 13, **Zoom** announced that it would provide its cloud video conferencing tools free for K-12 schools in Japan, Italy and the U.S. The country is also offering free basic accounts by request to schools in a number of other countries, including Austria, Denmark, France, Ireland, Poland, Romania and South Korea (forbes.com). As more and more people are forced to start working from home, Zoom is emerging as one of the most in-demand software tools, as evidenced by its current ranking as the #2 free app on the Apple App Store. Canadian telecommunications firms **Telus**, **Rogers** and Bell (**BCE**) are doing their part to help us work from home by waiving data usage caps on home Internet as well as long-distance and roaming fees (globalnews.ca).

Movies will start moving online as theatres start closing

As the closure of movie theatres across the country accelerates, Universal (**Comcast**) has made the radical decision to disrupt the traditional 90-day window, making *Trolls World Tour* available online when it debuts in the theatre on April 10. In addition, it will be making several movies that are in theatres now, such as *The Invisible Man*, *The Hunt* and *Emma* available online as early as Friday. But Universal is only following this simultaneous omnichannel distribution strategy for low to mid-tier budget movies as it has decided to push back the release date of its high-budget movie, *F9*, by a year to next April (cnbc.com).

Fitness classes will start moving online as gyms start closing

On Monday morning, I decided to skip Equinox — on Friday morning, I called to put my membership on hold. Although Equinox has yet to shut down, I am guessing all gyms will soon become ghost towns as they are forced to close. The good news is that Equinox is going digital — soon members will be able to access a streaming platform with on-demand fitness content such as yoga, HIIT and spin classes. On March 13, Equinox started beta testing the Variis app with its members in Austin (which I'm guessing was chosen to coincide with SXSW, which has been cancelled) and will then roll it out to all members. It is also directly competing with **Peloton** as it just started pre-selling its SoulCycle at-home bike for $2,500 (versus $2,950 for Peloton) and $40 for access to the Variis app (similar to the $40 monthly membership fee for Peloton) (refinery29.com).

U.S. Department of Defense is re-evaluating JEDI contract

On March 12, the U.S. Department of Defense stated that it wishes to re-evaluate its decision to award the JEDI (Joint Enterprise Defense Infrastructure) cloud services contract to **Microsoft**. This is material as the JEDI contract could be worth as much as $10 billion over the next decade (cnn.com). We note that on January 22 Amazon filed a motion to halt Microsoft's work on the JEDI contract until a court rules on its protest of the award, and on February 13 a federal court ordered a temporary block on Microsoft's work.

Chapter 8: WAR

March 24, 2020

The coronavirus pandemic is reaching panic stage here at home, with the number of cases exploding the past week by 10 times in the U.S. to over 43,000 and by five times in Canada to over 2,000. As the U.S. invokes the Defense Production Act, we are seeing more and more companies taking war-time measures, with auto and auto parts makers looking to re-tool their factories to produce ventilators, apparel manufacturers making masks and gowns, and brewers and distillers making hand sanitizers. We are also starting to see now vacant hotels, dorms, sports arenas and convention centres being turned into makeshift hospitals. Essential retailers, facing an unprecedented surge in demand, are calling in the troops, hoping to hire hundreds of thousands of recently unemployed service workers.

Tech companies are also being called to duty, launching R&D initiatives to combat coronavirus and voice assistants and chatbots to consult with us on if we have come down with coronavirus. We are also seeing an online cultural renaissance as educators, fitness instructors, musicians, comedians and performers migrate to livestreaming platforms. And Zoom is becoming a saviour — in addition to using it for work, you might want to try a Zoom dinner date or happy hour — we had a great catch-up visit on Zoom this weekend with our friends in San Francisco and Colorado (but if you have kids, make sure you put them on their IPad first!).

As our days get darker and the reality of our new dystopian ghost town world sets in, we should keep this quote (which went viral last week on Twitter) in mind: "Your grandparents were called to war. You are being called to sit on your couch and watch Netflix. You can do this."

Coronavirus cases explode the past week by 10x in U.S. to 43,214 & 5x in Canada to 2,046

In the past week, the coronavirus pandemic reached panic stage with the number of coronavirus cases exploding in the U.S. by ten-fold (from 4,287 to 43,214) and in Canada by five-fold (from 415 to 2,046). As of the time of writing (4:27pm Pacific Time on March 23), the number of total cases of coronavirus doubled in the past week to 375,458, while the number of related deaths more than doubled to 16,371, resulting in the death rate sharply rising from 3.9% to 4.4%. The coronavirus seems to have stopped spreading in Mainland China as there were only 464 new cases, with the total now at 81,496.

However, it is deadly scary how fast the coronavirus is spreading outside Mainland China as the number of confirmed cases nearly tripled from 100,095 to 293,962. More importantly, the coronavirus is starting to explode beyond the initial outbreak zones of South Korea, Italy and Iran, which now account for only a third of cases, down from over a half just last week. Europe is the epicentre of new outbreaks, with the number of coronavirus cases more than tripling in Spain (from 9,942 to 33,089), quadrupling in France (from 7,272 to 29,056) and more than tripling in France (from 6,650 to 20,123).

It continues to be absolutely terrifying what is happening in Italy as the number of cases more than doubled in the past week from 27,980 to 63,927, despite the government imposing a draconian lockdown on the entire country two weeks ago. What is even more frightening is that because of its more elderly population, it is experiencing a much higher related death rate of 9.5%, which is up from 7.7% last week. In

Iran, the number of cases rose by just over 50% to 23,049, although it is still expected the actual number could be much higher. South Korea's aggressive actions (which includes drive-up testing booths) have led to a peak in the virus as the number of coronavirus cases in the past week rose by only 9%, from 8,236 to 8,961.

Essential goods retailers are going on hiring sprees to meet surging demand

The labour force is quickly shifting down to the base functional level of the customer capital side of the value pyramid to retailers providing essential goods that are allowed to keep their stores open during lockdown. To keep up with the surge in demand, these retailers are going on hiring sprees:

- **Food Retail: Kroger** hired over 2,000 workers last week and currently has over 10,000 job openings, but this does only represent 2.2% of its current base of 460,000 employees. Kroger has reduced its store hours to provide time for additional cleaning and restocking of shelves (cnbc.com).
- **Drug Retail: CVS Health** is looking to immediately hire 50,000 people on a full-time, part-time and temporary basis to work in its stores, distribution centres, and as home delivery drivers and customer service professionals. This is the most ambitious hiring spree in CVS Health's history as it is looking to increase its labour force by 17%. It is also handing out one-time cash bonuses to its on-site employees of $150–$500 (cnbc.com).
- **General Merchandise Stores: Walmart** is looking to hire 150,000 temporary workers by the end of May to work in its clubs, stores, distribution centres and fulfillment centres, increasing its labour force by 10%. To meet this goal, it is expediting the application time from 2 weeks to 24 hours and it expects many of the temporary positions to convert to permanent over time. It is also handing

out one-time cash bonuses of $150-$300. **Dollar Tree** is hiring 25,000 employees, increasing its labour force by 13%. It is looking to hire full-time and part-time employees to work as cashiers and stockers at its 15,000 retail stores and equipment operators at its 24 distribution centres. 7-Eleven (**Seven & I Holdings**) is also looking to hire 20,000 employees to work in its stores (cnn.com).

Trump invokes Defense Production Act

On March 18, Trump invoked the Defense Production Act. This obscure wartime law was passed in 1950 in response to the Korean War to give government greater control to direct industrial production (cnn.com). The three sections of the Act are:

1. **Priorities & Allocations**: Will require companies to accept and prioritize contracts for essential services and materials.
2. **Expansion of Production & Capacity**: Authority to create incentives for industries to produce critical materials.
3. **General Provisions**: Enables government to strike agreements with private industry and create a volunteer block of executives to be called to government service.

On March 19, Trudeau stated that he might invoke Canada's Defence Production Act to ramp up the production of equipment for frontline healthcare workers. Like in the U.S., this act would give the government the authority to force companies to produce the needed equipment (ipolitics.ca).

Companies are re-tooling factories to produce hand sanitizers, ventilators and masks, and converting hotels into hospitals

We are seeing more companies start to take war-like measures to produce much-needed medical supplies and services:

- Auto and auto parts companies making ventilators
- Apparel manufacturers making masks and gowns
- Alcoholic beverage companies making hand sanitizers
- Hotels, dorms, sports arenas & convention centres being used as hospitals

Auto and Auto Parts Companies Making Ventilators

Medtronic PLC, Koninklijke Philips NV, Draegerwerk AG and **Getinge AB**, the biggest suppliers of medical ventilators and related respiratory equipment, are ramping up production to meet surging global demand (wsj.com). But they need help, so **GM** and **Ford**, which are closing their North American factories, are in talks with the White House about supporting the production of medical equipment like ventilators, which are in short supply. GM and Ford would not be looking to re-tool their factories but use the extra space in their factories to manufacture the ventilators (cnbc.com). Canadian auto parts makers like **Linamar, Magna International** and **Martinrea** are also in discussions with the Ontario government about how they could use their production facilities and workers to produce ventilators (finance.yahoo.ca). Elon Musk is also working on making ventilators. He said it will not be difficult as **Tesla** makes cars with sophisticated HVAC systems and SpaceX makes spacecraft with life support systems but warned they can't be produced instantly (usatoday.com).

Apparel manufacturers making masks and gowns

On March 18, California's Governor, Gavin Newsom, shared that hospitals are becoming so desperate that they are going to the LA garment district to ask seamstresses to make masks (businessinsider.com). We are starting to see apparel manufacturers switching their sewing production to making masks and gowns. For example, **Canada Goose** is in talks with the Ontario government to use its sewing production to make medical gowns (finance.yahoo.ca), while 1083, a French blue jeans producer, has shifted its production to makeshift sanitary masks to give to hospitals across France (wsj.com). Even companies that are experiencing a surge in demand are pitching in. **Razer**, the Irvine-based global gaming hardware manufacturing company, is converting some of its existing manufacturing lines to make surgical masks. Razer plans to donate up to a million surgical masks to countries around the world (forbes.com).

Alcoholic beverages companies making hand sanitizers

Labatt Breweries (**Anheuser-Busch InBev**) is re-tooling its beer-making facilities to make hand sanitizer. Initially, Labatt will produce 50,000 bottles to donate to Food Banks Canada, frontline workers and restaurant partners (cbc.ca). Meanwhile, **Pernod Ricard SA**, the French spirits giant, is now making hand sanitizer at its U.S. whiskey distilleries in Kentucky, West Virginia and Texas. In Sweden, Absolut Vodka is donating alcohol for the production of hand sanitizer (wsj.com). And Air Co., a NYC-based sustainable vodka start-up, is re-directing 100% of its production capacity to making hand sanitizer, which is made up of 70% ethanol. Air Co.'s award-winning technology pulls a pound of carbon dioxide from the air which it combines with water to turn into pure ethanol using solar energy. Air Co. is working with NYC officials to donate the hand sanitizer to local restaurants to give to their food delivery workers (techcrunch.com).

Hotels, dorms, sports arenas & convention centres being used as makeshift hospitals

In New York, the U.S. Army Corps of Engineers plans to take over as many as 10,000 hotel rooms, college dorms and even sports arenas in NY to re-purpose them into hospitals. Apparently, the Army Corps can turns these venues into ICU-like facilities in just a few days (nypost.com). In Baltimore, the city is turning the Convention Centre and adjacent **Hilton** Hotel into a field hospital. In Israel, the Defense Ministry has re-purposed two luxury hotels to serve as quarantine shelters (wsj.com).

A tsunami of retail bankruptcies is building as non-essential retailers are forced to close

The retail apocalypse is being fast-forwarded as we expect to see a tsunami of retail bankruptcies as non-essential businesses and malls are forced to close. **Simon Property Group** was slightly proactive as on March 18 it announced that effective 7 pm the next day it would be temporarily closing all its 200+ malls across the U.S. (cbsnews.com).

Coronavirus is attacking nursing homes

According to the Centers for Medicare and Medicaid Services (CMS), the coronavirus is taking a heavy toll on nursing homes, with at least 146 nursing homes in 27 states across the U.S. having at least one infected patient (wsj.com). Closer to home, the Lynn Valley Care Centre in North Vancouver now has 36 residents and 19 staff infected by the coronavirus with 10 deaths. We believe the fear being created by the outbreak of the coronavirus in seniors' homes could be long-lasting, accelerating the "aging-in-place" movement and negatively impacting Senior REITs.

Airlines repurpose passenger planes to carry cargo as DHL invokes "force majeure"

Airlines are using their empty passenger planes to transport cargo. As airlines have grounded their passenger planes, this has led to a huge loss of air freight capacity in the belly of these planes. For example, passenger planes account for 45% of air freight capacity in Asia and 80% on transatlantic routes. As a result, shipping costs and transit times have doubled. According to Neel Jones Shah, who runs air freight operations for Flexport, the cost of shipping cargo from Shanghai to Chicago has nearly doubled from $3.00–$3.50 to $6.00/kilogram while the time to ship cargo from Hong Kong to Chicago has doubled from 3–5 days to 8 days. Airlines are looking to make extra income by re-purposing their passenger planes to carry cargo but the problem is they are less efficient than cargo planes as a Boeing 777 can only carry 44,000 lb of air freight, one-third the capacity of 125,000 lb of a cargo plane (wired.com). This comes as DHL Global Forwarding (**Deutsche Post**) invokes "force majeure", warning customers that it may be unable to fulfill its ocean and air freight contracts. From a legal sense, this protects DHL from liability for non-performance based on events beyond its control (supplychaindive.com).

Demand surges for CPGs, freezers, desks & air filters as households prepare for lockdown

On March 19, **Amazon** Prime Pantry temporarily closed nationwide as it struggled to fulfill open orders and re-stock items after experiencing a surge in order volumes. Amazon Prime Pantry provides Prime members with access to discounted non-perishable food and household items (cnbc.com). Big-box retailers like Walmart, **Target** and **Best Buy** are also experiencing a temporary surge in demand for a number of different products as households prepare for the new reality of staying at home. With restaurants closing and people panicking over running out of food, people are rushing out to buy freezers to store frozen food. With offices closed, people are scrambling to set up at-home offices, buying workstations and laptops. With schools closed, people are starting to set up learning stations for their kids, buying desks, laptops and **Apple** iPads. And with concerns over catching the coronavirus, people are rushing out to buy air filters (cnbc.com). Best Buy is making a number of operational changes. It is now doing in-home consultations virtually and is limiting the number of customers in the store at a time to 10–15 (corporate.bestbuy.com). We are also seeing most essential goods retailers introduce special shopping hours for seniors, limit entry of people into the store and make sure they stand at least 6 feet apart while they are lining up or in the store (cnn.com). As a foreshadowing of how our food supply could be interrupted by travel bans, the German government is considering re-deploying newly unemployed workers like restaurant waiters to harvest the fields as border closures have blocked seasonal workers from Eastern Europe (wsj.com).

Costco acquires final-mile logistics firm for $1 billion in cash

On March 18, **Costco** acquired final-mile logistics operator Innovel Solutions for $1 billion in cash from Transform Holdco, the operator of Sears and Kmart. Costco has been a client of Innovel's since 2015, using it to deliver and install large and bulky products like appliances, furniture and mattresses. Innovel currently makes over 4 million deliveries per year, offering 24–48-hour delivery to 85% of U.S. households. Innovel will provide Costco with valuable structural capital in the form of its 11 distribution centres totaling more than 15 million square feet, over 100 final-mile cross-dock centres and dedicated call centres. More importantly, by owning its own e-commerce delivery company, it will enable Costco to take greater control of the delivery experience and customer relationship (businessinsider.com). But we believe Costco will need to make some changes to Innovel's culture as we see a bit of a red flag as it scores poorly on both Glassdoor (3.1 out of 5.0 based on 51 reviews) and Yelp (1.5 out of 5.0 based on 38 reviews in the San Francisco area).

Non-essential businesses are shutting down online too

Just like non-essential businesses are starting to be physically shut down, this is now happening online. Amazon is taking emergency measures as it has started to prioritize medical supplies, household staples and other high-demand products coming into its warehouses from third-party sellers. Third-party sellers can still sell goods on Amazon but will need to handle their own logistics, including storing their goods in other warehouses and arranging delivery for customers (wsj.com).

As restaurant traffic plummets 100% Domino's Pizza looks to hire 10,000 employees

As cities shut down restaurants during the past week, traffic fell off a cliff to zero. According to data shared by OpenTable (**Bookings Holdings**), restaurant traffic (including phone, online and walk-in diners), on a year-over-year basis, plummeted globally from 47% on March 15 to over 80% on March 17 to near 100% on March 19. Traffic followed this pattern in the U.S. and Canada too with all restaurant traffic currently down 100% (opentable.com/state-of-industry). The problem is that most restaurants can't survive by doing just take-out and delivery. The exception is pizza delivery king, **Domino's Pizza**, which is hiring 10,000 employees. It is looking to hire part-time and full-time employees for a number of positions, ranging from delivery drivers to pizza makers to customer service reps to managers to licensed truck drivers for its supply chain centres. Domino's Pizza is ideally positioned to fill the void created by restaurant closures given it employs its own delivery workers and 55% of its orders are delivery (cnbc.com).

To survive the lockdown, small businesses are starting to think out of the box, temporarily pivoting their business models. Balden Specialty Foods, a NY-based wholesaler and distributor, has seen an 85% drop in food service sales to restaurants and schools the past few days. So it is shifting from a B2B to a B2C business model, taking online orders from consumers with a minimum order value of $250. In the U.K., The Cauldron Restaurant, a Bristol-based restaurant, has changed its name to "The Cauldron Dispensary" and is selling takeout chilled ready meals, fruits and veggies and cleaning products and toilet paper (cnbc.com).

Uber & Lyft's ridesharing volumes are plummeting as cities come under lockdown

Uber's ridesharing volumes have dropped as much as 60–70% in cities like Seattle and we expect Uber's ridesharing volumes will continue to plummet as the world increasingly comes under lockdown.

But on the positive side, its multiple lines of business enable it to leverage its network of drivers to deliver food, medicine and basic goods. Uber Health is working with health officials to deliver coronavirus tests and Uber Freight is working with the government to make sure it is involved in the supply chain for critical items. On the financial side, Uber has a cushion of $8.5 billion in cash and the advantage of a highly variable cost structure (techcrunch.com). As **Lyft** is 100% ridesharing, it is in more dire straits than Uber. To attempt to survive, it is looking to expand into delivering medical supplies to the elderly. In addition, it is piloting a state-sponsored meal delivery service in the San Francisco Bay Area for seniors and kids. Lyft's drivers will pick up the meals from centralized distribution facilities and deliver them to specific home-bound seniors and low-income kids (techcrunch.com). As a red flag for both Uber and Lyft, they have yet to pull their scooters off the streets, unlike Lime and Bird. On March 17, Lime suspended service in California, Washington, Italy, France and Spain. On March 18, it suspended service in a further 18 European countries, 19 U.S. states and Canada. Bird has also suspended service across 20 European countries and in some U.S. cities (theverge.com).

CVS opens first drive-up testing location as healthcare industry turns to telemedicine for survival

On March 19, CVS Health opened its first drive-up testing location for coronavirus in the parking lot of one of its drugstores in Worcester County, Massachusetts. This service is available to first responders such as firefighters, police and healthcare workers, not the general public (cnbc.com). Meanwhile, the U.K. is in talks with Amazon and other companies about using their logistics services to ramp up the delivery of coronavirus tests to frontline health workers (reuters.com). The coronavirus pandemic has forced the healthcare industry to adopt telemedicine as a survival mechanism. Hospitals are offering telemedicine training sessions, health care providers are shifting to virtual consults, doctors are meeting with seniors enrolled in Medicare via FaceTime and Skype and hospitals are setting up chatbots, system checkers and telemedicine tools to triage patients (cnbc.com).

Philippine Stock Exchange closes as NYSE moves to fully electronic trading

We are also starting to see the closure of stock exchanges. On March 16, the Philippine Stock Exchange closed and suspended currency and bond trading citing its concern for the health of its traders (reuters.com). We note the NYSE (**Intercontinental Exchange**) has closed five other times in history:

- **World War 1**: *July 30–December 12, 1914*
- **Banking Holiday**: *March 3–5, 1933*
- **Kennedy Assassination**: *November 22–26, 1963*
- **9/11**: *September 10–17, 2001*
- **Superstorm Sandy**: *October 29–30, 2012*

Although the NYSE has not closed, it did move to fully electronic trading on March 23. The SEC states that this is a temporary measure to protect the health safety of traders; however, we wonder if this could mark the evolution of stock exchange markets from the physical to the digital layer (cnbc.com).

UPS and FedEx make changes to their business operations

UPS and **FedEx** are making changes to their business operations. FedEx has suspended collecting physical signatures while UPS is requiring its drivers to stick a notice on the front door and then ring the doorbell and stand at a distance while the person signs the form with their own pen. On the commercial side, many drivers are facing challenges entering businesses and starting to find alternative drop-off spots. Under pressure from the union, UPS and FedEx are also starting to make changes to improve the safety of working conditions in their package sorting centres and air hubs such as increased sanitation and social distancing between workers (wsj.com).

WeWork could soon be heading to the ICU unit as the coronavirus preys on its huge duration mismatch

On March 13, I cancelled my WeWork membership and with the world now coming under lockdown, WeWork's co-working locations are becoming ghost offices. Although I do miss WeWork and hope it survives, the chances are highly unlikely as the coronavirus preys on the biggest flaw in its business model — its huge duration mismatch which creates a massively high level of operating and financial leverage. For example, Work's average lease duration is 15 years but it sub-leases space on a short-term basis (individuals are month-to-month and enterprises average 15 months), with estimated annual lease costs per location of $2.8 million, or $52 per square foot. As over half of WeWork's members are on a month-to-month lease like myself, I am guessing that most of them have (or will) cancel their hot desk membership. The big red flag to me is that WeWork still refuses to close its co-working locations, claiming it is providing office space to essential insurance, healthcare and cleaning products supplies companies, but the reality is that if you can work out of a WeWork, you can likely work from home.

SoftBank is unlikely to save WeWork as it looks to back out of $3 billion share tender offer

It doesn't seem likely that SoftBank will bail out WeWork a second time. On March 18, **SoftBank** stated it is looking to use regulatory probes from the SEC and Justice Department into WeWork as a means to back out of the $3 billion tender offer it made for WeWork shares back in October. The $3 billion tender offer is for shares held by existing investors, including $970 million for Adam Neumann's shares. SoftBank still plans to extend the $5 billion in debt to WeWork (wsj.com). The new reality is that SoftBank has given up its plans for global domination and is shifting to survival mode — on March 23, it announced it will sell up to $41 billion in assets to shore up its balance sheet (cnbc.com).

Tech giants launch initiatives to combat coronavirus

AWS just launched the AWS Diagnostic Development Initiative and committed a $20 million initial investment to *"accelerate diagnostic research, innovation and development to speed our collective understanding and detection of COVID-19 and other innovate diagnostic solutions to mitigate future infectious disease outbreaks"*. The initiative is open to research institutions and private entities using AWS and already has participation from 35 global research institutions, start-ups and businesses (blog.aboutamazon.com). This comes as the White House issues a call to action to AI experts as it released the COVID-19 Open Research Dataset, a collection of 29,000 articles about COVID-19, SARS COV-2 and the coronavirus group. The government is hoping that AI experts will be able to work together to develop new text and data mining techniques to find answers to important questions to combat the coronavirus (whitehouse.gov). Facebook and Google are also in discussions with the U.S. government to use location and movement data to predict where the next coronavirus outbreak will be and where to locate additional health resources (cnbc.com).

If you think you have coronavirus, you can consult with Siri or use CDC's chatbot

"Siri, do I have coronavirus?" You can now consult with Apple's Siri about your symptoms and whether you have come into close contact with someone who tested positive for coronavirus. Using answers supplied by the U.S. Public Health Service and CDC, Siri will then suggest what steps you should take next and recommend telehealth apps you can download on the App Store for a virtual consultation (digitaltrends.com). Unfortunately, this service is only available in the U.S.; when I tried it, it just directed me to the Government of Canada's

website. If you don't want to talk with Siri, you can check out CDC's new "Coronavirus Self-Checker" chatbot which lets you assess your symptoms and risks for coronavirus and let you know whether you should seek medical assistance. CDC built the chatbot, named Clara, on **Microsoft**'s "Health Bot" platform and powers it using Azure (techcrunch.com). Another good, more general resource is Google's new "COVID-19 Information and Resources" website. The website provides health info, safety and prevention tips and data insights. But what I found most useful is the links to YouTube videos to survive our new stay-at-home reality, including kids' learning, working from home, working out and cooking at home (theverge.com).

Make it look like you're working out of your dream home on your next Zoom call

The next time you're on a **Zoom** call, you can make it look like you work out of your dream home. The Creative Team at West Elm (**Williams-Sonoma**) has created faux backgrounds for you to upload to Zoom. Just save one of the images on the Front + Mail blog and then upload it as a Virtual Background to Zoom (apartmenttherapy.com).

Hong Kong uses electronic wristbands to enforce quarantines

Hong Kong is putting electronic wristbands on all new arriving passengers to enforce its two-week coronavirus quarantine. The electric wristbands are connected to a smartphone and when people get home, they are required to walk around the corners of their house so the technology can precisely track the exact co-ordinates of their living space (cnbc.com).

Nike's "play inside" messaging is brilliant, fitness studios start livestreaming classes

"*IF YOU EVER DREAMED OF PLAYING FOR MILLIONS AROUND THE WORLD, NOW IS YOUR CHANCE. Play Inside, Play for the World*". **Nike** once again proved its social conscience prowess with this new message on its homepage that it shared on Twitter on March 21 with the tweet:

"*Now more than ever, we are on one team*" (twitter.com). With gyms closed, a number of fitness studios are offering free livestreamed and recorded digital classes to help us play inside. It's interesting as some like Blink Fitness, Orangetheory, **Planet Fitness**, 305 Fitness and Barry's Bootcamp are livestreaming classes at specific times on online platforms like **Facebook**, YouTube (**Alphabet**) and Instagram. Others like **Peloton** and Gold's Gym are offering free access to fitness classes on their app for the next 90 days while Crunch Fitness is limiting free access to its app to existing members. And CorePower Yoga is offering free access to 20 yoga classes on its website (cbsnews.com).

Streaming quality cut in Europe; musicians, comedians & performers migrate to livestreaming platforms

In Europe, video streaming platforms like **Netflix**, YouTube, Amazon, **Disney** and Facebook are temporarily switching their default from HD (high-definition) to SD (standard-definition) to ease the demand on Internet infrastructure (techcrunch.com). As lockdowns come into place across the U.S. and Canada, we expect to see the streaming quality reduced here. With theatres closed, Paramount (**Viacom**) is releasing its romantic comedy, *The Lovebirds*, on **Netflix** after canceling its April 3 theatrical release. This is significant as it marks the first time a cancelled movie has gone to a third-party video streaming platform (engadget.com).

Musicians are facing a crisis as they derive the majority of their income from live performances. To survive, they are quickly migrating to digital platforms like Instagram, YouTube and Amazon's Twitch and creating livestreamed performances that some are calling "quaranstreams" (theverge.com). On the positive side, we are witnessing a digital culture renaissance as musicians, comedians, performers and artists migrate up the structural capital side of the value pyramid from physical venues to livestreaming platforms like Instagram and YouTube (wsj.com). If you have kids at home, you might want to check out Khan Academy. The non-profit offers 10,000 free online classes in 42 languages for kids in pre-K to Grade 12. To help parents out, Khan Academy just added suggested daily timelines for four different age groups (forbes.com).

Rising wholesale chicken prices in China signals economy is starting to recover

As a potentially positive sign of how quickly our economy will be able to rebound once the coronavirus pandemic is over, the wholesale price of chicken in China, which fell over 50% between mid-December and mid-February, has started to slowly rise again as the growth in the number of new cases has abated. This data comes from Gro Intelligence, a NYC-based big data/SaaS platform focused on the global agriculture industry which tracks and forecasts demand for commodities by using its AI-powered tool to crunch 650 trillion data points daily. As Sarah Menker, the founder of Gro Intelligence states: *"At a very, very deep level, modeling macroeconomic behavior is modeling human behavior...in times of crisis, food is a very basic starting point"* (wsj.com).

Chapter 9: Future Shock

April 7, 2020

"Image an entire society...suddenly transported into this new world. The result is mass disorientation, future shock on a grand scale." – Alvin Toffler, Future Shock, 1970

We are experiencing future shock on a global scale. To survive the coronavirus pandemic both individuals and companies need to lockdown, which means leaving behind the physical world and adopting the digital world. As I shared in the call with many of you, when I started researching structural disruption developments over three years ago, I never imagined I would end up publishing such a dystopian research report like the one I did last week. And as I explored in "The Survival Guide to the New Ghost Town Economy", we are witnessing what Toffler deems as the "premature arrival of the future" and structural disruption is no longer just accelerating — it is now arriving in the form of quantum leaps. Most importantly, this shift into the future tense will not be temporary, but permanent.

If you look at the cover of my new e-book, "The New Cyber Decade: Are You Driving Towards Utopia or Dystopia?", you'll see I used an image of Tesla's Cybertruck to foreshadow the radical transformation of the corporate landscape. However, we're no longer just driving toward the New Cyber Decade, we're now driving through the New Cyber Year. Welcome to

Future Shock.

Coronavirus pandemic explodes to over 1 million cases as NY becomes the epicenter of the outbreak

It is deadly scary how fast the coronavirus is now spreading and how the death rate is turning out to be higher than we initially thought. In the past two weeks, the number of total cases of coronavirus exploded by 3.5 times, from 375,458 to 1,331,032, while the number of related deaths rose by more than 4.5 times, from 16,371 to 73,917, resulting in the death rate rising very sharply from 4.4% to 5.6%.

In the past two weeks, coronavirus has skyrocketed by 8 times in the U.S. and Canada, with the number of cases rising in the past two weeks from 43,214 to 356,942 in the U.S. and from 2,046 to 16,500 in Canada. In the U.S., the outbreak is hitting New York the hardest, which now has 130,689 cases, or one-third of all the cases in the country, while there are 41,090 cases in neighbouring New Jersey and 15,718 cases in Michigan. In Canada, Quebec is suffering the worst with 8,580 cases, accounting for over one-half the cases in the country, while there are 4,347 cases in Ontario, 1,230 in Alberta and 1,203 in B.C.

While the U.S. accounts for over one-quarter of total cases, Europe is also an epicenter of new outbreaks, with the number of coronavirus cases reaching over 100,000 in four European countries. Over the past two weeks, the number of cases has risen 5 times in France (from 20,123 to 98,957), more than quadrupling in Spain (from 33,089 to 135,032), more than tripling in Germany (from 29,056 to 101,806 cases) and doubling in Italy (from 63,927 to 132,547).

The good news is coronavirus has stopped spreading in Mainland China as there were only 1,169 new cases in the past two weeks, with the total now at 81,496. South Korea's aggressive actions also led to a peak in the virus as the number of coronavirus cases in the past two weeks rose by only 15%, from 8,961 to 10,284.

lululemon & Chipotle are continuing to invest in their people

A good way to determine which companies are antifragile (i.e., will not just survive, but thrive after the pandemic) is to make note of those that are continuing to invest in their people. For example, on April 2, **lululemon** committed to extending pay for all its employees to June 1. As Calvin McDonald, CEO of lululemon, discussed in a CNBC interview, this plays to the three guiding principles that lululemon has established for the pandemic: 1) to continue to support its people; 2) to strike the right balance between short-term and long-term decisions; and 3) to continue to invest in the future. Supporting our thesis that lululemon is meeting new needs for at-home athleisure, he stated it is seeing online sales shifting to comfortable clothing as well as at-home yoga accessories. He also shared lululemon is using the opportunity to further develop talent by leaning in on online development courses for employees (cnbc.com). **Chipotle Mexican Grill** is also continuing to invest in its people as it is distributing $6.5 million in bonuses for the first quarter to its field leaders and restaurant managers because it is the "right thing to do". Chipotle established this quarterly bonus program last June. It is also giving away 100,000 free burritos to health care workers (cnbc.com).

Food retail is being radically transformed

We expect the coronavirus pandemic will accelerate the emergence of "dark stores" in the food retail space as this next generation of the grocery store is purpose-built not for customers, but for fulfillment of online grocery orders. To meet high demand for its "click and collect" service, **Kroger** is testing turning one of its grocery stores in Ohio into a "dark store" (supermarketnews.com). We also expect to see the rapid expansion of online grocery delivery to lower-income households. To help keep residents safe from the coronavirus, the USDA is accelerating the two-year pilot program it launched in the state of New York last April that will enable SNAP (Supplement Nutrition Assistance

Program) food stamp recipients to buy groceries online from **Amazon** and **Walmart**. The USDA expanded the program to Seattle in January, just launched it in Alabama, and Iowa and Oregon are speeding up their state's enrollment. Currently, 42 million Americans, representing 13% of the population, receive a total of $65 billion in annual SNAP benefits, but this is expected to rise given the escalating pandemic-related layoffs. For example, the number of weekly SNAP applications jumped in Oregon from 1,000 to 3,000–4,000 and the state expects 20% of residents could soon rely on SNAP benefits to help them purchase food (foodandwine.com).

To meet the surging demand for grocery delivery, Uber is re-allocating its network of ridesharing drivers to deliver essential goods. In France, it has partnered with **Carrefour** to offer grocery deliveries from 15 of its stores in Paris. In Spain, it has partnered with **Galp** to offer essential goods delivery from its service station stores in 15 cities across Spain. And in Brazil, it has partnered with Pague Menos (pharmacy), Shell Select (**Royal Dutch Shell**) (gas store) and Cobais (pet supplies) (techcrunch.com). Although retail giants like **Target** and Walmart have had the advantage of being allowed to keep their stores open during the lockdown, they are starting to be ordered to start roping off aisles in their stores that sell non-essential goods like clothing, toys and video games (thedenverchannel.com).

Amazon is capitalizing on the surging demand for online media content

Amazon is collaborating with SXSW to host online the recently cancelled SXSW 2020 Film Festival. The participating filmmakers will receive a screening fee and the film festival will run on Amazon Prime Video for 10 days with free access to anyone with an Amazon account (forbes.com). You can now rent and purchase movies on the Amazon Prime Video app on your iPhone or iPad. This agreement between **Apple** and Amazon is significant as the payment process is not through Apple, which usually takes a 30% cut of in-app purchases, but Amazon using your credit card stored on its platform (cnbc.com).

Restaurant capacity expected to permanently decline by at least 14%

The National Restaurant Association estimates 30,000 restaurants have closed their doors for good and 110,000 are expected to follow suite next month. Given there are more than 1 million restaurants across the U.S., these 140,000 closures would represent a 14% permanent reduction in restaurant capacity (businessinsider.com). To try and survive, OpenTable (**Bookings Holdings**) is temporarily pivoting its business model from restaurant reservations to grocery store reservations. Although OpenTable is currently piloting this with a few restaurants turned pop-up markets and local grocery stores in San Francisco and LA, it is in discussions with national food retailers. This would be a brilliant solution to help solve the problem of store overcrowding and long grocery store line-ups (theverge.com).

WeWork is headed to the ICU ward as SoftBank pulls its life support

On April 1, **SoftBank** terminated the $3 billion tender off it made for WeWork shares back in October held by existing investors, including $970 million for Adam Neumann's shares. As part of this, SoftBank is no longer obliged to proceed with $1.1 billion in debt financing for WeWork (cnbc.com). As further evidence of its struggle to survive, WeWork is in discussions with some of its biggest landlords to reduce its lease payments by as much as 30%. One of the proposals is to restructure its existing leases to revenue-sharing agreements but it is meeting resistance from landlords (crainsnewyork.com).

Tesla prototypes a new ventilator; Facebook develops Disease Prevention Maps; IBM offers chatbot solution to help battle the coronavirus

Companies continue to take war-like measures to produce much-needed medical supplies and services to help battle the coronavirus. For example, **Tesla** is leveraging its engineering expertise to design and build a prototype for a new ventilator. The ventilator leverages Tesla's existing IP and technology as the infotainment screen and computer from its Model 3 is at the heart of this new device and it also uses the suspension system from its Model S (theverge.com). **Facebook**'s Data for Good team is launching new tools to collect anonymized location data collected from users to track if physical distancing is working. Facebook is also developing Disease Prevention Maps which features co-location data, movement range trends and a social connectedness index (cnbc.com). **IBM** is offering its coronavirus chatbot solution, Watson Assistant for Citizens, for free the next 90 days to government agencies, health care institutions and academic organizations. The chatbot uses CDC and local sources to answer coronavirus questions by text and phone (venturebeat.com). Interestingly, Arvind Krishna, the new CEO of IBM, expects the coronavirus pandemic to speed up companies' adoption of AI and the cloud. According to Krishna, only 20% of the world is in the cloud and only 4% has taken advantage of the potential for productivity from AI (cnbc.com). We note that Krishna, a 30-year IBM veteran, has been the Senior Vice-President of Cloud for the past five years.

Luckin Coffee plummets 75% on news the COO fabricated sales

On April 2, **Luckin Coffee**'s stock price plummeted 75% after it disclosed an internal investigation revealed the COO fabricated sales by $310 million from Q2 to Q4. This is significant given Luckin Coffee's sales for the first nine months of 2019 were only $413 million (cnbc.com).

Club Med reaches out to guests to bring the Club Med resort experience to them digitally

It's hard to believe it was only two months ago I was relaxing in the warmth of the Mexican sun at Club Med in Ixtapa. Although Club Med

(**Fosun International**) has closed many of its resorts, it is looking to maintain the emotional connection with its past guests by "Bringing the Club Med Resort Experience to You" digitally through sharing activities like a downloadable printable colouring sheet, a "Crazy Signs" dance competition on Instagram and the recipe for its famous White Chocolate Bread (clubmed.ca).

Chapter 10: The New Risk Factor

April 15, 2020

SAFETY... The bottom of Maslow's hierarchy of needs is still all that matters as the number of coronavirus cases globally reaches nearly 2 million with the number rising in the past eight days by 70% in the U.S. to over 600,000 and in Canada by 63% to over 27,000. But social distancing is starting to work, and as we peer over the abyss to the future re-opening of the physical economy, safety is emerging as the primary risk factor and the catalyst for radical industry transformation as it permanently distorts the value equation on all three sides of the value pyramid:

CUSTOMER CAPITAL SIDE (Value Origination): Safety is taking precedence over sustainability as outbreaks are leading to the closure of meat processing plants while the shutdown of restaurants, coffee shops and pubs is causing milk, crops and even beer to go to waste. Although the shift to renewable energy will continue, the shift to sustainable packaging and reusing containers might be halted as personally I've started to buy packaged fruits and vegetables in bulk from Costco. I'm also worried safety concerns will take precedence over physical experiences, which makes me question American Dream Mall's decision to pivot to more of a theme park.

STRUCTURAL CAPITAL SIDE (Value Capture): Physical spaces will be radically transformed by the adoption of new health and safety measures which will impact the value of real estate assets and increase operating and labour costs. The biggest drivers will be de-densification and the adoption of touchless technologies like Alexa and facial recognition. In offices, open floor plans could revert to cubicles (goodbye co-working?) and there will be a deep focus on better cleaning processes and ventilation systems. I also expect a rising labour safety rights movement, as evidenced by fast food workers in California going on strike to demand safety gear, hazard pay and paid sick leave.

ECONOMIC CAPITAL SIDE (Value Extraction): The coronavirus pandemic will bring an end to the gig economy as we know it as it has exposed the lack of a social safety net for independent contractors, which I expect will be reclassified as employees, threatening their underlying platform economy model. For example, facing a 94% drop in ridesharing trips, Uber has launched Work Hub to connect its drivers to its three other platforms (Uber Eats, Uber Freight, Uber Works) and is expanding into parcel delivery. Airbnb has also entered survival mode as it was just forced to raise $1 billion in debt at LIBOR+10%.

Coronavirus cases reach nearly 2 million as death rate rises from 5.6% to 6.4%

In the past eight days, the number of total cases of coronavirus rose by 48%, from 1,331,032 to 1,973,715, while the number of related deaths rose by 70%, from 73,917 to 125,910, resulting in the death rate rising from 5.6% to 6.4%.

The number of coronavirus cases rose by 70% in the U.S., from 356,942 to 605,193 and by 64% in Canada, from 16,500 to 27,035. The U.S. now accounts for over 30% of total cases, up from over one-quarter last week. In the U.S., the outbreak continues to hit New York the hardest, which saw the number of cases rise by 55% to 130,689, now accounting for just over 20% of all cases in the U.S., down from a third last week. The number of cases in neighbouring New Jersey rose by 68% to 68,824 and those in Michigan rose by 72% to 27,001 and Massachusetts overtook Michigan with 28,164 cases. In Canada, Quebec is suffering the worst with the number of cases rising by 67% to 14,248, still accounting for over one-half the cases in the country. The number of cases rose by 83% in Ontario to 7,953, by 52% in Alberta to 1,870 and by 24% in B.C. to 1,490.

The rate of spread is falling in the four most affected countries in Europe. Over the past eight days, the number of cases has risen by 33% in France (from 98,957 to 131,361), by 28% in Spain (from 135,032 to 172,541), by 29% in Germany (from 101,806 to 131,359) and by 23% in Italy (from 132,547 to 162,988). The other good news is the coronavirus has nearly stopped spreading in Mainland China as there were only 641 new cases in the past eight days, with the total now at 83,306. Likewise, South Korea's aggressive actions also led to a peak in the virus as there were only 280 new cases, bringing the total to 10,564.

Amazon hiring 75,000 more employees as it re-opens its marketplace to non-essential goods

Eric Schmidt, the former CEO of Google (**Alphabet**), is predicting the coronavirus pandemic will make Big Tech even bigger. True to our antifragile thesis, he states: *"The strongest brands and the strongest companies will recover more quickly"* (fortune.com). A perfect example is **Amazon**, who hired over 100,000 people in the U.S. in the past month and is now looking to hire 75,000 more to meet surging demand in its distribution centres and across its delivery network. This represents a 35% increase in its U.S. workforce base of 500,000 (wsj.com). As a result of this ramp-up, Amazon is able to start opening its marketplace to non-essential third-party sellers. On March 17, Amazon took emergency measures to prioritize medical supplies, household staples and other high-demand products coming into its warehouses from third-party sellers. Now it has started to allow third-party sellers to start shipping some non-essentials, although it is limiting product quantities (cnbc.com). Given the surge in its own customers' orders,

Amazon is suspending Amazon Shipping. But this isn't too material as this third-party delivery service, which picks up packages from businesses to deliver to customers, is still in beta stage as it has been testing it in London and LA (wsj.com).

Build-up in inventory of used vehicles could lead to a collapse in residual values

The auto industry is warning we could see a collapse in used car prices and residual values resulting from the paralysis of used vehicle auctions. The problem is we are seeing a build-up in the inventory of used vehicles as the collapse in demand for rentals leads rental car companies like **Hertz** and **Avis Budget** to sell off their fleet and passenger vehicles come off lease. To reduce the flood of used passenger vehicles, the finance units of **GM** and **Ford** are offering one-month extensions to customers. But the other problem is that the spike in unemployment has likely dampened demand for cars (new or used) once the pandemic is over (pennlive.com).

Office de-densification will be more than offset by shift to employees working from home

Based on the expectation that tenants will pay a premium for safe, clean and healthy buildings, building owners are creating new cleanliness and security protocols. In turn, this is leading to a demand for features like indoor air purification (nypost.com). The office itself will be transformed radically by the adoption of new health and safety concerns. The biggest driver will be de-densification as open floor plans revert back to cubicle farms and well-spaced desks with dividers while common areas such as conference rooms and kitchens will have half as many seats. This increase in the square footage per employee could offset some of the reduction of demand from employees who decide to continue working from home. We could also see the adoption of voice assistants like Alexa to open doors, operate the elevator and replace touch screens. There will be also be an increased focus on cleaning, including more frequent cleaning, the installation of better ventilation systems, the installation of UV lights to enable deep disinfecting of the office at night, and the introduction of furniture with antibacterial fabrics and materials (vox.com). The coronavirus pandemic will also transform how office buildings and companies track the entry and exit of workers. They will be forced to abandon current technologies like access cards and finger and thumb-biometric scanning and adopt new technologies like touchless facial recognition technology and thermal scanning (theedgemarkets.com). As further evidence of the permanent shift to working from home, **TD** expects to offer this as an option after the pandemic ends to its workforce of over 9,000 call centre employees from 15 U.S. and Canadian cities who are now working from home (bnnbloomberg.com).

WeWork didn't pay April rent, Knotel is trying to offload 1 million square feet of office space

We're starting to think that the end of open floor plans and increased health and safety concerns over common areas could foreshadow the death of co-working. As a further red flag that WeWork (**SoftBank**) is struggling to stay alive, it has stopped paying rent at some of its U.S. locations (wsj.com). This is ironic as WeWork still hasn't shut down its co-working locations and is insisting its enterprise tenants (which have an average lease duration of 15 months) continue to pay rent. Meanwhile, given the new health and safety concerns, Knotel is trying to shed its portfolio of office space located in buildings with small elevators and poor ventilation. Knotel is in talks with landlords to return 1 million square feet of office space, of which a large portion is in NYC, which accounts for half of its 5 million square foot office real estate portfolio (commercialobservor.com).

Retail and hospitality industries are becoming increasingly fragile

On April 7, S&P Global Market Intelligence published a report listing the top ten consumer industries with a median probability of default of at least 25%. This list of fragile industries includes non-essential retailers that have been forced to close their stores (department stores, apparel retail, houseware & specialties, home furnishings), travel and entertainment industries that have been forced to close their physical spaces (hotels & cruise lines, leisure facilities, casinos & gaming, restaurants) and auto-dependent industries (tires & rubber, auto parts & equipment). On the flip side, the antifragile industries with a median default rate of 5% or less include CPGs, food retail and education services (cnbc.com). As evidence of the fragility of the retail and hospitality industries, according to Trepp, the CMBS lodging loans not paid have risen from 1.5% in March to nearly 20% in April while CMBS retail loans not paid have risen from 1.7% in March to 9.0% in April (cnbc.com). For example, in the retail space, the Triple Five Group is concerned some of its tenants are not paying rent. And those who are paying rent, are asking landlords to take a smaller cut or delay the rent payment to a later date (cnbc.com). Even multi-residential REITs are becoming fragile as nearly one-third of tenants in the U.S. didn't pay their April rent during the first week of the month. According to the analysis of data from 13.4 million rental apartments, only 69% of tenants paid their April rent, which is down from 82% a year ago (wsj.com).

True Religion files for Chapter 11 as American Dream Mall pivots to more of a theme park

On April 13, True Religion filed for Chapter 11 for the second time (cnbc.com). We note that True Religion, which was acquired for $824 million in 2013 by TowerBrook Capital Partners, first filed for bankruptcy in July 2017. This could be the start of the building tsunami wave of retail and mall bankruptcies. For example, the American Dream Mall has decided to pivot toward more of a mega theme park and less of a mall. The Ghermizian family's Triple Five Group has decided to shift its leasing strategy for the mall, increasing the entertainment mix from 55% to 70% by adding new venues such as a trampoline park, experiential museum and hotels in place of cookie cutter retail outlets (cnbc.com). However, given the increased importance of safety and health, we are concerned that theme parks and entertainment venues will have to radically transform their spaces and how they operate.

Quantum leap in demand for warehouses will be offset by oversupply of commercial real estate

The quantum leap in the shift to online sales will lead to a quantum leap in demand for warehouse space, especially temperature-controlled warehouse space (wsj.com). However, as a result of increasing convenience expectations, warehouses will need to be built closer to population centres. And given the expected coming collapse in retail, office and hospitality commercial real estate markets, there will likely be an oversupply of buildings available to be re-purposed into warehouses.

Food supply disrupted as meat processing plants shut and perishables go to waste

On April 11, the governor of South Dakota ordered Smithfield Foods (**WH Group**) to close its plant in Sioux Falls indefinitely after 238 cases of coronavirus were linked to the plant, representing over one-half of the cases in the county. This is significant as in addition to employing 3,700 workers, the plant sources pork from 550 farmers and accounts for 4–5% of U.S. pork production. U.S. meat processing plants are becoming hot spots for the coronavirus as the close quarters on processing lines creates a high risk of infection spread. For example, **Tyson Foods** temporarily shut down its pork plant in Iowa after two dozen employees tested positive for coronavirus and Cargill and JBS USA Holdings (**JBS SA**) have temporarily closed their beef plants in Pennsylvania (wsj.com). The other disruption is happening with perishables. For example, the closure of coffee shops has led to an oversupply of milk, resulting in U.S. farmers now dumping an estimated 14 million litres of milk every day. Likewise, the closure of restaurants has resulted in current crops going to waste, and going forward there could be a shortage of crops if there are not enough workers to harvest the fields. And the closure of pubs could even lead to the expiration of undrunk beer. On the positive side, the rise in home baking has led to increased demand for flour, and rising demand for Vitamin C at home has led to greater demand for orange juice (bbc.com).

Streaming media viewing hours doubled in the past month & Netflix was the winner

According to Reelgood, streaming media viewing hours have doubled in the past month. Interestingly, just over one-half of the streaming is occurring between the workday hours of 8am to 6pm. **Netflix** appears to be winning the streaming wars as it accounts for 42% of the hours with Amazon at 22% and Hulu at 17% (forbes.com). Further to our thesis of the fast-forwarded obsolescence of the movie theatre, according to Universal (**Comcast**), *Trolls World Tour* was its highest-grossing video-on-demand (VOD) title, bringing in 10 times more on its opening day than its second biggest ever VOD release, *Jurassic World: Fallen Kingdom* (9to5mac.com). We note that on March 16, as the closure of movie theatres across the country accelerated, Universal made the radical decision to disrupt the traditional 90-day window, making *Trolls World Tour* available online when it was to debut in the theatre on April 10.

Hospitals are quickly adopting remote monitoring tools for COVID-19 patients at home

Hospitals are quickly adopting AI-powered remote patient monitoring tools to keep patients diagnosed with COVID-19 out of the hospital. For example, Baptist Health in Kentucky is tracking 20 COVID-19 patients while Providence health system in Washington is monitoring over 1,000 confirmed and suspected patients in their homes. And LSU Healthcare Network in New Orleans plans to start using AI this week to start remotely monitoring cardiac patients who are highly vulnerable to the coronavirus (wsj.com).

Amazon working with Canadian government to manage PPE delivery; Apple & Google partner to help track spread of coronavirus

Justin Trudeau announced that the federal government will be working with Amazon Canada to manage the delivery of medical PPE like masks, gloves, face shields and gowns to the provinces and territories (narcity.com). Other tech giants are also leveraging their capital to help battle against the coronavirus. On April 10, **Apple** and Google announced a partnership to provide tools to help track the spread of coronavirus. The two tech giants will launch APIs in May to enable interoperability between Android and iOS devices using apps from public health authorities. The apps will use Bluetooth technology for contact tracing to let you know if you've come into contact with someone diagnosed with COVID-19 (cnbc.com). We note that on March 20, the Singapore government rolled out TraceTogether, a coronavirus contact tracing app. The app works by exchanging short distance Bluetooth signals when users are near one another, with the data stored in their phones for 21 days. If a user is diagnosed with coronavirus, Singapore's health ministry can access the app data to identify people that came into close contact with the individual. Although this raises privacy concerns, the response seems positive as it was downloaded over 500,000 times within 24 hours of its launch. The good news for the rest of the world is that the government is making the technology behind the contact tracing app freely available to others (cnbc.com).

Walgreens opens drive-thru testing as Amazon builds its own coronavirus testing lab

Walgreens is opening 15 drive-thru testing locations across seven states. Walgreens is looking to test up to 3,000 people per day using **Abbott Laboratories'** rapid COVID-19 test (cnbc.com). Stanford Medicine built a new app in partnership with Apple to help connect first responders like firefighters, police officers and paramedics in California to drive-thru coronavirus testing sites. The First Responder COVID-19 Guide app uses Apple's ResearchKit and CareKit software. Stanford Medicine hopes to expand the app to frontline workers like grocery store employees (cnbc.com). Amazon is building its own coronavirus testing lab for its employees. Amazon plans to start testing small numbers of its front-line employees soon (bbc.com).

Amazon launches virtual "place in line" as Panera Bread & McDonald's pivot into grocery

Amazon has increased its online grocery order capacity by over 60% since the pandemic started and is looking to enhance its capabilities. A brilliant new feature it is launching is to help its grocery customers secure a virtual "place in line" to distribute grocery windows on a first come, first-serve basis. In addition, Amazon has expanded the number of Whole Foods locations offering pick-up from 80 to 150, representing just under one-third of its 487 stores in the U.S. In addition, it is temporarily transitioning its new grocery store in LA to a pure micro-fulfillment centre (reuters.com). We are also seeing restaurants pivot into selling groceries. For example, Panera Bread has temporarily transformed itself from a café into a grocery store. Customers can go onto the Panera Bread app or website or **Grubhub** to order perishable grocery items like breads, bagels, milk, yogurt, cream cheese and fresh produce for pick-up or delivery (cnbc.com). In Australia, **McDonald's** is pivoting to offer basic grocery items like milk, English muffins and gourmet bread rolls to its customers through takeaway or its drive-thru (insideretail.com.au).

Fast food workers in California go on strike to demand greater protection

Fast food workers in California are going on strike to demand greater protection against the coronavirus. Workers from QSRs such as **McDonald's**, Taco Bell and Pizza Hut (**Yum! Brands**), **Domino's Pizza**, Popeye's (**Restaurant Brands International**), Subway and **El Pollo Loco Holdings** are participating in the strike. Their three demands are: 1) safety gear (i.e., masks, gloves, soap); 2) hazard pay (an extra $3 per hour); and 3) paid sick leave (2 week's pay to workers exposed to the coronavirus) (vice.com). On the delivery front, Uber has fast-tracked the launch of Uber Eats for business, which it has been testing in the U.S. for the past 17 months. Uber is hoping this will meet the new needs of companies looking to support their employees while they are working from home or front-line workers at hospitals (venturebeat.com).

Uber launches Work Hub for its drivers and starts to pivot into parcel delivery

Uber's ridesharing platform has come to a screeching halt with journeys down 94% since the beginning of March. To help its drivers find other work, Uber has launched Work Hub which connects its driver to its three other platforms: 1) Uber Eats (meal delivery): 2) Uber Freight (trucking); and 3) Works (blue-collar temporary shifts). Uber is also posting job openings for companies that are ramping up their hiring during the pandemic, such as logistics delivery (**UPS** and **FedEx**), essential goods retailers (Walgreens, Albertsons, 7-Eleven (**Seven & I Holdings**), CPGs (**PepsiCo** and Land O'Lakes) and QSRs (McDonald's) (forbes.com). Uber is also pivoting into parcel delivery. In India, it is partnering with Flipkart (**Walmart**) to deliver essential goods in Delhi, Mumbai and Bangalore. Uber will be providing its drivers with the necessary safety equipment and is allowing them to keep 100% of the revenue (techcrunch.com). And in Australia, Uber will be launching contactless parcel delivery for businesses. Drivers will pick up and drop off items booked by business customers through its app. However, customers are restricted from shipping alcohol, tobacco, weapons, stolen items, money, jewelry and high-value items (7news.com.au).

Airbnb enters survival mode as it is forced to raise $1 billion in debt

Airbnb is so desperate for cash as it just raised $1 billion in debt at an interest rate of LIBOR+10% from private equity firms Silver Lake and Sixth Street Partners. As part of the funding, they will also receive warrants convertible into shares at an $18 billion valuation, representing a 40% discount to the $31 billion that Airbnb was valued at back in its last funding round in 2017. Airbnb has been hit with a tsunami of cancellations, resulting in plummeting revenue, a customer service nightmare and escalating host attrition as they seek long-term tenants or to sell their place. On March 13, Airbnb rolled out a new policy that allows guests to cancel reservations for bookings made before then for check-out dates between March 14 and May 31. But it is making it difficult for guests to do this as to get a full cash refund, they need to provide documentation with screenshots such as an official government site or a doctor's letter to explain why they can't travel. Otherwise they are just given a travel credit. Although Airbnb has the benefit of a highly variable cost structure, to try to appease its hosts, which have to deal with revenue loss from cancelled bookings, it has committed to spend $250 million to reimburse its hosts for 25% of the fee (wsj.com). On top of this, we note that in November, Airbnb committed to spend $150 million this year on safety initiatives to verify all 7 million homes listed on its platform following the Vice expose and Halloween party shooting. In addition, Airbnb faces escalating regulatory risk as Ontario has temporarily banned Airbnb and VRBO short-term rentals during the pandemic. The only exception is for individuals in need of housing during this emergency period (nowtoronto.com).

Chapter 11: The Parade

April 21, 2020

> *On September 19, 1918, flu arrived at the Philadelphia Navy Yard
> and within days, 600 sailors had caught the disease. Nine days
> later the Fourth Liberty Loan Campaign rally brought 200,000
> Philadelphians together in the streets...Philadelphia lost about
> 12,000 people and had about 47,000 reported cases in just four
> weeks.*

— *Penn and the 1918 Influenza Epidemic*, University of Penn archives

*As I watched the crowds standing together shoulder-to-shoulder proudly
waving American flags protesting shut-in orders., I couldn't help but think
of the fate that met the flag-waving crowds at the parade in Philadelphia
just over a century ago. For "those who cannot remember the past are
condemned to repeat it".*

*But the problem is that the Spanish Flu of 1918, which killed a staggering
50 million to 100 million people in the two years between March 1918
and March 1920, has been largely forgotten. When I asked my Mom this
weekend if my Grandma, who was born in Victoria, B.C. in 1902, had ever
spoken about it, she said she hadn't, which was surprising because the
Spanish Flu led to the deaths of 55,000 Canadians and 675,000 Americans.*

While the protestors are still stuck in the first and second stages of the grieving process — denial and anger — the good news is that most of us have already advanced to the third stage — bargaining. Interestingly, the underlying themes of my research notes since the coronavirus pandemic hit here at home in early March seem to reflect society's progression through the first three grieving stages:

- **Stage 1: Denial:** *The Next Ten Years*
- **Stage 2: Anger:** *The New Ghost Town Economy, LOCKDOWN, WAR*
- **Stage 3: Bargaining:** *Future Shock, The New Risk Factor*

We are still in the bargaining stage as companies are adjusting their operations and pivoting their business models as they re-imagine how to survive this new ghost town economy. For example, we are seeing the implementation of taking employee temperatures at Walmart, meat processing plants and the partially re-opened Shanghai Disney Resort, while Emirates is conducting rapid on-site COVID-19 testing for passengers before they board the plane. Meanwhile, Uber is pivoting to grocery and package delivery to stay alive, restaurants are pivoting to selling groceries to survive the lockdown and Heinz is capitalizing on people being shut-in at home with the launch of Heinz to Home in the U.K.

But the bad news is that fragile entities like JC Penney, Neiman Marcus and 24 Hour Fitness aren't in any position to bargain as they look to file for bankruptcy. Which takes us to the fourth stage — depression.

Coronavirus cases reach nearly 2.5 million as death rate escalates to 6.9%

In the past six days, the number of total cases of coronavirus rose by 25%, from 1,973,715 to 2,473,209, while the number of related deaths rose by 35%, from 125,910 to 170,042, resulting in the death rate escalating from 6.4% to 6.9%.

In the past six days, the number of coronavirus cases rose by 30% in the U.S., from 605,193 to 784,599, and by 39% in Canada, from 27,035 to 37,710. The U.S. now accounts for nearly a third of total cases. In the U.S., the outbreak continues to hit New York the hardest, which saw the number of cases rise by 94% to 253,191, now accounting for nearly a third of all cases in the U.S. The number of cases in neighbouring New Jersey rose by 29% to 88,806 and those in Massachusetts rose by 41% to 39,643. In Canada, Quebec continues to suffer the worst with the number of cases rising by 36% to 19,319, still accounting for over one-half the cases in the country. The number of cases rose by 41% in Ontario to 11,184, by 56% in Alberta to 2,908 and by only 14% in B.C. to 1,699.

The rate of spread continues to fall in the four most affected countries in Europe. Over the past six days, the number of cases has risen by 19% in France (from 131,361 to 156,480), by 16% in Spain (from 172,541 to 200,210), by 12% in Germany (from 131,359 to 147,065) and by 11% in Italy (from 162,988 to 181,228). The coronavirus has nearly stopped spreading in Mainland China as there were only 511 new cases in the past six days, with the total now at 83,817. Likewise, South Korea's aggressive actions also led to a peak in the virus as there were only 110 new cases, bringing the total to 10,674.

JC Penney, Neiman Marcus & 24 Hour Fitness consider filing for bankruptcy

JC Penney, which is weighed down by its $3.7 billion debt load, is evaluating strategic alternatives, including a potential bankruptcy filing. JC Penney just missed a $12 million interest payment to bondholders which kicks off a 30-day grace period before it officially defaults on its debt. It missed the payment on its $388 million 6.375% bonds, which have traded down to 8.5 cents on the dollar (wsj.com). Likewise, Neiman Marcus, which was forced to shut down all of its 43 locations and furlough 14,000 employees nearly a month ago, is preparing to file for bankruptcy as early as this week. The luxury retailer is weighed down with $4.8 billion in debt as a result of its leveraged buyout in 2013 by Ares Management and the Canadian Pension Plan Investment Board. To avoid the fate of Neiman Marcus and JC Penney, department stores like **Macy's** and **Nordstrom** are rushing to secure new financing by borrowing against some of their real estate (reuters.com).

According to Global Data, the coronavirus pandemic has resulted in the closure of 4.8 billion square feet of U.S. retail space, or 55% of the total. Ironically, this new ghost town economy is exposing the complete dependence on the physical layer for categories previously valued for their Internet-resistant characteristics, like restaurants, fitness companies and discount apparel (cpexecutive.com). For example, 24 Hour Fitness, which was forced to shut down all its nearly 450 clubs in the U.S. a month ago, is considering filing for bankruptcy (cnbc.com). The mid-priced gym chain, which is weighed down by a heavy debt load, was struggling even prior to the pandemic as it had fully drawn the entirety of its $120 million revolving credit line on March 24 (wsj.com).

Meat processing plants in U.S. and Alberta become coronavirus hot spots

On April 15, the CDC arrived at Smithfield Foods' (**WH Group**) pork processing plant in Sioux Falls, which has become the largest coronavirus hot spot in the U.S. with 518 employees now testing positive (usatoday.com). We note this is more than double the 238 cases four days ago when the governor of South Dakota ordered the indefinite closure of the plant. And this is not an isolated incident as employees have tested positive for the coronavirus at Smithfield Foods' plants in Wisconsin and Missouri. These plants are being closed for the next two weeks to be cleaned and when they re-open employees will be offered PPE and will be scanned with thermal scanning technology to detect fevers (wsj.com). As evidence of the fragility of the supply chain, the Missouri pork processing plant needs pork supplies from the Sioux Falls plant to operate.

In Canada, on April 17, Cargill's meat processing plant in High River, Alberta, became the largest coronavirus hot spot in Canada with 358 employees testing positive, up from only 38 five days earlier. Unlike the Smithfield Foods' three pork processing plants, Cargill's plant has remained open, although it has taken a number of new safety protocols like removing a second shift on April 14, resulting in the temporary furlough of half of its 2,000 workers, as well as checking employees' temperatures, giving them face masks, increasing the physical distance between employees and enhancing cleaning. Like in the U.S., this is not an isolated incident as employees have tested positive for the coronavirus at two other meat processing plants in Alberta, JBS' (**JBS SA**) plant in Brooks and the Harmony Beef plant in Balzac. These three plants, which represent three-quarters of beef suppliers in Canada, have not closed as they are classified as essential services as part of the food supply chain (cbc.ca).

Temperature scanning, masks, plastic shields, physical spacing & COVID-19 testing will be the new normal

"The happiest place on earth" will look a bit dystopian when it re-opens, as evidenced by the new safety protocols being implemented as **Disney** re-opens a portion of its Shanghai Disney Resort in China. In addition to limiting the operating hours and capacity, guests that wish to gain entry will need to have their temperature checked and present the government-controlled QR code on their phone indicating they are virus-free, and then wear a mask at all times, except for eating. Likewise, restaurants are looking to operate at half capacity, install new features like plexiglass shields between booths, switch to disposable menus and seal silverware in plastic and go completely cashless. Stores are also looking to change their operating practices

by eliminating testers and sanitizing items after customers try them on. Meanwhile, Major League Baseball is looking at the idea of playing in a ghost stadium.

In addition to staggering shifts for workers and giving them PPE like masks, manufacturing companies are taking additional safety measures. For example, **Tyson Foods** has installed walk-through temperature scanners for its workers while **Toyota Motor** is looking to slow down its assembly lines to maintain social distancing between workers. To maintain social distancing in offices, companies are installing transparent shields to divide desks and adding markets to direct foot traffic. And as a foreshadowing of the foreseeable future for airline travel, Emirates has started conducting rapid on-site COVID-19 testing for passengers through a blood test that provides results in just 10 minutes (wsj.com).

Pandemic leading to fastest labour redeployment shift in postwar history

The coronavirus pandemic is resulting in one of the fastest labour redeployment shifts in postwar history. On the customer capital side of the value pyramid, the labour force is quickly shifting down to the base functional level to retailers providing essential goods that are allowed to keep their stores open during lockdowns. For example, nearly a month ago, **CVS Health** embarked on its most ambitious hiring spree as it looked to increase its labour force by 17%, hiring 50,000 people on a full-time, part-time and temporary basis to work in its stores, distribution centres, and at-home delivery drivers and customer service professionals. To achieve this, CVS has partnered with a dozen of companies to employ their laid-off workers, including **Gap**, Hilton (**Hilton Worldwide Holdings**) and **Delta Air Lines**. Likewise, **Kroger**, who is looking to hire 10,000 workers, has created an exchange with its suppliers (i.e., food service companies like **Sodexo SA** and **Sysco** and hospitality companies like

Marriott International). Companies are also internally redeploying their workforce, retraining their employees to move them up from the physical to the digital layer of the structural capital side of the value pyramid. For example, **Verizon Communications** is temporarily moving its in-store employees to customer service and sales roles. And **TD** has temporarily shifted over 2,000 of its employees into new roles (wsj.com).

Luxury goods are back in vogue in China

The Chinese market for luxury goods is rebounding as consumers emerge from the lockdown. **LVMH** reported that sales started turning positive in the second half of March. As evidence of the pent-up demand, LVMH's sales are showing very high growth rates in April, with sales for some brands up over 50% compared to a year ago (wsj.com).

Container shipping companies have cancelled 458 sailings to keep rates up

Freight rates have not declined, but only because container ship-ping companies are reducing shipping capacity. According to Sea-Intelligence, container shipping companies like **Maersk** have cancelled a total of 458 sailings since the Chinese New Year, with 89 related to the Wuhan shutdown in February and March and 369 related to reduced import demand in Europe and the U.S. in April and June. This reduced capacity equates to a total reduction of 6.4 million TEUs (20-foot equivalent units), which represents 4% of the annual shipping capacity (freightwaves.com).

Oil price future contracts go negative for first time in history

The coronavirus shock led oil price futures contracts to tumble into negative territory for the first time ever, with the May contract for WTI declining by over 300% to -$37.63 at the close on April 20 and even the June contract declining by 16% to $22.27 (cbc.ca). The new ghost town economy doesn't run on oil as the coronavirus has idled our factories, taken cars off the road, and grounded planes, resulting in demand for oil in the U.S. falling to the lowest level in 30 years. On the supply side, inventory is building with pipelines filling up, storage tanks brimming and ships being used to store oil (wsj.com).

Alibaba investing $28 billion in cloud over next three years

Alibaba will invest $28 billion in its cloud computing division over the next three years. Alibaba will be investing in technology related to operating systems, servers, chips and networks. Although Alibaba is the leading cloud player in China, it ranks behind Amazon and **Microsoft** in terms of global market share (cnbc.com). Speaking of Alibaba, **Tesla** has opened a store on Taobao.com, Alibaba's online marketplace. Although you can't buy an actual Tesla car on the site, you can request a test drive and buy Tesla car parts and related merchandise. Tesla started delivering its China-made Model 3 cars in January (wsj.com).

Heinz finally goes DTC with launch of Heinz to Home in U.K.

Heinz is finally going direct-to-consumer. In the U.K., Heinz just launched Heinz to Home, offering home delivery of its Essentials Bundle to customers looking for comfort food as they self-isolate at home. The bundle consists of 16 cans: eight cans of baked beans, four cans of cream of tomato soup and four cans of spaghetti loops. The bundle costs £10 plus £3.50 for shipping and will be delivered in three days (heinztohome.co.uk).

Restaurants pivot to grocery delivery, farmers re-direct unwanted food to food banks

Prior to the pandemic, we saw the lines blurring between grocery stores and restaurants with grocery stores moving into meal delivery — now we are seeing some restaurants pivot to grocery delivery as they struggle to survive during the lockdown. This is a smart strategy as it enables restaurants to leverage their supplier capital by unbundling bulk supplies they receive from their food distributors like **Sysco** to meet their customers' growing need for groceries, toilet paper and even alcohol (nationalpost.com). For example, Earls has launched Earls Grocery which sells bundles of groceries like a produce pack for $45 or a dairy and egg pack for $55, as well as specialty items like brunch kits (earls.ca). But the problem is that it is too hard for some restaurants to pivot their operations and their business interruption policies might not cover pandemics. So the founder of Napa Valley's French Laundry and the founder of Wolfgang Puck have created a new restaurant alliance called the Business Interruption Group (BIG) to begin a public opinion and lobbying claim to pressure insurers to pay claims and for government to reimburse insurers. With 15 million workers, the restaurant industry is the largest U.S. employer (wsj.com). With restaurants closed, food on the farm is going to waste, so the California Association of Food Banks is connecting farmers with food banks to re-direct perishables that are going to waste now that restaurants and coffee shops are closed. Last week, in a single day, they connected 4 million pounds of food (fastcompany.com).

Walmart struggles to staff stores with 10% of workers on leave, is it time for stores to go "dark"?

Walmart is struggling to staff its stores as 150,000 workers, or 10% of its base of 1.5 million employees, are currently on leave, with 2,000 having tested positive for the coronavirus and at least 18 having died from it. To protect its employees and customers, Walmart is mandating that all employees start wearing masks and is now checking temperatures at the start of each shift (wsj.com). But Marc Perrone, the President of the United Food and Commercial Workers' (UFCW) union, is becoming concerned it is too dangerous to let customers browse aisles as 85% of his members are reporting that customers are not practicing social distancing in grocery stores. He believes it is time for grocery stores to go "dark", meaning closing their stores to the public and converting to curbside pick-up and delivery. For example, in NYC,

Amazon's Whole Foods has transformed its store in Bryant Park to a "dark" store" (cnn.com). We note that prior to the pandemic, we were seeing the emergence of "dark" grocery stores — now the rising safety risk to grocery workers could accelerate this structural shift. To meet the rising need for at-home delivery of prescriptions, **Costco** is expanding its partnership with Instacart that it started testing back in November. Costco is expanding the prescription delivery service with Instacart to 200 locations in eight states and plans to expand nationwide in the coming months (techcrunch.com).

Uber pivots to package delivery and expands Uber Eats to grocery delivery

Uber is pivoting to package delivery with the official launch of Uber Direct and Uber Connect. Uber Direct is its B2C delivery platform for retail items while Uber Connect is its P2P (peer-to-peer) delivery platform for individuals (techcrunch.com). Uber is also expanding Uber Eats, which saw orders on its grocery delivery platforms across Europe rise 59% from February to March as a result of new store sign-ups and higher demand from existing stores. Uber is working with nine of the largest convenience stores in the U.K., including Costcutter, which has seen its sales on the platform rise 350% in the past month with 100 of its stores now offering this service. Uber Eats recently partnered with **Carrefour** in Paris and is in talks with other grocery stores to join its platform. Uber Eats now has 1,000 convenience and grocery stores on its platform in Europe and 3,500 globally (uk.reuters.com). To make its restaurant delivery platform more accessible to elderly people shut in at home who don't have a smartphone or feel comfortable using apps, Uber is piloting a dial-an-Uber Eats service in NYC and Miami and plans to expand it into more states. This follows the pilot just two months ago of its dial-an-Uber ridesharing service in Arizona (reuters.com). Although this service may expand Uber's total addressable market (TAM), it will also increase its fixed cost structure, making the incremental deliveries less profitable.

Weddings and politics move online

"NEW: 'I am issuing an Executive Order allowing New Yorkers to obtain a marriage license remotely and allowing clerks to perform ceremonies via video conference.'" This tweet on April 18 from Andrew Cuomo, Governor of New York, illustrates how quickly the world is moving from the physical to the digital layer as now people are not just dating online, they can even get married online. Even politics is moving online: for the first time in its 700-year history, Britain's House of Commons will be sitting remotely. The hybrid approach will see 50 members sit in the chamber under strict physically distancing guidelines while 120 MPs connect via Zoom **(Zoom Video Communications**.) (straitstimes.com).

Amazon wants us to buy less

Amazon is making a number of unprecedented moves to encourage us to buy less. The company is re-tooling its website to keep customers focused on buying essential items by no longer upselling items or encouraging impulse buys. In addition, Amazon has quietly cancelled its Mother's Day and Father's Day promotions and has indefinitely postponed Prime Day, which it usually holds in mid-July and sold 175 million items over a 48-hour period last year (wsj.com). In France, Amazon has temporarily closed its warehouses after the court forbid it from shipping non-essential goods as a result of the risks to its workers from the coronavirus. However, it will still continue to ship to France from warehouses outside the country (wsj.com).

Chapter 12: The Digital Abyss

April 28, 2020

A new civilization is emerging in our lives, and blind men every-where are trying to suppress it...Pieces of this new civilization exist already today. Millions are already attuning their lives to the rhythms of tomorrow. Others, terrified of the future, are engaged in a desperate futile flight into the past and are trying to restore the dying world that give them birth. The dawn of this new civilization is the single most explosive fact in our lifetimes.

— Alvin Toffler, *The Third Wave*, 1980

The coronavirus pandemic is acting as a catalyst to catapult us into the new civilization I call the New Cyber Age. I'm no longer talking about "The New Cyber Decade" — in the past six weeks, the digital divide has deepened into a digital abyss. And we're starting to see the reckoning as coronavirus attacks those stranded on the wrong side of the abyss while the digital world thrives.

Coronavirus is attacking department stores and apparel retailers as Lord & Taylor has joined JC Penney and Neiman Marcus in looking to file bankruptcy while Macy's is looking to raise up to $5 billion in debt and Gap is warning of a cash flow shortfall. Coronavirus is also preying on *the crowded working conditions of meat processing plants, with outbreaks leading to the closure of Cargill's beef processing plant in Alberta and United Poultry Company's two poultry-processing plants in Vancouver. And the closure of factories, stores and restaurants in the physical world is resulting in demand falling off a cliff in the trucking industry as the initial panic buying for essential goods has subsided.*

Meanwhile, the digital world is thriving as the Internet grows and becomes a bigger part of people's lives. People are turning to video conferencing platforms like Zoom, which saw its daily users skyrocket by 50% to 300 million in less than a month, and up from only 10 million in December. People are also escaping to Netflix for entertainment, and we are seeing the emergence of virtual music festivals on Minecraft and Fortnite. As the restaurant industry faces an existential crisis, Chipotle and Domino's Pizza are seeing their digital investments pay off as is Walmart which hired 150,000 people in the past month and is looking to hire 50,000 more. And although physical experiential retail is dead for now, we are seeing the emergence of virtual experiential retail.

Walmart hired 150,000 people in the past month and is looking to hire an additional 50,000

In the past month, **Walmart** has hired 150,000 people and now it is looking to hire 50,000 more. It's fascinating as Walmart met its hiring goal six weeks ahead of schedule — it received over 1 million applications by partnering with over 70 companies in hard-hit industries, like restaurants and hotels, looking to redeploy their furloughed workers, and it also expedited its application time from 2 weeks to 24 hours. Walmart is now looking to hire people in mainly temporary and part-time positions to work as drivers for its fleet and pickers in its warehouses to meet the sustained demand in its e-commerce distribution channel (cnbc.com). To complement its delivery efforts, Walmart is partnering with Nextdoor, a neighbourhood hub app, to launch "Neighbors Helping Neighbors". The new feature on the neighbourhood hub app will show the closest Walmart stores and enable neighbours to connect online so those making a trip to Walmart can volunteer to also pick up groceries for those that can't make it to the store (techcrunch.com). We note that Nextdoor has raised $455 million since launching in San Francisco in 2010.

Chipotle & Domino's Pizza's investments on the digital layer start to pay off

Chipotle Mexican Grill provided a number of insights during its Q1 2020 conference call on April 21 into how it is positioned to not just survive the coronavirus pandemic, but also thrive after it. The investments it has been making on the digital layer are starting to pay off. Although in-store ordering is down 75%, delivery is up 150% and order ahead is up nearly 120%, with digital now accounting for nearly 70% of its sales. Going forward, Chipotle plans to keep investing in its digital infrastructure. Although it is deferring all new basic re-models, it is pulling forward those where it is adding a digital make line or a Chipotlane. The value of Chipotle's digital loyalty program is also increasing as membership in its rewards database increased 50%, from 8 million to nearly 12 million. Chipotle is also seeing a shift in demand from lunch to dinner as pantry loading has slowed and people are experiencing a fatigue in cooking.

Domino's Pizza provided further evidence to our thesis that it is also uniquely positioned to not only survive the pandemic, but also thrive during and after it on its Q1 2020 conference call on April 23. The investments that Domino's has been making in its digital channel are paying off as 75% of its orders are now digital and it is adding new customers as plenty of people are trying delivery for the first time. It continues to innovate as it just rolled out the Pizza Pedestal, a simple cardboard pedestal for its delivery workers to put your pizza on as part of the contactless delivery service. Domino's is also well positioned to hire 10,000 new workers given the tens of millions of people recently let go and that it is a much more attractive employer than the food delivery platforms as it is looking to hire people as employees, not just as independent contractors. Like Chipotle, Domino also expects to see a rise in orders with pantry loading slowing and cooking fatigue setting in. As further evidence of Domino's antifragile nature, it is giving away 10 million pizza slices across the U.S. as part of its new Feed the Need program.

As insight into the performance of food delivery platforms, as a result of the lockdown in India, Swiggy and Zomato have seen orders plummet by two-thirds, from nearly 3 million to under 1 million. To survive, they have expanded their platforms to grocery delivery. In addition, to cut costs, Swiggy is reducing its monthly burn rate on customer acquisition from $20 million to $5 million and cutting 1,000 jobs from its cloud kitchen division (techcrunch.com).

Lord & Taylor explores bankruptcy as Macy's looks to raise up to $5 billion in debt

Lord & Taylor, which was forced to close all its 38 department stores a month ago, is exploring filing for bankruptcy protection (reuters.com). Interestingly, back in August, **Hudson's Bay Company** sold the iconic nearly 200-year-old luxury department store brand for $100 million to Le Tote, a seven-year-old online fashion subscription rental service. But part of the payment was in the form of a $25 million secured two-year promissory note, and as Hudson's Bay Company kept ownership of some of the real estate assets, it is still responsible for the rent payments, which amount to tens of millions a year. **Macy's**, which was forced to shutter all its 775 department stores on March 18, is looking to raise as much as $5 billion in debt, using its inventory and real estate as collateral (cnbc.com). And Sycamore Partners is trying to back out of its recent deal with **L Brands** to acquire a 55% stake in Victoria's Secret for $525 million. On April 22, Sycamore Partners filed a lawsuit in a Delaware court stating that L Brands violated the terms of the transaction when it closed Victoria's Secret's stores and skipped the rent payment in April and that the pandemic triggered a "material adverse effect" clause (cnbc.com). This could be bad news for L Brands as Victoria's Secret has become increasing irrelevant for maintaining its sexy image in the wake of the #metoo movement and, more importantly, the lockdown will accelerate the disruption by new DTC entrants such as Third Love.

Gap warns of cash flow shortfall while department store bankruptcies could trigger a tsunami of co-tenancy clauses

With **JC Penney** and Neiman Marcus, and potentially Lord & Taylor, looking to file for bankruptcy, this could trigger a tsunami of co-tenancy clauses (cnbc.com). As I warned in my research note back on March 21, 2017: *"According to Morningstar, $48 billion in loans backed by mall property are at risk of default. When an anchor tenant, like Macy's, Sears or JC Penney, vacates, the mall loses not just income from the anchor tenant, but also shopper traffic. There is the risk this could trigger a co-tenancy clause which would allow the remaining mall tenants to exercise their right to terminate their lease or renegotiate terms with lower rents until another retailer occupies the vacated anchor space."* In addition, retail REITs face a growing tsunami of store vacancies. For example, on April 23, **Gap** warned that it might not have enough cash flow to fund its operations. In April, Gap stopped paying rent on its shuttered stores, which totals $115 million per month. Gap is also negotiating with its landlords, of which the largest is **Simon Property Group** which has 412 Gap stores in its malls, and is negotiating with its landlords to defer rent payments or agree on an abatement. Gap also stated that it plans to terminate leases and permanently close some stores (cnbc.com). As we advised in our April 1 research report, *The Survival Guide to the New Ghost Town Economy*, a good way to determine the survivors is to make note of which retailers were the most proactive to shut down, which means they are confident in the loyalty of their community and their ability to shift their sales online. And one of the retailers we red flagged was Gap, which did not proactively close its stores, only its hours of operations.

Patagonia was first retailer to close stores and had foresight to suspend its online operations

On the positive side, not only did Patagonia show its genuine care for its customers and in-store employees by being the first retailer to proactively close its stores on March 13, but it also had the foresight to suspend its online operations on that day as well to protect the safety of its warehouse employees. As Todd Soller, head of global logistics and supply planning at Patagonia, stated on April 21 as Patagonia announced it was re-opening its online store: *"We knew we needed to take ample time to assess and design our new workplace procedures and layouts to address the threat of COVID-19"*. As a foreshadowing of the precautions that all companies will need to take in their workplaces, Patagonia is re-opening its one distribution centre in Reno with new safety protocols, including giving masks and gloves to all its workers, installing temperature scanning at all building entrances and staggering employee start times (forbes.com).

Meat processing plant closures lead to rising meat prices and build-up in livestock

The temporary closure of meat processing plants owing to the coronavirus outbreaks has led to a sharp drop in meat production. According to CoBank, production in the U.S. was down the week of April 13 by 24% for beef, 20% for pork and 10% for poultry. With outbreaks continuing, inventory is expected to tighten within two weeks, resulting in rising meat prices (wsj.com). In addition, the reduced production is leading to an oversupply of livestock, resulting in price reductions. For example, the market price of a hog in the U.S. has recently fallen 20%, from $55 to $45. In Canada, the reduced capacity of the 13 pork processing plants resulted in a 16% decline in the volume of hogs being slaughtered the week ending April 14. In addition to a reduction in cash flow from selling less hogs, farmers are also seeing higher operating costs as they have to keep feeding the hogs (financialpost.com).

Canada faces meat shortage as Cargill's plant shuts down and cases rise at JBS plant

On April 20, **Cargill** finally decided to temporarily shut down its meat processing plant in High River. But it has been slow to act as a worker just died and the number of employees testing positive has escalated in the past week from 38 to 484, making it Canada's worst coronavirus outbreak hot spot. This could start to impact Canada's beef supply as it processes 4,500 head of cattle a day, accounting for over one-third of Canada's beef processing capacity. Coronavirus has also spread to Alberta's two other meat processing plants, with the number of employees testing positive rising from 3 to 67 in the past week at JBS' (**JBS SA**) plant in Brooks (cbc.ca). As an update, as of April 25, there were 798 cases linked to Cargill's plant in High River and 540 people infected in the community of Brooks where the union is now calling for the shutdown of JBS' plant.

United Poultry Company's two Vancouver poultry-processing plants shut down

On April 21, the United Poultry Company's poultry-processing plant in Vancouver was immediately shut down after it was discovered as a new outbreak hot spot, with 28 workers testing positive for coronavirus, or just under 40% of the plant's workforce. The danger is that the plant is located in the heart of the city's densely packed homeless population as it is only a half block from Oppenheimer Park tent city. From a food supply perspective, the shutdown is not material as the plant only processes 4% of the chickens in B.C. but it adds to the growing number of meat processing plants being hit by coronavirus outbreaks (vancouversun.com). On April 24, its sister plant in Coquitlam was shut down by the government after two employees tested positive.

GM shuts down Maven car-sharing platform as Hertz works with debt restructuring advisors

GM, which suspended its Maven vehicle-sharing platform in March, is now shutting it down completely. GM will be redeploying Maven's 45 employees within the company and transferring the assets to its Global Innovation organization to develop "new fleet services" and "mobility solutions" (cnbc.com). This decision is not surprising as GM had already started to scale down its unprofitable Maven operations last May, and with the coronavirus pandemic car-sharing is now totally taboo. GM launched Maven in January 2016 to meet the shifting demand for Millennials opting for on-demand transportation alternatives in cities where car ownership is expensive. On the legacy car-sharing front, **Hertz** is laying off 10,000 employees and working with debt restructuring advisors as it struggles to survive with its $17 billion debt load in this new ghost town economy where nobody wants to rent a car. The layoffs are significant as they equate to over one-quarter of its base of 38,000 employees. In addition to revenue drying up, Hertz is being hit by plummeting residual values for the vehicles in its fleet (ca.investing.com).

Trader Joe's e-commerce weakness exposed as Amazon preps to launch Ultra Fast Fresh in U.K.

"Creating an online shopping system for curbside pickup or the infrastructure for delivery, it's a massive undertaking. It's something that takes months or years to plan, build and implement and it requires tremendous resources." Although Trader Joe's has been able to create an amazing in-store experience and an incredible emotional connection with its customers by investing in its people, this admission by Matt Sloan, VP of marketing, underlines how coronavirus is exposing the weaknesses

of companies that have avoided investing in the e-commerce layer (inc.com). At the same time, coronavirus is bringing to fruition the strengths of companies that have been investing heavily in the e-commerce layer, like Amazon. For example, **Amazon** is preparing to launch Ultra Fast Fresh in the U.K. to bring grocery delivery service to almost 40% of households by the end of this year. To achieve this, Amazon is retrofitting nine of its existing depots to handle fresh produce and fulfill grocery orders within hours (reuters.com). This is similar to the free Prime Now two-hour grocery delivery service that Amazon started to roll out in the U.S. at the end of October for Prime members. We are seeing a shift in food shopping behaviour as people return to the middle and frozen aisles as they stock up on comfort foods. Big CPG brands are seeing a resurgence in demand for processed and frozen foods such as frozen pizza, pasta sauce and mac 'n cheese (wsj.com).

UPS partners with CVS Health to launch prescription drone delivery to retirement community

UPS is partnering with **CVS Health** to launch drone delivery services of prescriptions to The Villages in Florida. This showcases how drones can be used to deliver urgent medicine to "high-risk populations" as The Villages is the largest retirement community in the U.S. with over 135,000 residents (businessinsider.com). We note that UPS was granted a certificate from the FAA in October to operate limited drone delivery services across the U.S. in partnership with Matternet, a drone delivery company that has raised $26 million since launching in Menlo Park in 2011.

Facebook buys strategic 9.99% stake in Indian telecom operator for $5.7 billion

Facebook just invested $5.7 billion for a 9.99% stake in Indian telecom operator Jio Platforms Ltd. (**Reliance Industries**). This is Facebook's largest overseas investment and the second-largest behind its $22 billion WhatsApp acquisition in 2014. This investment is strategic as it will enable Facebook to partner with Jio Platforms to offer more services through its WhatsApp messaging service, which has become the default digital town square in India with over 400 million users, or nearly one-third of the population. For example, Facebook is looking to enable people to buy products via WhatsApp to advance Jio Platform's e-commerce effort to connect millions of mom-and-pop grocery stores (wsj.com).

Zoom's daily users skyrocket 50% to 300 million in less than a month

On April 22, **Zoom** disclosed it has passed over 300 million daily users, up 50% from 200 million earlier this month and from only 10 million daily users in December. The company is actively addressing security and privacy concerns as it has implemented a 90-day feature freeze and is releasing Zoom 5.0, which includes passwords by default, improved encryption and a new security icon to control meetings (theverge.com). In response to the rising demand for video conferencing, Facebook has created a competitor to Zoom called Messenger Room which will allow up to 50 people to participate in a video chat through a link. Although Messenger Room provides privacy features such as the ability to "lock" a room and block and report people, the problem is that it follows the same data collection policies as Facebook, which includes sharing your info with third parties (forbes.com). To survive, both individuals and companies need to leave behind the physical world, which means embracing technologies like messaging, e-mail, voice and video on the digital layer. In his annual letter to shareholders, Jeff Lawson, co-founder & CEO of **Twilio**, shares how he believes Twilio was built for these challenges created by the coronavirus pandemic: *"We provide three things the world has needed during this crisis: digital engagement, software agility, and cloud scale."*

Netflix thrives during lockdown as Spotify rolls out curated pod-

cast playlists

"The things we are certain of is the Internet is growing. It's a bigger part of people's lives, thankfully. And people want entertainment. They want to be able to escape and connect, whether times are difficult or joyous." These comments by Reed Hastings on **Netflix**'s Q1 2020 conference call on April 21 showcase how the digital platform economy is thriving during the coronavirus pandemic. What I loved about the call is how honest management was, admitting that the increase in subscriber growth in March is essentially the result of pull-forward of demand for the rest of the year, and how they aren't looking to exploit this opportunity by raising prices, but rather looking to add value for members by continuing to improve the content and make sure Netflix has a steady stream of titles. The good news for everyone is that Netflix's content will not suffer as it has largely physically shot its slate of series and films for 2020 and is pretty deep into its 2021 slate, which are in post-production in locations remotely all over the world. **Spotify** is advancing its aspiration to become the "Netflix of Audio" with the roll-out of human-curated podcast playlists. This is brilliant as it will enable podcasters to reach new listeners and solve the discovery problem of the long tail of podcasts. Spotify is rolling out three weekly playlists titled "Best Podcasts of the Week", "Brain Snacks" and "Crime Scene", which will be localized to the individual countries. To start with, Spotify is rolling this out to six countries, including the U.S., Germany, Sweden, Mexico, Brazil and the U.K. (theverge.com).

Virtual music festivals emerging on Minecraft and Fortnite

As young people escape to the virtual worlds of Minecraft and Fornite, we are seeing the emergence of virtual music festivals. On April 26, Club Matryoshka is hosting a 24-hour virtual music festival on Minecraft, **Microsoft**'s sandbox video game. The Infinite Summer music festival will feature three stages showcasing performances from a wide range of musicians. Admission is free but a $10 donation to WHO's COVID-19 Solidarity Response Fund is suggested (vice.com). Interestingly, Club Matryoshka debuted its exclusive virtual club on Minecraft back in August. And on April 23, over 12 million people attended Travis Scott's Astronomical virtual concert hosted on Fortnite (cnn.com). The Houston-based rapper, singer, songwriter and record producer has sold over 45 million records in the U.S. and has been nominated for six Grammy Awards and won a Billboard Music Award

Alphabet stops talks to lease over 2 million square feet of office space in San Francisco

As a foreshadowing of the coming collapse in demand for office real estate, **Alphabet** has apparently stopped talks to buy or lease over 2 million square feet of office space in the Bay Area. This includes plans to potentially lease over 1.5 million square feet at **Brookfield Property Partners'** new development at Pier 70 in San Francisco (bisnow.com).

Expedia raises cash to survive the pandemic

Expedia is raising $3.2 billion in cash to survive. In addition to $2 billion in new debt financing, the company is raising $1.2 billion in a private placement of perpetual preferred stock from private equity firms Silver Lake and Apollo Global Management, which will each get a spot on the company's board (cnbc.com). OTA companies like Expedia and **TripAdvisor** are being hit hard by travel restrictions and the lockdown with airline traffic down 95% and hotels near empty, except for those that have been repurposed into healthcare facilities (wsj.com).

Demand is falling off a cliff in trucking industry as initial essential goods panic buying subsides

Demand is falling off a cliff in the trucking industry as a result of the shutdown of factories, retail stores and restaurants. Although the initial panic buying by households to stock up on essential goods in March led to a 50% growth in trucking shipments to grocery and discount stores, they have now re-stocked and demand is back to normal. As a result, loads that paid $1,000 last month are now paying $300 or less, which is not enough to cover the pay for drivers, fuel and other costs (wsj.com).

Western Europe recruits students and unemployed for a "great agricultural army"

Western European countries are redeploying students and newly unemployed workers like flight attendants and restaurant staff for a "great agricultural army" to harvest the fields as border closures have blocked seasonal workers from Central and Eastern Europe. Europe, which has a patchwork of over 10 million farms, relies on low-cost labour as many of the farms are focused on specialty crops like white asparagus and Champagne grapes that require manual labour. Germany is looking to recruit 10,000 domestic workers while the U.K. is looking to hire 70,000 British people for its newly launched "Pick for Britain" campaign. Although restrictions on migrant farm workers from Mexico may result in shortage of labour in the U.S., the situation won't be as bad in Europe as U.S. farms are much bigger and grow bulk crops which are easier to plant and harvest with machinery (wsj.com).

Nearly 1 million kegs of beer going stale in abandoned bars and restaurants

According to the National Beer Wholesalers Association (NBWA), there are 10 million gallons of beer (equivalent to nearly 1 million kegs of beer) abandoned in closed venues such as bars, restaurants, stadiums and concert halls across the U.S. and even more stuck at distributors' warehouses and breweries. In the U.K., where nearly one-half of all beer is drunk outside the home versus 20% for the U.S., there are an estimated 50 million pints of beer going to waste. The problem is that beer is perishable, with a 2–6-month shelf life, and you can't just pour large volumes down the drain as it would disturb the pH balance. Downstream, some venues are starting to sell DTC while others are searching for third-party logistics operators to dispose of the beer safely. Upstream, brewers are shifting their packaging to cans to sell to consumers through liquor and grocery stores, and some are sending expired beer to craft distillers to turn into hand sanitizer (wsj.com).

Physical experiential retail is dead for now, but virtual experiential retail is emerging

Although the physical experiential retail is totally dead for now, we are seeing the emergence of virtual experiential retail. For example, Burrow, which just opened its flagship 2,200-square-foot furniture store in NYC in February, has launched virtual consultations through Burrow at Home and is hosting weekly Instagram Live sessions called "The Wind Down" in which it interviews people across industries to see what they are doing with their new evening routines. Meanwhile, Camp NYC, a family experience store, has rolled out free virtual 30-minute birthday parties on its website with help from sponsors like **Ally Financial** (wsj.com).

Trump threatens to not approve $10 billion loan to USPS

On April 24, President Trump stated he won't approve the $10 billion loan to the USPS unless the company raises delivery charges by 4–5 times the current rates for Amazon and other large shippers (apnews.com). Obviously Trump is using the coronavirus pandemic to advance his personal vendetta against Jeff Bezos and The Washington Post. We note that two years ago, Trump went absolutely postal against Amazon in series of tweets like this one he posted on March 29, 2018: *"I have stated my concerns with Amazon long before the Election. Unlike others, they pay little or no taxes to state & local governments, use our Postal System as their Delivery Boy (causing tremendous loss to the U.S.), and are putting many thousands of retailers out of business!"*

Chapter 13: INFLECTION POINT!

May 5, 2020

It had been a decade since I had set foot in a boardroom and my Ubernomics presentation was quite a radical departure from most sell-side equity research, so I was quite nervous when Ed and I embarked on our first marketing trip in Toronto in September 2016. But it was fun and, more importantly, the portfolio managers from the dozen investment firms we met with gave us valuable feedback and I realized there was real demand to figure out how to capitalize on the emerging disruption and when this disruption would reach the inflection point. As one portfolio manager observed: "...the key for us will be figuring out how to make money from it — and maybe even more importantly how not to lose money as companies/perception gets shifted through these trends."

- Barbara Gray, *Secrets of the Amazon*, 2017

As I was reading through the conference call transcripts from the tech giants last week, I realized the coronavirus pandemic is acting as a catalyst to fast-forward structural disruption to hit this inflection point. It's interesting as an inflection point is defined as "a point on a continuous plane curve at which the curve changes from being concave (concave downward) to convex (concave upward), or vice versa". If you remember from my April 1 research report, "The Survival Guide to the Ghost Town Economy", this corresponds to the concept of antifragile (convex) versus fragile (concave) that Nicholas Nassim Taleb discusses in his book, "Antifragile: Things that Gain from Disorder", that we can use to gain insight into which companies are headed for the ICU ward and which ones will be able to survive the lockdown.

The coronavirus continues to prey on the fragile, claiming the lives of J. Crew and Roots USA and sending Reitmans and Hertz to the ICU ward. But tech giants, who exist in the digital realm, are not just immune from the coronavirus but starting to capitalize on society's mass exodus from the physical world to provide us with new ways to help us socialize, learn, work, shop, and even meet our healthcare needs.

Tech CEOs: The coronavirus pandemic is acting as catalyst to accelerate digital transformation

"We have seen 2 years' worth of digital transformation in two months."
- Satya Nadella, CEO of Microsoft

"It's now clear that once the emergency is past, the world will not look the same... Ultimately, we'll see a long-term acceleration of movement from businesses to digital services, including increased online work, education, medicine, shopping and entertainment. These changes will be significant and lasting." – Sunar Pichai, CEO of Alphabet

"At this time of social distance, of shuttered school and gathering places, of delayed plans and new ways of socializing, we have seen significant evidence that our products have taken a renewed importance for customers." – Tim Cook, CEO of Apple

As evidenced by these statements made by CEOs from the world's biggest tech companies, the coronavirus pandemic is acting as a catalyst to accelerate the digital transformation of society. More importantly, based on the insights we gained from last week's conference calls for Alphabet, Amazon, Apple, Facebook and Microsoft, we believe the pandemic is creating a unique opportunity for them to completely disrupt how we socialize, learn, work, shop and meet our healthcare needs, enabling them to expand their total addressable market (TAM) and gain wallet share.

SOCIALIZE: Digital platforms are thriving as they become an essential part of the social infrastructure:

- **Alphabet**: *"People are spending significantly more time on their Android apps with downloads of apps from Google Play rising 30% from February to March. YouTube watch-time has also significantly increased. One area in particular is live streams."*
- **Facebook**: *"So, we're seeing major increases in use of our services. For the first time ever, there are now more than 3 billion people actively using Facebook, Instagram, WhatsApp, or Messenger each month...In many of the places that have been hardest hit by the virus, messaging volume has increased more than 50%, and voice and video calling has more than doubled across Messenger and WhatsApp...Between WhatsApp and Messenger, there are more than 700 million daily actives participating in calls...whether that's the Pope's weekly mass on Facebook Live or DJs hosting dance parties on Instagram, every day more than 800 million daily actives are engaging with live streams, across workout classes, concerts and more."*
- **Microsoft**: *"People everywhere are turning to gaming to sustain human connection while practicing social distancing. We saw all-time record engagement this quarter, with nearly 19 million active users of*

Xbox Live, led by the strength on and off-console."

- **Apple**: *"services like FaceTime and Messages set new all-time records for daily volume during this quarter as users relied on their devices to stay connected in a new reality... App Store revenue grew by strong double digits, thanks to robust customer demand for both in-app purchases and subscriptions. Our third-party subscription business grew across multiple categories and increased over 30% year-over-year, reaching a new all-time high. Our first party subscription services also continued to perform very well. Apple Music and cloud services, both set all-time revenue record and AppleCare set a March quarter record. Paid subscriptions for all three of these services were up strong double-digits."*

LEARN: Tech giants are powering the new virtual classroom:

- **Alphabet**: *"100 million students and educators are using Google Classroom, double the number from the beginning of March. We have seen a massive increase in demand for Chromebooks. Analysts have reported 400% increase during the week of March 21 year-over-year."*
- **Microsoft**: *"More than 183,000 educational institutions now rely on Teams."*
- **Apple:** *"Teachers and students around the world are relying on our technology to teach, learn, and stay connected with each other. We are in the process of deploying major orders of iPads to school systems working to keep learning going strong at a distance, including tens of thousands in Ontario, Canada; Glasgow, Scotland and Puerto Rico, a 100,000 to the city of Los Angeles and 350,000 to New York City, our largest educational iPad deployment ever."*

WORK: Tech giants are powering the office-less world:

- **Microsoft**: *"We saw more than 200 million meeting participants in a single day this month, generating more than 4.1 billion meeting minutes. Teams now has more than 75 million daily active users...20 organizations with more than 100,000 employees are now using Teams, including Continental AG, Ernst & Young, Pfizer, and SAP...We're accelerating Teams innovation, adding new capabilities each week, and now support meetings of all sizes, meetings that scale from 250 active participants to live events for up to 100,000 attendees to streaming broadcasts."*
- **Apple**: *"In the enterprise market businesses everywhere have been making the transition to working remotely. We've created content to assist our customers in this transition including an on-demand video learning series focused on topics like remote deployments of iPad and Mac and security."*

SHOP: We are seeing a quantum leap in the shift to online sales:

- **Amazon**: *"We see our Prime customers are shopping more often and they have larger basket sizes."*
- **Alphabet**: *"Last week, we announced that merchants can list products in Google shopping for free. It's been widely rolled out in the U.S. with more countries to come and the response has been positive."*
- **Facebook**: *"with so many businesses forced to close their physical storefronts, more are looking to build their digital presences and those which already invested in their digital presences are increasingly viewing them as the primary storefronts... while there may be some short-term spike, I do think plays into a pre-existing long-term trend."*
- **Apple**: *"as stores shift to become fulfillment centers for online orders, organizations are leveraging apps for remote shoppers and food delivery to reduce foot traffic."*

MEET HEALTHCARE NEEDS: Tech giants are leveraging their capital to fight against the coronavirus, positioning them to take a quantum leap in the disruption of healthcare:

- **Alphabet**: *"Verily has tested thousands of people in California and has partnered with Rite Aid to bring free testing to 8 additional states. Google Cloud is forming deep partnerships, such as with leading healthcare provider, HCA Healthcare to understand data around ICU bed availability, ventilator supplies and test results."*
- **Amazon**: *"AWS is helping healthcare workers, medical researchers, scientists, and public health officials working to understand and fight COVID-19 by providing a centralized repository of curated, up-to-date, pre-processed, and publicly-readable datasets focused on the spread and characteristics of the virus."*
- **Apple**: *"With new FDA guidance on non-invasive remote patient monitoring, for example, the ECG app on Apple Watch is increasingly being used to facilitate remote ECG measurements and recordings for telemedicine usage, reducing patient and healthcare provider contact and exposure. Many hospitals such as Geisinger Health System, NYU Langone Health, and Stanford Health Care are using apps on iPad and iPhone to support communication and video conferences between hospitalized patients and their care teams. This enables the care teams to keep a close watch on patients without entering isolation rooms, which helps to minimize exposure and reduces some of the need for personal protective equipment."*

AMC's fight against Universal highlights how the lockdown is fast-forwarding the obsolescence of movie theatres

On April 28, the Academy of Motion Pictures announced it is changing its Oscar eligibility rules to include streamed films while theatres are closed (cnbc.com). Although this is a temporary measure and the film had to be scheduled for theatrical release, we believe this is another sign of how the coronavirus pandemic will fast-forward the obsolescence of movie theatres. For example, the same day, Jeff Shell, head of NBCUniversal (**Comcast**) stated he expects to release movies on both formats once theatres re-open, based on the success of the online debut of *Trolls World Tour*, which generated nearly $95 million in rental fees from nearly 5 million rentals in the first three weeks since it was released online on April 10. The digital distribution channel is more attractive for studios from a revenue cut perspective, as they get to keep 80% of digital rentals versus only 50% of box office sales. NBCUniversal plans to deploy the same release strategy for its upcoming new comedy, *The King of Staten Island*, which is scheduled to hit theatres on June 19. Other studios are following suite: Warner Bros. (**AT&T**) will release its upcoming children's movie, *Scoob!*, direct to digital on its scheduled theatre debut date of May 15 (wsj.com).

However, the theatres are starting to fight back against the elimination of the traditional 90-day window as that evening, Adam Aron, CEO of **AMC Entertainment Holdings**, threatened to not book any of NBCUniversal's movies in theatres and published an open letter stating: *"AMC believes that with this proposed action to go to the home and theatres simultaneously, Universal is breaking the business model and dealings between our two companies...It assumes that we will meekly accept a reshaped view of how studios and exhibitors should interact, with zero concern on Universal's part as to how its actions affect us...It also presumes that Universal in fact can have its cake and eat it too"* (wsj.com).

Amazon launches Prime Video Cinema in the U.S. as its viewers nearly double

But the reality is that **Netflix** and Amazon Prime Video are the new movie theatres. For example, on Amazon's Q1 2020 conference call, the company disclosed: *"We're also seeing a lot more use of our video benefits and our digital benefits. So in March, for the first time viewers* *nearly doubled"* and added: *"We launched Prime Video Cinema in U.S., U.K. and Germany where movies are going direct to pay-per-view because of lack of theaters."* Amazon has also renewed its exclusive streaming partnership with the NFL for "Thursday Night Football" games for another three years. Amazon is apparently paying more than the $65 million per year it paid to the NFL when it signed the initial two-year partnership back in July 2017. This time, Amazon will also receive exclusive national rights to one Saturday game (wsj.com). The games will be available to Amazon's +150 million global Prime members.

Simon Property Group's and Macy's desperate rush to re-open is a red flag

Just like a good way to determine the survivors back in mid-March was to make note of those most proactive to shut down, we believe the best way to determine which ones are the most fragile are those that desperately decide to re-open. For example, on April 28, **Simon Property Group** (SPG) announced that it will be re-opening nearly one-quarter of the 200+ malls and outlet centres it closed on March 19. Over three-quarters of the 49 re-openings across the 10 states are in only 3 states (21 in Texas, 10 in Indiana, 7 in Georgia). SPG is taking a number of safety precautions, including limiting operating hours and occupancy to one person per 50 square feet; however, we believe it falls short as it is only making temperature checking and mask wearing voluntary for customers (cnbc.com). We believe SPG is motivated to quickly re-open its malls so it can force its tenants to pay rent. We note that Taubman (which SPG acquired for $3.6 billion in cash on February 11) played hardball with its tenants in a memo on March 25 when it told them they need their rent payments to make their own utility and mortgage payments.

Another desperate retailer is **Macy's**, which announced on April 30 that it will be re-opening 68 department stores on Monday in five states that have eased restrictions, with the plan to open another 50 stores on May 11 and have all its 775 stores re-opened in six weeks if allowed by state and local governments. As a foreshadowing of what safety measures retailers will need to implement, Macy's will be taking the temperatures of its employees and requiring them to wear masks, offering "no touch" consultations in its beauty department, requiring customers to use hand sanitizer before trying on jewelry and watches, only opening a few fitting rooms and putting a 24-hour hold on items that have been tried on (wsj.com).

We prefer the more cautious approach being taken by Kimco Realty and Best Buy

On April 30, **Kimco Realty** announced that it will be rolling out permanent designated curbside pick-up spaces at 23 of its shopping centres, or at just over 5% its portfolio of +400 shopping centres and mixed-use developments. We expect other retail REITs will follow suit as the Retail Industry Leaders Association and National Retail Federation just released a blueprint for retailers to think about returning to business and Phase 1 calls for ramping up online sales and offering curbside pick-up. In Phase 2, stores will re-open to the public but implement safety measures such as social distancing and limiting capacity (cnbc.com).

Best Buy, which closed all its stores in early April as it shifted to curbside pick-up, will now allow customers to start to schedule in-store consultations to discuss their tech needs of potential kitchen appliance purchases. Best Buy is rolling this out slowly, starting in 200, or 20%, of its +1,000 stores. In addition, Best Buy will resume in-home delivery, installation and repairs, but with new safety precautions. In mid-March, the company experienced a temporary surge in demand for a number of different products as households prepared for lockdown but its sales have since levelled off and declined, leading it to furlough 51,000 employees on April 15 (cnbc.com).

Roots USA and J. Crew file for bankruptcy as Reitman warns it may

be next

The bankruptcies of apparel retailers are beginning. On April 29, **Roots** filed for Chapter 7 bankruptcy protection for its Roots USA Corp subsidiary and permanently closed seven stores in the U.S. However, it will continue to sell to U.S. customers through e-commerce (globeandmail.com). On May 4, J. Crew, which operates 182 J. Crew and 140 Madewell stores, filed for Chapter 11 bankruptcy protection (cnbc.com). **Reitmans Canada**, which was in a fragile state even before it was forced to close its stores on March 17, warned on May 1 that it might not be able to continue as a going concern if it is unable to obtain additional funding (financialpost.com).

Bezos' long-term mindset shines through as he commits to spend $4 billion to get products to customers and keep employees safe

Bezos' long-term mindset shone on Amazon's Q1 2020 conference call as he shocked investors with the news that Amazon spent $600 million in Q1 on COVID-19-releated expenses to get products to customers and keep employees safe and he expects this could grow to over $4 billion in Q2. The expenses include the purchase of 100 million face masks, 1,000 thermal cameras and 31,000 thermometers, investment of $300 million to build a coronavirus testing lab for its employees, and the cost of productivity headwinds in its facilities as it implements social distancing and ramps up the 175,000 new employees it has just hired. Amazon is also helping to keep low-income communities safe as the USDA has expanded the SNAP (Supplement Nutrition Assistance Program) for food stamp recipients to buy groceries online from New York, Washington and Alabama to seven more states (Arizona, California, Florida, Iowa, Kentucky, Nebraska, Oregon) with additional states to come online soon.

Amazon's net sales rose 26% in Q1 2020 to $75.5 billion but its EPS declined by 29% to $5.01 as a result of business disruption and higher costs related to the coronavirus pandemic. Amazon's profit driver continues to be its high-margin AWS division, where net sales rose 33% to $10.2 billion and its operating margin rose 120 bp to 30.1%. AWS is now up to a $41 billion run-rate. The company's overall operating margin fell 210 bp to 5.3% as its operating margin in North America, which accounts for 61% of its net sales, declined 350 bp to 2.8% and its International operating margin declined 150 bp to -2.1%. Amazon's "Other" revenue, which is mainly advertising revenue, rose 44% to $3.9 billion. Its negative shipping delta widened by $2.4 billion in Q1 to $5.4 billion as the 49% increase in its shipping costs to $10.9 billion more than offset the 28% increase in its subscription services revenue to $5.6 billion.

Sun Country Airlines speeds up plan to start flying cargo planes for Amazon

Sun Country Airlines' decision to partner with Amazon back in late December is now looking brilliant. With its passenger demand down 95%, Sun Country Airlines is moving quickly on its plans to start shipping cargo for Amazon. Sun Country will start flying its first cargo plane on May 7 with the plan to have all 10 of its converted **Boeing** 737-800 jets flying by the end of July, instead of the end of the summer as originally planned (cnbc.com). We note that in June, Amazon leased 15 of these jets from **GE** Capital Aviation Services.

U.S. SAAR drops to 30-year low of 7.7 million in April as Hertz prepares for potential bankruptcy filing

U.S. auto sales hit a 30-year low in April as auto buyers stayed home. According to Edmunds, U.S. auto sales declined by 53% in April to 633,260, which translates into a SAAR of 7.7 million versus 16.3 million a year ago (edmunds.com). This comes as **Hertz** prepares for a potential bankruptcy filing after it failed to make lease payments to preserve cash (wsj.com).

Ford cancels Lincoln-branded EV; online auto shopping set to

snowball; Tesla applies for licence to supply electricity in U.K.

Ford, which idled its factories in mid-March, announced on April 28 that it plans to re-open in Europe next week and partially re-open in the U.S. on May 18. As evidence of how the coronavirus pandemic is slowing down investment in autonomous vehicles, Ford is pushing back the target date for the autonomous vehicle service it is developing with Argo AI from 2021 to 2022. In addition, Ford is canceling plans for the Lincoln-branded electric vehicle which it is developing with Rivian (wsj.com). We note that last April, Ford made a $500 million strategic investment in Rivian and announced plans to develop a new vehicle using Rivian's skateboard platform.

Honda Canada, which idled its three Ontario plants and most of its 4,200 workers in late March, is looking to resume production on May 11, depending on inventory and demand levels. Like all manufacturers, it will be implementing safety measures on the plant floor. The biggest takeaway though is this statement from Jean Marc Leclerc, head of Honda Canada: *"Online shopping in our industry is going to snowball."* (windsorstar.com), which underlines how the coronavirus pandemic is pushing the auto industry up to the digital layer of the structural capital side of the value pyramid.

We note it was only back in March 2019 that Elon Musk had to compromise and close only half as many **Tesla** stores as previously announced after facing strong pushback from Class A retail REITs such as Simon Property Group, **Macerich** and Taubman Centers. But he didn't change his strategy to shift all sales online as the Tesla stores would just function as showrooms. Speaking of Tesla, it applied for a license to supply electricity in the U.K on April 28. Although the details are still unknown, it is reported that Tesla may be looking to introduce its Autobidder software that it developed to sell surplus energy back to the grid and is using at its Hornsdale Power Reserve in Southern Australia (uk.reuters.com).

Unions call for workplace safety regulations as Trump orders meat processing plants to stay open

On April 28, President Trump invoked the Defense Production Act to order meat processing plants to stay open by classifying them as critical infrastructure for the national meat and poultry supply chain. According to the UFCW, outbreaks at meat processing plants have led to the closure of 22 plants, reducing pork and beef production by 25% and 20% respectively. Although the CDC released guidelines for meat and poultry processing workers and employers two days earlier, we are concerned that Trump doesn't care about the safety of workers. At least 20 plant workers have died from the coronavirus and by invoking the Act, Trump provides liability protections for big employers like Smithfield Foods (**WH Group**), **Tyson Foods** and JBS USA Holdings (**JBS SA**), which account for the majority of the plant closures (cnbc.com).

The same day, unions representing over 6 million American workers, joined together to call for the OSHA to implement enforceable emergency coronavirus workplace regulations to ensure the safety of workers. In their statement, they criticize the OSHA, the agency that polices workplace safety within the Department of Labor, for leaving workers to fend for themselves (cnbc.com). The unions' concerns echo those of Representative Rosa DeLauro, former assistant secretary of Labor for OSHA, who introduced legislation on April 21 to the House of Representatives for the *"COVID-19 Every Worker Protection Act of 2020"* (congress.gov/bill).

Lyft & Uber shift into survival mode: Lyft cuts 17%, Careem cuts 31%, Uber Eats exits 7 markets

On April 29, **Lyft** announced it would be laying off 982 employees, or 17% of its employee base. In addition, it will be furloughing 288 employees and cutting salaries for hourly employees for the next three months (cnbc.com). Although Lyft's platform economy model provides it with the benefit of an asset-light and highly variable cost business model, this decision to reduce fixed operating costs shows how it is moving into survival mode. Although Uber hasn't announced any job cuts yet, its Chief Technology Officer, Thuan Pham, who is its longest serving top executive, just stepped down and it is rumoured that **Uber** is considering laying off over 5,000 employees, which would equate to nearly 20% of its global employee base (theverge.com). In addition, on May 4, Uber's new Middle East subsidiary, Careem, which it acquired in March 2019 for $3.1 billion, is cutting 536 jobs, equating to 31% of Careem's workforce (financialpost.com). The same day, Uber announced that Uber Eats is exiting seven markets (Czech Republic, Egypt, Honduras, Romania, Saudi Arabia, Uruguay, Ukraine) and transferring its operations in the UAE to Careem. This strategic move indicates that Uber is accelerating its strategy to cut its global losses in areas where it is not the #1 or #2 player as these markets account for 1% of Uber Eats' gross bookings but 4% of its adjusted EBITDA losses (techcrunch.com).

lululemon advances its community-driven mission through offering free access to digital meditation tools

lululemon continues to advance the company's original mission to *"create components for people to live a longer, healthier, and more fun life,"* as it is now helping its community find peace of mind through digital meditation tools (shop.lululemon.com). On April 30, Calvin McDonald, CEO of lululemon, tweeted: *"Together @lululemon & @unfoundation are proud to expand the Peace on Purpose program for everyone to use, offering digital mindfulness tools originally created to support the mental & emotional health of UN humanitarian workers."*

TikTok reaches 2 billion downloads

TikTok has reached 2 downloads just five months after it passed 1.5 billion downloads as millions migrate to this short-form video sharing app to connect with others as they escape the physical world (

cnet.com).

Zoom partners with Oracle to scale as it meets new competition from Facebook & Google

Zoom is partnering with **Oracle** Cloud Infrastructure to meet its sky-rocketing need for immediate additional cloud capacity. Zoom selected niche cloud player Oracle for *"its advantages in performance, scalability, reliability and superior cloud security"*, which signals that Zoom is looking to go more after enterprises than SMEs (techcrunch.com). But Zoom is facing new competition from Facebook and Google.

On Facebook's Q1 2020 conference call on April 29, Mark Zuckerberg, shared: *"We are doubling the size of WhatsApp video calls from four to eight... For video rooms we announced a completely new product called Messenger Rooms. And the idea here is that you can create a room for any active event you want, send the link to your friends or have them discover your room on Facebook and then they can just drop in and hang out for a bit..."* The day prior, on Alphabet's Q1 2020 conference call, the company disclosed it has seen a 30-fold increase in usage since January and has reached over 100 million daily Meet meeting participants and is still adding 3 million new users each day. The next day (April 29), Google announced that it is opening up its Google Meet videoconferencing service for free to anyone with a Google account. Previously Google Meet was only available for its enterprise and education clients via G Suite. Although Google offers a superior service to Zoom in terms of call time (unlimited versus a 40-minute restriction per call for Zoom's free service) and to Facebook in terms of the number of participants (100 versus 50), it is not as user-friendly as you need to login to join a meeting, you can't just click a link to join. But the big advantage it has is that it will be able to capitalize on its existing customer and structural capital by integrating it into Gmail (verge.com).

Facebook plans to hire 10,000 employees as it sees signs of stabil-

ity in ad revenue

Based on insights we gained from Facebook's Q1 2020 conference call, it is proving to be antifragile as has committed to continue to pay all its employers and contractors, with over 95% being able to work from home, and, more importantly, it plans to hire at least 10,000 more people in engineering and product roles this year. Although Facebook experienced an initial steep decrease in ad revenue in March, with big hits in the travel and auto verticals, it has seen signs of stability in April, with relative strength in gaming technology and e-commerce.

Could virtual showrooms on Zoom be the future of retail?

In Sweden, a menswear stores called Tres Bien has launched a virtual version of its store on Zoom. Although you can't buy anything on Zoom (yet!), customers can call in and talk to sales associates one-on-one. The concept is popular as there is always someone lined up in the virtual waiting room during the store's operating hours (vogue.com). This is a brilliant concept as it enables Tres Bien to enhance its emotional connection with its customers and build a community. From a strategic perspective, it advances my thesis that the future of retail is stores that don't sell goods, but function as showrooms — for this is possible no longer just in the physical world, but now the virtual world.

Shopify launches new shopping app called Shop

On April 28, **Shopify** launched a new consumer shopping app called Shop. Shop was built off the foundation of its Arrive package tracking app, which has been used by 16 million customers. Unlike most shopping platforms, Shop does not have ads as the feed of recommended products is based on brands you have previously bought through the Shopify store or those you decide to follow. Shop enables you to learn more about each brand and then buy it through Shop Pay using one-click. To support merchants through these tough times, Shop added a feature that enables you to browse local merchants to see which ones currently support delivery (techcrunch.com).

Coronavirus pandemic has necessitated the rapid adoption of telemedicine

On Teladoc Health's Q1 2020 conference call on April 29, Jason Gorevic, CEO of **Teladoc Health,** shared insights into three ways the coronavirus pandemic has necessitated the rapid adoption of telemedicine. On the demand side, consumer awareness and adoption around virtual care has risen, as evidenced by a 125% increase in registrations and a 90% year-over-year growth in total visits to over 2 million, with over 60% of the visits coming from first-time users. On the supply side, physicians and hospital systems are embracing virtual care as a delivery methodology, as evidenced by the more than doubling of the number of licensed physicians in its network. In terms of the service itself, health plans and employers are now viewing virtual care across all specialties, as evidenced by over half of bookings in Q1 being multi-product.

FDA grants emergency use authorization to Gilead for antiviral drug remdesivir

On May 4, the World Health Organization announced it will discuss with the U.S. government and **Gilead Sciences** on how to make remdesivir more widely available. This follows three days after the FDA granted emergency use authorization to use the antiviral drug to treat COVID-19 following positive results from the National Institute of Allergy and Infectious Disease's clinical trial that showed remdesivir sped up patients' recovery time from 15 to 11 days. Gilead is looking to produce over 140,000 rounds by the end of May, over 1 million by year-end and several million next year (cnbc.com).

Pandemic drone could help fight against spreading of coronavirus

Draganfly, a firm founded in Saskatoon in 1998, is collaborating on developing "pandemic drones" with the Australian Department of Defense and the University of Southern Australia. The drones use computer vision to fly above a crowd and detect people who are sneezing and coughing and monitor peoples' vital signs such as temperature, heart rate and respiratory conditions (businessinsider.com). Although the initial budget for this project is only $1.5 million, we believe it could foreshadow the deployment of drones into an AI army to fight against the spreading of the coronavirus.

Air pollution drops in the new ghost town economy

The new ghost town economy has resulted in air pollution dropping to levels not seen in 70 years. For example, with factories shut down and cars off the road, nitrogen dioxide ($NO2$) levels have declined by 30% in areas like the Northeast U.S. and San Francisco (wsj.com).

U.S. Supreme Court livestreams its first ever teleconference hearing

On May 4, for the first time in its 230-year history, the U.S. Supreme Court will sit remotely. After canceling scheduled cases in March and April, the U.S. Supreme Court will be hearing ten cases via teleconference over the next two weeks. As the cases will be livestreamed for the public, this will democratize access to the hearings as only fifty seats are set aside in the physical courtroom for the public (wsj.com). We note this follows the recent move by Britain's House of Commons to sit remotely, which seems more progressive as it is using Zoom videoconference, not just teleconference.

Chapter 14: Home Sweet Home

May 12, 2020

> *Today it takes an act of courage to suggest that our biggest factories and offices may, within our lifetimes, stand half empty, reduced to use as ghostly warehouses or converted into living space.. A return to the cottage industry – a new emphasis on the home as the center of society.*

\- Alvin Toffler, *The Third Wave*, 1980

In the past two months, the home has emerged as the centre of society — the place from which we go online to socialize, learn, work, shop and even meet our healthcare needs. Once we met our basic physiological needs by stocking up our pantries and freezers, we advanced up the customer capital side of the value pyramid to meet our emotional needs by investing in our homes. Last month I decided to transform our backyard and went onto Wayfair and bought a turquoise outdoor mat and matching lounge cushions for our deck and a badminton set. And I'm not alone as Wayfair just revealed that home is becoming an area that we're disproportionately investing in right now. But, more importantly, Wayfair expects this could turn into a new multi-year tailwind for home improvement and home spending. And this societal shift runs even deeper as we're starting to develop new needs and desires for a home.

On Zillow's conference call, Rich Barton discusses how the lockdown experience has "uncorked new aspirations and hopes of what home can be and needs to be...Whether they are dreaming about an extra room for an office, a bigger yard, a less dense neighborhood, or for many of you maybe, a new second home." He also discusses how all these factors are creating the catalyst for a "great reshuffling". On Redfin's conference call, the company shares how it is even seeing signs of a demographic shift toward small cities. As Twilio shares on its conference call, digital transformation has been fast-forwarded from years to a weekend as "developers and companies, big and small, got to work, reconfiguring the world for a work from home and nearly 100% e-commerce reality." According to MIT, nearly half of the U.S. workforce is now working from home and companies are investing in this new work from home environment, as according to a new Deloitte survey, 60% of CFOs are looking to increase spending over the next twelve months on tech for virtual work and automated processes. The tech giants are once again leading the way as Facebook and Google just announced they will allow most of their employees to work from home through the end of this year.

Target's opportunistic acquisition of Deliv will help it further enhance Shipt

On May 7, **Target** opportunistically swooped in to buy the technology assets of Deliv, the same-day delivery platform for large national multichannel retailers. Interestingly, the prior day, Deliv announced it was closing shop and would be winding down its operations over the next 90 days. As part of the deal, Target is bringing on board Deliv's CEO, Daphne Carmeli, who founded Deliv back in 2012, and some of her team members (cnbc.com). We believe Deliv's technology will provide Target with valuable structural capital to help it further enhance its Shipt same-day delivery service and grow its e-commerce distribution channel, which has become increasingly valuable as shopping online becomes the new normal.

It's ironic as back in January 2017, in my first research report, *Where Do the Ubernomic Fault Lines Lie in Your Portfolio?*, I cautioned investors that the retail fault line is creating a high level of structural risk for retail REIT companies. My thesis was based on the fact that in February 2014 and February 2016 Class A retail REITs (i.e., General Growth Properties, Macerich, Simon Property Group, Taubman Centers and Westfield) invested in and partnered with goods delivery company Deliv to deliver their merchandise to their customers. I viewed this as evidence of the shifting consumer dynamic toward the acceleration of online shopping that threatened to render both the core activities (leasing space to retailers) and core assets (the shopping malls) obsolete.

Wayfair sees multi-year tailwind emerging for home improvement and home spending

Wayfair is hiring 1,000 additional frontline workers, increasing its employee base by 6%, to meet the increased demand for its indoor and outdoor home furnishings and accessories from people looking to improve the experience of being stuck at home. The key insights we gained from Wayfair's Q1 2020 conference call on May 5 are:

· **Rapid E-Commerce Adoption Is Driving a Secular Shift to Online:** *"likely that e-commerce adoption is going to step change across a wide swap of categories. In our case, millions of new customers shopped at Wayfair over the last several weeks...what we are seeing is a huge secular shift from off-line to online. And there's no question. Part of it is temporary, but we do think part of it is permanent."*

· **Lockdown Led to Increased Home Spending Across a Wide Number of Categories:** *"If you think about the seven-week period now the first couple of weeks in kind of mid- to late March, there were* *certain categories that accelerated first. And these are ones you associate with staying at home and working at home and the kids being at home, home office and cooking at home, home office, kitchen, large appliances, small electrics, storage and organization, children's playroom, children's furniture, outdoor recreation. But what we saw during that period is we saw then it start to spread pretty widely. The outdoor category started to take off, the decor category started to take off, the renovation category started to take off."*

- **New Multi-year Tailwind Could Be Emerging for Home Improvement and Home Spending**: *"home is becoming an area that customers are disproportionately investing into right now. And I would expect that to persist for a while. After 9/11, which was, I would say, not as big a persistent long duration shock as this is proving to be, there was actually a multiyear tailwind into home improvement and home spending that was unlocked through that."*

BAM launches $5 billion retail revitalization program to delay fast-forwarded mall obsolescence

"What we're going to see is what all of us expected to play out over the next five to 10 years is going to play out over the next one to two years." This statement by Brian Kingston, CEO of **Brookfield Property Partners** (BPP), reflects how the coronavirus pandemic is fast-forwarding the retail apocalypse. But the reality is the tsunami wave of retail and mall bankruptcies has already started hitting the shore and we expect this will play out much faster than one to two years. It's interesting as on Brookfield Property Partners' Q1 2020 conference call on May 8, Kingston also discussed how retail collections were 20% in April and are tracking close to this in May but he is optimistic the vast majority of these retail rents will be ultimately collected. But it seems like the source of funding will be capital coming from BPP's parent itself. On the call, Kingston shared that he estimates that between two-thirds

and three-quarters of his retail tenant base will qualify for the retail revitalization program announced the day prior by **Brookfield Asset Management** (BAM).

BAM is making a desperate move to delay the fast-forwarded obsolescence of the mall with the launch of a $5 billion retail revitalization program. Under the program, which is being led by Ron Bloom, a managing director of BAM's private equity arm, BAM will provide capital to medium-sized retailers with at least $250 millon in annual revenue pre-COVID-19 in exchange for a non-controlling stake (bnnbloomberg.ca). But propping retailers up with cash does not solve the underlying disease facing retailers as this is not a cyclical economic issue, but structural. But clearly BAM remains in denial about this as it continues to raise the stakes. For example, in March 2018, Brookfield Property Partners bought the remaining 66% stake in GGP, in a deal that valued GGP at $15.3 billion and then in February, it paid $81 million, along with **Simon Property Group**, for Forever 21, the teen apparel retailer that filed for bankruptcy on September 29.

Gold's Gym, Neiman Marcus & Aldo file for bankruptcy

The bankruptcies keeping coming. On May 5, Gold's Gym filed for Chapter 11 bankruptcy protection. Gold's Gym had already permanently closed 30 of its corporate-owned gyms last month but expects to keep its 700 gyms worldwide open as it looks to restructure (cbsnew.com). On May 7, Aldo filed for bankruptcy. The Canadian-based shoe retailer operates 3,000 stores worldwide (financialpost.com). The same day, Neiman Marcus filed for bankruptcy. This follows less than two months after the luxury retailer was forced to furlough 14,000 employees as it shut down its stores (43 Neiman Marcus stores, 2 Bergdorf Goodman stores, 22 Last Call discount stores). Neiman Marcus is in the process of permanently closing half of its Last Call discount stores but is not planning any asset sales or mass store closings as part of the restructuring. But it is seeking to eliminate $4 billion of its $5.1 billion in debt as its creditors take majority ownership from Ares Management and the Canadian Pension Plan Investment Board, which led its leveraged buyout in 2013 (wsj.com).

Lord & Taylor and JC Penney look to be next in line

It seems like Lord & Taylor, which is exploring filing for bankruptcy protection, does not expect to survive the pandemic as it plans to liquidate inventory in all of its 38 department stores as soon as it is able to re-open (cnbc.com). As we previously noted, back in August, **Hudson's Bay Company** sold the iconic nearly 200-year-old luxury department store brand for $100 million to Le Tote, a seven-year-old online fashion subscription rental service. But part of the payment was in the form of a $25 million secured two-year promissory note, and as Hudson's Bay Company kept ownership of some of the real estate assets, it is still responsible for the rent payments, which amount to tens of millions a year.

JC Penney could file for bankruptcy as soon as May 15. On April 15, JC Penney missed a $12 million interest payment to bondholders which kicked off a 30-day grace period before it officially defaults on its debt (cnbc.com). We note JC Penney has 846 department stores and 90,000 employees. On May 5, JC Penney filed a temporary restraining order against Sephora (**LVMH**) who "threatened an imminent termination" of their joint enterprise operating agreement which has been in place since February 2009. Basically, Sephora, which operates shop-in-shop boutiques in 650 of JC Penney's department stores, didn't want to re-open when JC Penney did. However, the two seem to have settled their differences— two days later, they announced they had agreed to "mutually beneficial revisions" to their existing agreement (footwearnews.com).

Early store re-openings by Nordstrom, Gap & Kohl's are red flags

On May 5, **Nordstrom** announced it will permanently close 16 department stores as part of its restructuring process to reduce costs.

These closures represent 14% of its base of 116 department stores. Nordstrom also plans to do a phased re-opening, implementing new safety protocols similar to **Macy's**. The big difference is that Nordstrom plans to host styling appointments virtually, offer curbside pick-up at more locations and add parking spaces for returns outside some stores. (seattletimes.com).

On May 6, **Gap**, which did not proactively close its stores, announced it plans to re-open 800 of stores by the end of May, or nearly one-third of its base of 2,750+ stores in North America. Gap is desperate to re-open as on April 23 it warned it might not have enough cash flow to fund its operations and last month, it didn't pay the $115 million total monthly rent on its shuttered stores. On the positive side, Gap is expanding its e-commerce distribution channel, doubling the number of ship-from-store locations to 2,000 and expanding curbside pick-up beyond its current 75 locations (cnbc.com). As a further red flag, five days prior, the retailer announced that it had entered into a multi-year licensing deal with IMG. Although Gap is pitching this deal with the positive spin that it will enable it to access new markets, categories and distribution channels, we believe this is more about Gap trying to monetize its iconic brand names of Gap, Banana Republic and Janie & Jack in order to survive (franchising.com). We note that it was only back in March 2019 that Gap acquired the Janie and Jack high-end kids clothing brand for $35 million from Gymboree.

On May 7, **Kohl's** announced that it expects to have one-quarter of its 1,100 department stores re-opened across 14 states by Monday. But the big differentiator for Kohl's is its nationwide curbside pick-up it launched on April 2, which it will continue to offer (cnbc.com). Although IKEA has an amazing in-store experience, its weak capabilities in e-commerce have been exposed by the coronavirus pandemic. The stores remain closed (which we view as a positive indicator), but the good news for IKEA fans is that IKEA Canada, which closed all its stores on March 16 and suspended its online Click & Collect service, launched a new contactless Click & Collect curbside pick-up service on May 11 for a $5 flat rate (calgary.ctv.news).

Why is Walmart launching a premium-tier grocery delivery service in the midst of a pandemic?

In the middle of a pandemic, when it's next to impossible to even find a grocery delivery time slot, why is **Walmart** launching a premium tier grocery delivery service? Walmart is launching a new delivery service called "Express" that will enable you to pay $10 on top of the standard delivery charge to receive your groceries in under two hours. Apparently Walmart has been piloting Express in 100 stores across the U.S. since mid-April with plans to expand it to nearly 1,000 stores in May and nearly 2,000 in the weeks after (usatoday.com). It is clearly trying to compete with Amazon's free Prime Now two-hour grocery delivery service. But the problem is in the timing as Amazon started to roll this out at the end of October (prior to the pandemic). More importantly, Express completely violates Walmart's values of its accessibility-driven mission *"to save people money so they can live better"*.

Twilio sees digital transformation being fast-forwarded from years to a weekend

Investors are discovering that **Twilio** was built for the challenges created by the coronavirus pandemic, with a 25% increase in average daily sign-ups from March 18 through April 20 compared to the first 11 weeks of the quarter. But it shouldn't be any surprise that Twilio is on the right side of the digital abyss as in our April 28 research note we discussed how Jeff Lawson, co-founder & CEO of Twilio, shared in his April 22 annual letter to shareholders: *"We provide three things the world has needed during this crisis: digital engagement, software agility, and cloud scale."* We gained the following new insights from Twilio's Q1 2020 conference call on May 6:

- **Digital Transformation Is Being Fast-forwarded from Years to a Weekend**: *"this environment is showing companies that they need to really double down and accelerate on their digital transformation...Digital transformation projects that could have taken years such as transitioning from an on-prem contact centre to the cloud instead took a weekend. Developers and companies big and small got to work, reconfiguring the world for a work from home and nearly 100% ecommerce reality."*
- **Importance of Digital Communication Channels**: *"we all need to be communicating with our customers and digital channels more than ever. And that could be messaging that could be WhatsApp, that could be video. And that could also be voice and in the contact center. All of these channels are incredibly important this period of time."*
- **Emerging Use Cases for Digital**: *"six used cases that are opportunistically coming forward for us in under COVID. And the six are remote contact centre, self-service, contact list delivery, distance learning, telehealth and mass notifications."*
- **Telehealth Is Becoming the New Normal**: *"With shelter in place and social distancing going into effect, demand for telehealth solutions has soared. Virtual care became a new reality for doctors, nurses, clinicians and millions of patients around the world... I think that many doctors' visits for example, are going to stay as telehealth visits after COVID is over."*
- **Emergence of the Virtual Home Technician**: *"Over the course of just a few weeks, developers at Comcast integrated Twilio voice into their homegrown customer database, enabling technicians and customer care to contact customers for service requests remotely. They also initiated a pilot to incorporate Twilio video into the same database, which can enable a customer to use the camera on their phone to show a Comcast technician their setup and the technician can walk them through a self-diagnosis and repair without ever setting foot in their*

home."

- **Permanent Shift to Online Shopping as New Behaviours Become Normalized**: *"And I think that many more e-commerce or food delivery or curbside pickup like a lot of these things that are getting normalized right now will start to become even more normal. And so it is the social distancing that is going on right now is changing our behaviors, and I think many of those behaviors will change permanently."*

Zillow moves into offense mode as agents and homebuyers finally embrace virtual tools

On Zillow's Q1 2020 conference call on May 7, we gained a number of new insights into how the coronavirus pandemic is impacting the needs of homebuyers and agents and the home shopping experience. **Zillow** is proving to be antifragile as it had $2.6 billion in cash and investments at the end of Q1 and is giving most of its employees the option to continue to work remotely through the end of the year. More importantly, it has moved from survival to offense mode as it is unfreezing Zillow Offers home buying and accelerating its technology to deliver virtual real estate shopping transaction experiences.

- **Seeing a Quantum Leap in Tech Adoption**: *"Our vision of Zillow 2.0 is becoming a reality even sooner than we have had planned...you are seeing years of technology progress get accelerated down in a month."*
- **Virtual Tools Necessary for Safety Today Will Become Expectations for Convenience Tomorrow**: *"Our proprietary 3D tours and floor plans appointment based virtual tours, physical self-tours, e-signings and remote closings are providing necessary solutions for social distancing today. Adoption is accelerating. Agents used Zillow's proprietary tech to create 525% more 3D home tours in April than in February."*

- **New Needs and Desires for a Home:** *"According to MIT, about half the U.S. workforce is now working from home and they are not just working from home, they are teaching their kids, eating each meal, conducting their social lives all from home. Whether they are dreaming about an extra room for an office, a bigger yard, a less dense neighborhood, or for many of you maybe, a new second home, there is evidence that the experiences uncorked new aspirations and hopes of what home can be and needs to be."*
- **Increased Home Turnover:** *"all of these factors are leading to what I am thinking of is this great reshuffling. Now, we more clearly see that people have an innate desire to move and that this period may even be a catalyst for many who change their address for a variety of reasons."*

On its Q1 2020 conference call on May 7, **Redfin**'s CEO, Glenn Kelman, provided us with further insights into home buying demand:

- **Home Buying Demand Has Rebounded to Nearly Pre-Pandemic Levels:** *"the week ending on April 5, home buying demand was at about 68% of our January and February levels... By May 3, home buying demand was at 96% of its January and February level"*
- **Seeing Signs of a Demographic Shift toward Smaller Cities:** *"Since March 15, searches for homes and towns with population under 50,000 up — under 50,000 people, increased 71%, while over the same period, searches for homes in cities with populations greater than 1 million increased by only 38%..."*

Zoom acquires Keybase as companies look to increase spend on tech for virtual work

Zoom just acquired Keybase to add end-to-end encryption to its video calls. This is the first acquisition that Eric Yuan made since he founded Zoom in San Jose in 2011. Importantly, the addition of Keybase's technology and its 25-person team will advance the 90-day plan he implemented on April 1 to address security problems, which included the hiring of Alex Stamos, Facebook's former security chief, as a consultant. Zoom plans to offer end-to-end encryption to paid subscribers and choosing this option will prevent anyone from calling in by phone and also disable cloud-based recording of the call (cnbc.com). We note Keybase has only raised $10.8 million in a July 2015 Series A round since it was launched in NY in 2014. This is a wise move by Zoom as according to a new Deloitte survey, 60% of CFOs are looking to increase spending over the next 12 months on tech for virtual work and automated processes. In addition, nearly 60% don't expect operations to return to "near-normal" levels this year (zdnet.com).

Facebook and Google allow employees to work from home until end of the year

For example, on May 7, Mark Zuckerberg announced that **Facebook**, which will start re-opening many of its offices on July 6, will allow most of its employees to continue to work from home until the end of the year. In addition, Facebook will not hold any gatherings of over 50 people until at least July 2021 (cnbc.com). The same day, Google (**Alphabet**) extended its work from home policy from June 1 to the end of the year (bbc.com). Interestingly, the day prior, Google told its employees they can no longer expense food or other perks like fitness, home office furniture, decoration or gifts while they are working from home. In addition, teams working from home are not allowed to pay for perks or make charitable donations using unused internal event or travel budgets (cnbc.com). To help less digitally savvy companies navigate their return to the workplace, **Salesforce** introduced a new platform called Work.com. Work.com provides tools that enable employers to track employee health through surveys, organize employee shifts to maintain social distancing and do manual contact tracing (cnbc.com).

AMC Entertainment spikes 30% on speculation of Amazon takeover

On May 11, the stock price of **AMC Entertainment Holdings** spiked by 30% on speculation that Amazon may be looking to acquire AMC following rumours reported by The Daily Mail (dailymail.co.uk). It's ironic as in last week's note we discussed how AMC's fight against Universal highlights how the lockdown is fast-forwarding the obsolescence of movie theatres as **Amazon** launches Prime Video Cinema in the U.S. after its viewers nearly double. Before the pandemic, it made sense that video-streaming companies might look to move down the structural capital side of the value pyramid to the physical layer, as evidenced by **Netflix** taking over the iconic Paris Theatre in NYC in November 2019 and Amazon being in the running to acquire Landmark Theatres back in August 2018. But we question whether the economics will work in this new world of physical distancing which will reduce theatre capacity. In addition, unless Amazon sees value in AMC's real estate, it doesn't make sense for it to acquire the biggest movie theatre chain in the world as part of the attraction of Landmark was how it was similar to Whole Foods in terms of offering a high-fidelity venue to deepen the emotional connection with its Prime members as Landmark's theatres are more like art houses featuring coffee bars and lounges.

Fortnite emerges as a virtual social venue as it passes 350 million players

On May 6, Fortnite disclosed that it now has over 350 million registered players, with players spending 3.2 billion hours in the game during April. More importantly, with the recent addition of party royale, a gun-free social space where players can hang out with friends and watch concerts from big acts like Travis Scott, Fortnite is emerging as a virtual social venue (verge.com).

Norwegian cruises toward bankruptcy while Carnival hopes to set sail on August 1

On May 5, **Norwegian Cruise Line Holdings** warned it might seek bankruptcy protection as it has "substantial doubt" about its ability to continue as a "going concern". Norwegian Cruise Line's cruise ships have been sitting empty since the CDC issued a no-sail order for all cruise ships on March 14; on April 9, the ban was extended to July 24 (cnbc.com). On May 5, **Carnival** announced that it will resume its cruise line service beginning August 1, with eight cruise ships setting sail from the ports of Galveston, Miami and Port Canaveral. However, it is cancelling all its other North American and Australian cruises through August 31, which represent over 90% of its fleet of 109 cruise ships (cnbc.com).

Google cancels plans to develop Quayside smart city on Toronto waterfront

On May 7, Sidewalk Labs LLC (**Alphabet**) announced that as a result of the economic uncertainty and pressure on the local real estate market because of the coronavirus pandemic, it is cancelling its plan to develop a 12-acre digital district on the Toronto waterfront (cbc.ca). We note that it was back in October 2017 when Sidewalk Labs and Waterfront Toronto unveiled plans to build the Quayside smart city, which included moving both "people and goods autonomously through the district using bike-like vehicles, vans, delivery trucks and even garbage trucks."

Yelp adds virtual services to platform as Apple launches "Today at Apple at Home"

As society migrates from the physical to digital world, **Yelp** is adding a new category to its platform — virtual service offerings. Yelp will showcase businesses in categories such as home services, fitness, gyms, health and real estate that now offer virtual services such as consultations, classes, tours and performances. Yelp is also adding the ability for restaurants to identify that they offer curbside pick-up (techcrunch.com). **Apple** has brought its Genius Bar to our homes. In addition to being able to chat online with specialists, we can attend its new "Today at Apple at Home" online classes which feature its Creative Pros from Apple Stores around the world. For example, you can learn how to "turn your home into music with Garage Band" from Rosie in London or how to "capture striking photography with the iPhone" from Cameron in Singapore (apple.com). What I love about these videos is that they resonate with us on an emotional level as they are being recorded now, in the midst of the pandemic, by Apple's Creative Pros from their own homes.

Dr. Gawande looks to step down as Haven CEO

Dr. Atul Gawande is in advanced discussions to step down as CEO of Haven and take on a less operational role as Chairman. Dr. Gawande is looking to shift roles away from the day-to-day management of Haven so he can focus on policy and advocacy work related to the coronavirus pandemic (wsj.com). We note that it was less than two years ago, in June 2018, when Dr. Gawande, a well-known surgeon, Harvard Medical School professor of Public Health and best-selling author, was selected as the CEO for the not-for-profit healthcare venture between Amazon, **Berkshire Hathaway** and **JPMorgan Chase.**

Google Nest Cameras being used for remote patient monitoring in hospitals

Mount Sinai in New York is using Google Nest Cameras in patient rooms to enable hospital staff to communicate with COVID-19 patients and remotely monitor and track their symptoms and vital signs. In addition to reducing exposure to patients with coronavirus, this enables the hospital to preserve scarce PPE supplies. Google is installing Google Nest Cameras in over 100 rooms at Mount Sinai and plans to provide up to 10,000 of them to hospitals across the U.S. (techcrunch.com).

Airbnb shifts into survival mode as it lays off 25% of its employees

On May 5, Airbnb announced it was laying off 1,900 employees, or 25% of its workforce, as it shifts into survival mode. But as a testament to the true heart and soul of the company, Brian Chesky, co-founder & CEO of Airbnb, penned a genuinely heartfelt note to the departing employees. As a foreshadowing of the uncertain fate facing all travel and hospitality companies, Chesky shared: *"While these actions were necessary, it became clear that we would have to go further when we faced two hard truths: 1. We don't know exactly when travel will return. 2. When travel does return, it will look different."* He also discussed how Airbnb is going back to its core of home sharing as it pauses its efforts in Transportation and Airbnb Studios and scales back its investments in Hotels and Lux. Airbnb is also treating its employees on their way out well in terms of severance (14 weeks of base pay plus a week for every year), continuing health benefits (12 months of COBRA health insurance) and helping connect them with new job opportunities (news.airbnb.com).

Uber cuts 3,700 employees while it invest in Lime

On May 5, **Uber** announced it was cutting 3,700 employees, or 14% of its workforce, as it shifts into survival mode. However, this is just an initial restructuring step, as Dara Khosrowshahi shared in the memo he sent to employees: *"this is one part of a broader exercise to make the difficult adjustments to our cost structure (team size and office footprint) so that it matches the reality of our business (our bookings, revenue and margins). We are looking at many scenarios and at each and every cost, both variable and fixed, across the company"* (cnbc.com). But Uber continues to make strategic investments — on May 7, it led a $170 million venture round in Lime, which included Alphabet as a strategic investor. This is a strategic investment for Uber as it is integrating its app with Lime and merging its Jump electric bike and scooter division into Lime. To cut costs, Uber is also expected to lay off some of Jump's 500 employees after they move over to Lime. This round reportedly values Lime at just over $500 million, nearly an 80% discount to its previous valuation (cnbc.com).

Lyft and Uber's highly VC structure threatened as they're sued by California AG

Last week, **Lyft** and Uber reported their Q1 2020 results. Although the coronavirus pandemic has driven ridesharing off a cliff, their highly variable cost structure and cash cushion provides them with an antifragile business model. As Lyft shared on its call, two-thirds of its costs are variable. However, the rising gig economy labour rights movement could threaten their underlying platform economy business model. For example, on May 5, California's AG partnered with San Diego, LA and San Francisco to sue Uber and Lyft for allegedly misclassifying drivers as independent contractors instead of employees (wsj.com).

Ridesharing is slowly starting to recover

Lyft and Uber's rides plummeted 75% and 80%, respectively, year-over-year in April but the encouraging news is that ridesharing is slowly starting to recover as Lyft has seen three consecutive weeks of week-on-week growth, albeit with rides still down 70% year-over-year, and Uber reporting U.S. gross bookings up last week by 12% week-on-week. More importantly, Uber reported that Hong Kong is back to 70% of pre-crisis gross bookings levels, and on May 6, Jean Liu, President of Didi Chuxing, shared that ride volume in China has reached 60–70% of pre-coronavirus levels (cnbc.com). In addition, we believe ridesharing could gain share from transit, as evidenced by this comment made by Dara Khosrowshahi on Uber's Q1 2020 conference call on May 7: *"I wouldn't be surprised if there's some share shift from transit...a recovery led primarily by commute trips will open up exciting new prospects for Uber for business, as companies look to move their employees to and from offices, as well as partnership opportunities with transit agencies to move essential workers."*

Uber Eats and Cornershop acquisition provide Uber with market expansion opportunities

We continue to believe Uber is better positioned than Lyft given these two new insights we gained on Uber's conference call:

- **Uber Eats Provides Diversification and Customer Retention/Acquisition Benefits:** *"We've seen an enormous acceleration in demand since mid-March, with 89% year-over-year gross bookings growth in April...tremendous increase in restaurant signups...Eats has also allowed us to maintain high engagement with our existing customers and to bring in new customers onto our platform. This positions us to have a faster recovery than Rides-only players."*
- **Cornershop Acquisition Provides Foundation for Accelerated Expansion into Grocery Delivery:** *"From early March levels, grocery and convenience gross bookings increased 117% over the same period... in the next few months, we expect to closer our acquisition of Cornershop, one of the largest grocery delivery platforms in Latin America... we look forward to creating an integrated product across Cornershop, Uber, and Uber Eats apps."*

Chapter 15: Corona Summer

May 20, 2020

The coronavirus pandemic is propelling us into the future while trans-porting us back to the past. This weekend my boys went live for the first time on Amazon's Twitch, broadcasting their play-by-play of Microsoft's Minecraft in front of the (non-essential) green screen my husband ordered just a few days ago from Amazon. And Brady and Adam are not alone as livestreaming is exploding during the lockdown, with 1.5 billion hours viewed on Amazon's Twitch in April, up 100% from a year ago. While our boys escaped to their virtual world, we hopped onto Zoom to chat over a glass of wine with our friends in San Francisco.

"What do you think about doing an RV vacation?" asked Jason. It's hard to believe how quickly the world has changed as it was only back in early March that we were discussing the idea of meeting up with them in Italy this summer. But it's a new reality as apart from borders being closed off and planes grounded, the thought right now of staying at a hotel or eating out absolutely terrifies me. I smiled at his mention of RV'ing as this brought back nostalgic memories of my favourite childhood vacation — driving across Canada in a Triple E motorhome with my cousins. Although we've stayed at KOA campgrounds with our boys, we've never done a motorhome trip with them. But with summer camps cancelled and gas prices at all-time recent lows, I'm starting to think an RV might be the perfect mobile

quarantine option for the Corona Summer...

Apple acquires NextVR, Facebook acquires Giphy and introduces Facebook Shops

Apple is capitalizing on the coronavirus pandemic to move into the virtual reality space with the acquisition of NextVR for a reported $100 milion (cnbc.com). NextVR has raised $116 million since it launched in Newport Beach in 2009 but the coronavirus pandemic has wreaked havoc on its business model of broadcasting and producing live and recorded events in virtual reality, like sporting events and concerts. **Facebook** is also going on the offense, acquiring Giphy for a reported $400 million The GIF (graphic interchange format) animated image platform start-up has raised $151 million since launching in NY in 2013. Facebook actually tried to acquire Giphy in 2015 and Facebook is Giphy's largest customer, with Facebook, Messenger, Instagram and WhatsApp accounting for half of its total traffic. Facebook plans to integrate Giphy into Instagram first and then into its other apps (cnbc.com). Facebook has also just introduced Facebook Shops, a new feature that makes it more convenient for small businesses to upload their catalog to make their product listings available across Facebook's portfolio of apps. Initially, Facebook Shops works with Facebook and Instagram but in the future, businesses will be able to sell through the chat features of WhatsApp, Messenger and Instagram Direct (cnbc.com).

Could this be the summer of the RV?

This might turn out to be the summer of the RV, benefiting **Thor Industries** and **Winnebago**, as the WSJ highlights in its May 16 article, *"RV Vacations: The Safest Way to Travel This Summer"*. Although there was an initial spike in RV cancellations, especially from international travelers, the recreational vehicle is emerging as an attractive all-in-one safe transportation, accommodation and dining option for people looking to avoid the crowds of planes, hotels and restaurants. Demand is skyrocketing from domestic travelers as national parks and camp-grounds start to re-open, with RV rental marketplaces Outdoorsy and RVShare reporting a 450% and 650% increase in bookings since early April (wsj.com). These RV marketplaces were founded to disrupt the $32 billion RV market by increasing the utilization of RVs, which are an expensive asset and sit idle 97% of the time. RVShare, which has over 100,000 RV listings, has raised $50 million since launching in Akron in 2013. Last January, Outdoorsy, a peer-to-peer RV marketplace founded in Austin in 2014, raised a $50 million Series C round to double its listings to 65,000.

Amazon re-opens its marketplace to non-essential sellers

Just like non-essential businesses are starting to re-open, this is now happening online. On May 9, **Amazon** removed quantity limit restrictions on non-essential items for third-party sellers. In addition to restoring quantity of choice, Amazon is starting to improve convenience as next-day delivery is coming back for select cities in the U.S. Furthermore, Amazon is starting to encourage us to buy again by adding back its featured deals section and coupons to its site and restoring the "frequently bought together" widget on its product listings (cnbc.com). As you'll remember, on March 17, Amazon took emergency measures to prioritize medical supplies, household staples and other high-demand products coming into its warehouses from third-party sellers. It relaxed some of these restrictions on April 13, allowing third-party sellers to start shipping some non-essentials, but limiting product quantities.

Amazon expands Amazon Care to its Seattle warehouse workers

Amazon is expanding Amazon Care, its private healthcare offering, from its office employees to its warehouse workers in Seattle. In addition, Amazon is waiving costs for all health concerns until May 31 (cnbc.com). We note that Amazon started to pilot Amazon Care in

September, and in October acquired Health Navigator, a digital health-care start-up that routes patients to the right place by using online symptom checking and triage tools, which it has since integrated into the digital layers (i.e., care chat, video care) of Amazon Care.

JC Penney and Reitmans file for bankruptcy as Pier 1 Imports liquidates

On May 15, **JC Penney**, the 118-year-old department store retailer with 90,000 employees, filed for Chapter 11 bankruptcy protection. As part of its restructuring process, JC Penney plans to shrink its fleet of department stores by nearly 30%, from 846 to 604, by next year. In addition, JC Penney will be closing two distribution centres, reducing its corporate overhead by 25% and cutting $1 billion in expenses. JC Penney is also looking at spinning off its real estate assets into a real estate investment trust (cnbc.com). In addition, on May 18, Women's Wear Daily reported that Amazon is in talks with JC Penney (pymnts.com). On May 19, **Reitmans** filed for bankruptcy protection. As part of the restructuring process, Reitmans plans to optimize its retail footprint, which includes 576 stores across Canada with over 6,800 employees. Reitmans operates a number of brands, including 259 Reitmans, 106 Penningtons, 80 RW & Co., 77 Addition Elle and 54 Thyme Maternity stores (cbc.ca). The same day, Pier 1 Imports announced it will permanently shut its 942 stores across the U.S. and Canada and sell off its inventory and remaining assets after being unable to find a buyer (finance.yahoo.com). Pier 1 Imports filed for bankruptcy on February 17, just prior to the coronavirus pandemic, and was planning to use the bankruptcy process to complete the closure of the 450 stores it announced in January.

U.S. retail sales drop 16.4% in April as non-essential retailers were forced to close

According to the Census Bureau of the U.S. Department of Commerce, total retail and food services sales in April were down 16.4% from a year ago and dropped 21.6% from March to April. The worst hit were non-essential stores that were forced to close, with year-to-year sales down sharply for clothing stores (-89%), furniture stores (-67%), electronics and appliance stores (-65%), sporting goods and hobby stores (-49%), and department stores (-47%). The closure of restaurants and bars, except for take-out and delivery, led to a 49% decline in sales at food services and drinking establishments. With everyone under lockdown, there were a lot fewer cars on the road, as evidenced by the 43% decline for gasoline station sales and 33% decline for motor vehicles and parts dealers. Essential goods stores fared better as some of these were allowed to remain open, as evidenced by the sales performance for general merchandise stores (-15%), health and personal care stores (-10%), building material and garden stores (0%), and food and beverage stores (+12%). However, sales decelerated at these essential retailers from March to April as evidence of consumers stocking up ahead of the lockdown. The best performer, not surprisingly, was non-store retailers, which saw a 22% increase in sales.

SPG's aggressive mall reopening is a red flag as IKEA starts to circle the ruins

On May 12, **Simon Property Group** (SPG) announced that it has re-opened 77 locations and expects to have 100 open by the end of this week. SPG is moving aggressively to re-open as this represents half of its 200+ malls and outlet centres that it closed on March 19 (cnbc.com). As we previously mentioned, we believe SPG is motivated to re-open its malls quickly so it can force its tenants to pay rent. As David Simon, Chairman, CEO & President, commented during Simon Property Group's Q1 2020 conference call on May 11: "*the re-ality is, we have a lease and they have to pay... obviously if they decide they are in bankruptcy, then that's when they get the right to reject a lease...I do think for the retailers that are opening, they're gaining market share,* *they're taking advantage of pent-up demand and I think others that aren't ready are missing that opportunity.*" It's interesting as he was quite evasive about Taubman, which SPG made the untimely acquisition of on February 11 for $3.6 billion in cash: *"So, I have nothing to say on the further on Taubman. We'll let you know when we have information to provide.*" When asked about the impact of the accelerating shift to e-commerce, he conceded: *"I am sure there will be some retailers that will get the sense that the fleet, the store network is not as important as it was three months ago.*"

Meanwhile, IKEA is starting to circle the ruins of inner-city dystopian ghost department stores and malls in the U.S. IKEA's shopping mall arm, Ingka Centres, which owns 45 shopping centres in Europe, Russia and China, is actively searching for commercial real estate in NYC, LA, San Francisco and Chicago (reuters.com). We note that in January, Ingka Centres bought the Hammersmith's King Mall in west London for £170 million from Schroders. This was notable as it marked the first time that IKEA had taken over a shopping mall and even pre-COVID-19, highlights how it was capitalizing on the decline in the value of retail real estate to advance its strategy of establishing smaller-format urban centres to bring IKEA closer to customers.

Chipotle Mexican Grill and Starbucks start to play hardball with landlords

Unlike most restaurants, **Chipotle Mexican Grill** and **Starbucks** paid their rent in April and May but now they are playing hardball with landlords, capitalizing on their strength as a strong tenant to lobby to renegotiate their leases or defer rent payments. Under accounting rules, landlords can still book income if they defer rent, but not if they renegotiate leases and cut rent, which would lead to a decline in the valuation of their real estate assets (wsj.com).

Tapestry takes conservative approach to re-opening

On May 1, **Tapestry** re-opened 40 of its Coach, Kate Spade and Stuart

Weitzman stores and it has since expanded this to 300 stores. But unlike many retailers that have been desperate to open their doors, Tapestry is taking a more conservative approach by only offering in-store or curbside pick-up of online orders. (forbes.com). The key insight is that the pandemic is forcing Tapestry to rapidly climb up the structural capital side of the value pyramid as it looks to shift its physical/digital mix which stood at 90%/10% pre-COVID-19.

Amazon converts more Whole Foods into "dark stores"

To meet unprecedented demand for grocery delivery and navigate safety measures, Whole Foods continues to convert more of its stores into the "dark store" format (businessinsider.com). Although Whole Foods says these conversions are temporary, we expect the coronavirus pandemic will accelerate the emergence of "dark stores" in the food retail space as this next generation of the grocery store is purpose-built not for customers, but for fulfillment of online grocery orders.

PepsiCo goes DTC to meet snacking needs of customers stuck at home

On May 13, **PepsiCo** launched two new DTC websites, Snacks.com and Pantryshop.com, which it put together in less than a month (forbes.com). On Snacks.com you can select over 100 different varieties of chips, pretzels and tortilla chips from PepsiCo's 17 snack brands like SunChips, Dorito's and Lays, with free two-day shipping on orders over $15. On Pantryshop.com, you can choose from seven different themed pantry kits, like "Rise and Shine", which includes Aunt Jemima pancake mix, Quaker oats porridge and Tropicana juice, with free two-day shipping on the kits, which are priced between $30 and $50.

FedEx partners with Microsoft as it deals with flow disruption as retailers ship from stores

On May 18, **FedEx** announced that it has entered into a multi-year partnership with **Microsoft** to help "transform commerce" by leveraging FedEx's logistics network with Microsoft's cloud. Their first service, FedEx Surround, will offer customers real-time analytics into the supply chain and delivery. However, it won't be available until later this year (cnbc.com). Meanwhile, FedEx is temporarily limiting the number of packages that a dozen retailers can ship directly from their stores. The problem is that FedEx's shipping flow has been disrupted and overwhelmed as retailers have turned their closed stores into makeshift online mini-fulfillment centres. The list of retailers includes newly bankrupted Neiman Marcus, **Kohl's**, **Nordstrom** and **Abercrombie & Fitch** (wsj.com).

Twitter sets precedent as first company to allow employees to work from home forever

On May 12, **Twitter** set the precedent as the first company to now allow employees to work from home forever. As a further positive sign, Twitter is conservatively waiting until September to open its offices and allow business travel to resume while banning in-person company events for the rest of the year (cnbc.com). We believe this will accelerate the work-from-home movement and raise the bar, especially for tech giants looking to attract talent. It's interesting as just five days earlier, Google and Facebook extended the ability for their employees to work from home until the end of this year. And now **American Express** is joining Google and Facebook…"*American Express is more than a series of buildings with our name on the door. We are more than 60,000 colleagues strong, serving our customers and helping each other no matter where we are sitting.*" This proclamation comes from Stephen Squeri, CEO of American Express, in a video message to employees on May 18 as he announced that those who can do so will be able to now work from home for the rest of the year. In the video he spoke about how American Express will treat offices as an alternative workspace for people, phasing in occupancy from 10% to 50% by the end of this year, opening them up on a location-by-location, floor-by-floor and colleague-by-colleague basis (linkedin.com).

Softbank slashes WeWork's valuation by another 60% to $2.9 billion

On May 18, **SoftBank**'s CEO, Masayoshi Son, admitted his investment in WeWork was "foolish" as he disclosed that SoftBank is now valuing WeWork at $2.9 billion. This is down 60% from $7.3 billion at the end of the year and, more significantly, down a staggering 94% from its $47 billion pre-IPO valuation just a year ago. In total, SoftBank posted an $18 billion loss in the quarter ended March 31 for the $100 billion SoftBank Vision Fund. In his presentation, Son shared a series of slides illustrating unicorns trying to leap over the "Valley of Coronavirus" and predicted that 15 of his 88 unicorns, or 17%, could fall to their deaths amidst the pandemic (cnbc.com).

Role of CIO is changing while the manager role is becoming obsolete

The role of the Chief Information Officer (CIO) is changing during the coronavirus pandemic. When the lockdown started, the CIO was focused on the functional level — deploying technology to enable employees to work from home. Now their job is moving up to the emotional level — helping monitor and manage the impact of working from home on their employees with a focus on their mental well-being and wellness (wsj.com). In addition, the forced rapid adoption of the shift to work-from-home environment is leading to greater empowerment of employees, many of whom might decide they want to keep working from home. If this happens, it could lead to the obsolescence of the manager role (forbes.com). Events planners wishing to survive the pandemic will need to go digital. Bevy is raising a $15 million Series B round as it capitalizes on the explosion in demand for its virtual events platform. Bevy offers an end-to-end virtual experience for event organizers, providing tools for event creation and user registration and integrating into platforms like **Zoom, Salesforce,** Marketo and Meetup (techcrunch.com). We note

Bevy, an enterprise-grade virtual and in-person community events platform, had previously raised $6 million since being launched in Palo Alto in 2017.

Spotify signs exclusive $100 million podcasting deal with Joe Rogan

On May 19, **Spotify** announced that it has signed an exclusive multi-year podcast licensing deal with Joe Rogan that is reported to be worth more than $100 million. This is a big win for Spotify as it provides it with valuable supplier capital (*The Joe Rogan Experience* is currently ranked #2 on Apple's Podcast and Spotify gains exclusive access to the full library dating back to when it launched in 2009) and customer capital (Joe Rogan has a huge fan base with 8.41 million YouTube subscribers, 6 million **Twitter** followers and 9.4 million Instagram followers). The content will hit Spotify on September 1 and will become exclusive before the end of the year (wsj.com).

Disney will stream *Hamilton* on Disney+ as Amazon secures rights to seven Indian movies

On May 12, **Disney** announced it will release *Hamilton* on its new Disney+ streaming platform on July 3. Disney, who bought the distribution rights for *Hamilton* for $75 million last year, had originally planned to debut *Hamilton* in movie theatres in October 2021 (forbes.com). As further evidence of how the coronavirus pandemic is fast-forwarding the obsolescence of movie theatres, Amazon has secured rights to premiere seven Indian movies on Prime Video that were initially scheduled for theatrical release. Amazon Prime Video will be releasing the movies over the next three months, starting in May. Just like in the U.S., India's two large theatre chains, PVR and INOX, are alarmed by this move (techcrunch.com). We note that in November, Amazon entered into a five-year exclusive partnership with BookMyShow, a local Indian online movie ticketing giant that sells 15 million tickets per month. Amazon users can book tickets from the new "movie tickets" category on the website or through the Amazon Pay tab.

Livestreaming explodes and animation thrives during the lockdown

Livestreaming exploded during the lockdown. According to a new report from StreamElements and Arsenal, livestreaming hours reached 3.9 billion in April, up 99% from a year ago. The three biggest platforms all saw increased usage, with Amazon's Twitch up 100%, **Alphabet**'s YouTube Gaming up 65% and Facebook Gaming up 238%. Twitch maintained its 38% viewing share while YouTube Gaming's share fell from 14% to 12% and Facebook Gaming's share increased from 4% to 7% (forbes.com). Animation is also thriving during the coronavirus pandemic, both on the demand side and the supply side. According to Reelgood, animation viewership has risen 22% during the lockdown, likely owing to demand for entertaining content from kids stuck at home. On the supply side, animation is a digital, not physical, production process, so it is immune from the coronavirus. For example, **Netflix** sent personal recording studio kits to its voice actors so they could work from home, containing an iPad, USB microphone, popscreen, microphone and script stand. But the pandemic has wreaked havoc on the physical film industry, with the International Alliance of Theatrical Stage Employees union estimating that 120,000 film-industry workers lost their jobs in March, and in April the Writers Guild advised members to pursue animation projects (wsj.com).

NYC votes to cap delivery fees at 15% while Uber seeks to acquire Grubhub

On May 13, New York City Council voted to cap delivery fees at 15% the cost of the order during states of emergency like the coronavirus pandemic. Recently, similar mandates have been passed in San Francisco, Seattle, D.C. and Jersey City (cnbc.com). On May 14, over 40 U.K. MPs co-signed a letter addressed to Will Shu, CEO of Deliveroo, expressing their concerns on how Deliveroo's riders, which are classified as independent contractors, are: *"deprived of any minimum wage protection, holiday pay or sick pay provision under the law"* (techcrunch.com). Amidst this risk of rising regulation, we are seeing signs of more consolidation among food delivery platforms. On May 12, **Grubhub**'s stock price skyrocketed 29% on rumours that it was being acquired by **Uber** in an all-stock deal. This would be a strategic acquisition for Uber as it would give Uber Eats over 50% share of the food delivery market. However, the two companies are still in discussions over valuation as Grubhub is looking for a ratio of 2.15:1 shares whereas Uber has only offered 1.9:1 (wsj.com).

GM cuts 8% of workforce at Cruise

GM is cutting 8% of its workforce at Cruise, its autonomous driving start-up. Cruise is letting go of 144 employees across its engineering, recruiting and human resource departments (cnbc.com). We note this follows just weeks after **Ford** pushed back the target date of its autonomous vehicle service it is developing with Argo AI from 2021 to 2022, indicating that investment is starting to slow down in autonomous vehicles. This is also a continuation of GM's cost-cutting strategy — on April 28, it completely shut down its Maven vehicle-sharing platform.

Uber cuts 3,000 additional jobs as it moves deeper into survival mode

On May 18, Uber's CEO, Dara Khosrowshahi, announced Uber was shutting or consolidating 45 offices around the world and cutting 3,000 more jobs. On top of the 3,700 job cuts he announced on May 5, this brings the total cuts to 6,700, representing over one-quarter of Uber's employee base. These drastic moves are evidence of how Uber is quickly resizing to the new reality and re-focusing on its core of helping people move (Ridesharing) and delivery of things (Uber Eats, Grocery, Direct) as it winds down Incubator and AI Labs. In addition, Uber is pursuing strategic alternatives for Uber Works and is considering cuts to other businesses, like Uber Freight and autonomous driving (cnbc.com).

Micro-mobility emerging as attractive alternative as cities ease lockdown

Although scooter companies suspended service as the world started to go under lockdown in mid-March, solo micro-mobility solutions such as electric bikes and scooters may start to emerge as an attractive transportation alternative as the lockdown eases for commuters wishing to avoid crowded buses and subway cars. For example, as part of its new Streetspace program to enable physical distancing, London is converting some of its streets into "car free zones". The city is hoping this will encourage people to walk and cycle instead of taking the bus or use the London Underground (cnbc.com). Bolt is looking to capitalize on this behavioural shift and is expanding its new electric scooter service to 45 cities. Last March, the Estonian-based ridesharing firm re-branded itself from Taxify as it expanded into shared motorbikes and scooters and food delivery (cnbc.com).

We just witnessed the world's first drive-in concert

In Denmark, Mads Langer played to a crowd of 2,000 fans — except they weren't squeezed together — they sat socially distanced, in cars. To hear him play, fans could tune in their car radios to a dedicated channel. But he discovered what really resonated was playing while having social conversations on **Zoom** with individual groups in vehicles broadcast on a massive jumbo stage display (abc.net).

Walmart sees gains of 10% same-store and 74% e-commerce sales in Q1

Walmart is proving to be antifragile as it has hired 235,000 associates since the pandemic started and saw a 10% gain in U.S. comparable store sales and a 74% increase in e-commerce sales for Q1 2021. Walmart is shutting down Jet.com, which it acquired for $3.3

billion in September 2016, but this is not unexpected as last June it announced it would start integrating Jet.com into its e-commerce layer. We gained the following new insights into how the coronavirus is changing shopping habits from <u>Walmart's Q1 2021 conference call</u> on May 19:

- **Consumer Buying Quickly Shifted from Safety to Desire**: *"We experienced unprecedented demand in categories like paper goods, surface cleaners and grocery staples... As the quarter progressed, we saw a second phase related to entertaining and educating at home... We can see customers looking to improve their indoor and outdoor living spaces...Discretionary categories really popped towards the end of the quarter."*
- **Customers Rapidly Adopted Online Ordering**: *"The number of new customers trying pickup and delivery has increased 4x since mid-March...Store pickup and delivery spiked in March and remained elevated in April with sales growth of nearly 300% at peak...Sam's app added 700,000 members in the quarter."*
- **Customers Are Consolidating Shopping Trips**: *"April comp sales increased 9.5%. We saw customers consolidate shopping trips and purchase larger baskets in stores, which drove a ticket increase of about 16% while transactions decreased about 6%."*

Home Depot sees gains of 6.4% in total comp and 79% e-commerce sales in Q1

Home Depot is also proving to be antifragile as it saw a 6.4% gain in total comp sales and a 79% growth in e-commerce sales, with penetration jumping to just under 15%. We gained the following new insights into how the coronavirus is changing shopping habits from <u>Home Depot's Q1 2020 conference call</u> on May 19:

- **Customers Are Consolidating Shopping Trips**: *"During the first quarter, comp average ticket increased 11.1% and comp transactions decreased 4%."*
- **Customers Rapidly Adopting Online Ordering:** *"We saw our digital businesses accelerate from approximately 30% growth in early March to triple-digit growth by the end of April... Sales leveraging our digital platforms increased approximately 80% in the quarter and more than 60% of the time our customers opted to pick up their orders at a store."*

Chapter 16: Driving Into the Abyss

May 26, 2020

"Driving into the Abyss". As those of you who have been traveling with me on my intellectual journey through the land of structural disruption will remember, this was the title of the highly controversial research report I published back on February 17, 2017 in which I warned the auto fault line was creating deep structural cracks for Avis Budget and Hertz. My biggest worry was that they were "facing radical industry transformation that has the potential to create obsolescence for both companies' core activities (renting vehicles) and core assets (their car rental franchise)."

Likewise, as I warned a few months later in my April 3, 2017 research report titled "Auto and Retail Fault Lines Deepening: Avis Budget & Hertz Look Like Casualties": "We are becoming increasingly concerned about retail REITs as the acceleration toward online shopping threatens to render both the core activities (leasing space to retailers) and core assets (the shopping malls) with obsolescence."

It turns out my alarmist stance was justified as on Friday, Hertz drove into the abyss as it filed for bankruptcy and, in the past week, I learned that Mall of America, the largest shopping mall in the U.S., has fallen delinquent on its $1.4 billion mortgage. Although the ghost town economy has fast-forwarded the obsolescence of these physical activities and assets, the bottom line is the structural cracks were deepening years before the *coronavirus came along.*

Hertz's bankruptcy filing could lead to a collapse in used car prices
On May 22, **Hertz Global Holdings** filed for Chapter 11 bankruptcy protection after struggling to survive with its $19 billion debt load in this new ghost town economy where nobody wants to rent a car. Hertz had already laid off and furloughed 20,000 employees, equal to half of its workforce, as its fleet of nearly 700,000 rental vehicles has sat mostly idle for the past two months. On April 29, Hertz failed to make a lease payment on its vehicle-backed bonds to preserve cash (wsj.com).

In its Q1 2020 8-K report on May 12, Hertz disclosed: "*As of March 31, 2020, we had approximately 85% non-program vehicles in our worldwide fleet.*" If we apply this 85% to Hertz's fleet of over 500,000 vehicles as of March 31, it implies that Hertz has over 400,000 vehicles non-program at-risk vehicles, which has securitized into a $14.4 billion ABS that is not part of the bankruptcy filing. But these ABS holders only have to wait 60 days until they can do a forced liquidation and foreclose on and sell these vehicles. As Hertz warned less than two weeks ago in its 8-K: "*The slowing demand in the used-vehicle market due to current conditions in the economy has negatively impacted vehicle values and the value declines are expected to continue, which could result in a substantial loss on the sale of our non-program vehicles.*" The potential flood of Hertz's used fleet vehicles into the market could lead to an overall collapse in used car prices and residual values.

Largest shopping mall in America falls delinquent on its $1.4 billion mortgage
The Mall of America, the largest shopping mall in the U.S, is delinquent on its $1.4 billion mortgage. The Mall of America, which has been closed since March 18, missed making the payments on its CMBS for April and May. The Mall of America is not alone; according to Trepp, the percentage of loans in U.S. CMBS deals that are over 30

days overdue has risen from 2.3% in April to 7.3% now. In addition, the percentage of loans on the watchlist has risen from 12% to over 20% (ft.com). The problem is that the Ghermezian family mortgaged nearly half of its stake in the Mall of America and the West Edmonton Mall to spend $5.7 billion on the new American Dream Mall.

On May 21, **L Brands** announced that it will be closing 250 Victoria's Secret and Pink stores in the U.S. and Canada this year, equating to just under one-quarter of its retail fleet of 1,070 stores (cnbc.com). In Canada, Victoria's Secret is shutting down 13 of its 38, or one-third, of its stores (ctvnews.ca). This drastic move isn't surprising as Sycamore Partners was able to use the "material effect cause" triggered by the pandemic to back out of the deal that it signed with L Brands in February to acquire a 55% stake in Victoria's Secret for $525 million. Victoria's Secret faces an uphill battle as it has become increasingly irrelevant for maintaining its sexy image in the wake of the #metoo movement and, more importantly, the lockdown has accelerated its disruption by new DTC entrants such as Third Love. And another bankruptcy could be coming soon. Tuesday Morning, the discount home goods retailer, is preparing to file for Chapter 11 bankruptcy protection. Tuesday Morning, which furloughed most of its 9,000 employees last month, has been struggling to survive after the coronavirus pandemic forced it to shut down two months ago its only means of distribution — its 700 physical stores (wsj.com).

Fortnite debuts as the new movie theatre as Amazon Games launches its first PC game

In the age of lockdown and physical distancing, the drive-in movie theatre is making a comeback. However, there aren't many of them left as the number of drive-in movie theatres in the U.S. has fallen from a peak of 4,062 in 1958 to only 305 (wsj.com). And this represents less than 0.1% of the over 40,000 movie theatre screens. But we no longer need to head to a physical theatre to catch a new movie.

On May 22, Focus Features announced that *Irresistible* will go direct to video-on-demand and video streaming platforms like Amazon Prime Video on June 26. Its new political comedy movie starring Steve Carell was originally scheduled to hit the theatres on May 29 (mashable.com). But now the disruptors are starting to be disrupted. On May 21, Fortnite, the online video game with over 350 million registered players, announced that it will screen Christopher Nolan's latest film this summer. Fortnite is hosting the movie within Party Royale, its gun-free social space where over 12 million people attended Travis Scott's Astronomical virtual concert on April 23 (reuters.com).

No one seems better positioned to capitalize on the collision of video streaming and gaming platforms than Amazon. On May 20, **Amazon** launched *Crucible*, its first PC game published by Amazon Games. Amazon Games plans to follow this up with the launch of *New World*, a massively multiplayer online role-playing game, in August and is also developing a game based on the *Lord of the Rings* franchise. Amazon is following Fortnite's strategy, making *Crucible* free to play (finance.yahoo.com). Amazon's aggressive push into producing original gaming content is timely as its Twitch livestreaming gaming platform, which leads the market with 38% share, saw a 100% viewership increase in April to 1.5 billion hours.

Shopify unveils Shopify Balance, Shop Pay Installments & Local Delivery for merchants

At Reunite, **Shopify**'s first virtual event for its global merchant community, it unveiled a number of new and updated products that it has pulled forward to better support its merchants through the pandemic. This includes Shopify Balance, a business account for merchants, and Shop Pay Installments, a new "buy now, pay later" option for merchants to offer customers, which it plans to roll out in the U.S. later this year. Shopify also introduced Local Delivery to offer an improved and simplified local delivery experience which could be of great value given Shopify has seen average daily local orders skyrocket 176% since the pandemic started, with the percentage of merchants using local pick-up and delivery rising from 2% to 26%. Shopify is also partnering with **Facebook** on Facebook's newly launched Facebook Shops (financialpost.com).

Amazon launches designer digital storefront in partnership with Vogue

On May 14, Amazon launched "Common Threads: Vogue x Amazon Fashion" in partnership with Vogue and the Council of Fashion Designers of America to enable independent fashion designers to sell directly to consumers. The Common Threads site provides each designer with a digital storefront to showcase themselves and their spring collections. The initial cohort includes 20 designers but Amazon expects to add more in the coming weeks (vogue.com). It seems like Amazon is capitalizing on the pandemic to move deeper into the fashion industry as it was only back on March 27 that Amazon Prime Video debuted *Making the Cut*, a shoppable fashion design competition series hosted by fashion icons Heidi Klum and Tim Gunn in which the winning designs are available to buy after each episode on Amazon's new "Making the Cut" store.

Is the future of shopping an AI-powered shopping app?

Julie Bornstein, the former COO of **Stitch Fix**, couldn't have picked a better time to debut "The Yes", her new AI-powered shopping app. The app learns your personal style through simple yes/no questions and then provides you with a daily curated personal shopping feed of new apparel products that you can buy with one tap. In addition, the app is social as you can invite friends to it and see their Yes lists. Bornstein is a digital retail veteran, having spent seven years as the CMO & CDO at Sephora, and previously the head of e-commerce at Urban Outfitters and Nordstrom. Her co-founder, Amit Aggarwal, brings a strong background in search, having worked at Groupon,

Google and Bing (fortune.com). We note The Yes has raised $30 million since being founded in San Francisco in 2018.

Target leverages its stores to drive digital sales

"We've accelerated our digital fulfillment awareness with a guest and fulfillment capabilities by upwards of three years." As evidenced by this statement by Brian Cornell, CEO, **Target** has been able to really leverage its physical capital (i.e., stores) to drive digital sales during the pandemic. Looking forward, Target's new acquisition of Deliv will provide it with the opportunity to add capacity it its fulfillment network and reduce the cost of last-mile delivery. We gained the following new insights from Target's Q1 2020 conference call on May 20:

- **Target's Stores Stayed Open But Digital Drove Sales**: Target's total comp sales rose 10.8% but this was all driven by digital (up over 140%) as store comp sales were only up 0.8%. Target's overall comp growth escalated from 3.8% in February (with digital comp growth at 33%) to 16% in April (with digital comp growth at 282%).
- **Target Is Leveraging its Stores to Drive Digital Sales**: Target saw exponential sales growth in all its channels: pick-up (up nearly 150%), Shipt (over 300%) and drive-up (up over 600% with 5 million guests and up over 1,000% in April).
- **Target.com Is Gaining New Customers:** Target.com gained 5 million new guests and 2 million made their first Drive-Up trip.
- **Customers Are Consolidating Their Shopping Trips:** Comparable traffic declined 1.5% but average ticket rose 12.5%.

Lowe's outperforms as an essential retailer with a rural store footprint & DIY exposure

Lowe's achieved an 11.% gain in total comps, nearly double the 6.4% reported by **Home Depot,** as it benefited from having a more rural store footprint (one-quarter of its stores are in rural locations with only 10% in big cities) and less dependence on professional contractors. It is a good thing that Lowe's was deemed an essential retailer in the U.S. — although its e-commerce sales rose by 80% (in line with Home Depot), its e-commerce penetration is half of Home Depot's, at 8% versus just under 15%. We gained the following new insights into how the coronavirus is changing shopping habits from Lowe's Q1 2020 conference call on May 20:

- **Sales Increased During the Quarter**: *"U.S. monthly comps increased as we moved through the quarter with 5.1% in February, 8.9% in March, and 20.4% in April."*
- **Lowe's Is Leveraging its Stores to Fulfill Digital Orders**: *"90% of our dot-com sales are fulfilled or picked up at a store...over 60% of our orders are picked up in store... we rolled out curbside pick-up in a matter of days."*
- **Sales Hit an Inflection Point in April with the Lockdown**: *" lowes.com sales also increased significantly in April with comps of over 150% in the month, while our installed sales declined approximately 50% as many customers were unwilling to allow installation work in their homes."*

OpenTable forecasts 250,000 restaurants in the U.S. won't survive the pandemic

OpenTable (**Booking Holdings**) is forecasting that one-quarter of the restaurants in the U.S. will not survive the pandemic. Given there are more than 1 million restaurants across the U.S., this represents 250,000 closures, which is nearly double the National Restaurant Association of America's forecast in early April of 140,000 closures. The restaurant industry is being severely impacted by the pandemic, losing sales of $30 billion in March and $50 billion in April (mercurynews.com). But now there's the risk that insurers will have to foot part of this bill. On May 22, a Paris court ruled that **Axa** must pay a restaurant owner two months of coronavirus-related revenue losses as the decision to close his restaurants qualified for insurance coverage as a business interruption loss. This could set a precedent for restaurants, cafes and nightclubs seeking legal action against insurers who have refused to pay out business interruption policies (reuters.com). We note that a month ago, the founder of Napa Valley's French Laundry and the founder of Wolfgang Puck created a new restaurant alliance in the U.S. called the Business Interruption Group (BIG) to begin a public opinion and lobbying claim to pressure insurers to pay claims and for government to reimburse insurers.

Shopify & Facebook declare the end of office centricity

On May 21, Tobi Lutke, CEO of Shopify, tweeted: *"As of today, Shopify is a digital by default company. We will keep our offices closed until 2021 so that we can rework them for this new reality. And after that, most will permanently work remotely. Office centricity is over."* The same day, Mark Zuckerberg announced that Facebook will aggressively open up remote hiring in July and he expects half of Facebook's workforce will work remotely over the next 5-10 years. But remote employees will not be able to benefit from salary arbitrage as starting on January 1, Facebook will localize salaries, essentially adjusting them downward for the cost of living (reuters.com). We note that on May 7, Facebook set a precedent as it was one of the first companies to announce that it would let its employees work from home for the rest of this year. As physical conferences remain taboo, Run the World, a virtual events platform, has raised an $11 million Series A round. Run the World was founded in San Francisco less than a year ago but hit the ground running when it launched in February and waived all set-up fees for events impacted by the coronavirus. Since then, it has grown rapidly, doubling the size of its team to 30 people and hosting 2,000 events (techcrunch.com). A flood of venture capital is starting to flow into the virtual event space, as the week prior, Bevy raised a $15 million series B round.

Apple & Google launch contact tracing APIs, Amazon Business opens up PPE site

The tech industry's efforts to fight the coronavirus are positioning it to capitalize on the quantum leap in tech adoption in the healthcare industry. On the digital layer, on May 20, **Apple** and Google (**Alphabet**) launched APIs to enable interoperability between Android and iOS devices using apps from public health authorities to help track the spread of coronavirus. The apps use Bluetooth technology for contact tracing to let you know if you've come into contact with someone diagnosed with COVID-19 (wsj.com). We note it only took these two tech giants 40 days to develop this technology together. On the e-commerce layer, Amazon has delivered over 100 million PPE items such as N95 masks, ventilators, surgical gloves and large-volume sanitizers to over 20,000 front-line healthcare and government organizations since it launched its dedicated site on Amazon Business in late March. Now that demand for PPE from these entities has stabilized, Amazon is preparing to open up this site to businesses that are starting to re-open to the public (cnbc.com). And as evidence of how Amazon is still overwhelmed with the surge in demand as a result of the quantum leap to online shopping, it is postponing Prime Day, which it usually holds in mid-July, to September (cnbc.com). We note last year Amazon sold 175 million items over the 48-hour period.

Google pledges to stop making customized AI tools for oil & gas companies

Google has pledged to stop making customized AI tools for oil and gas companies. Greenpeace is hoping this could put pressure on Microsoft and Amazon to follow suit, which it criticizes in its new report, *Oil in the Cloud: How Technology Companies are Helping Big Oil Profit from Climate Destruction.* In its report, Greenpeace discusses how

Microsoft has the most contracts with energy firms in all phases and Amazon has contracts mostly in the mid and downstream phases, with pipelines, shipping and storage companies. Greenpeace believes these cloud contracts undermine the climate commitments made by the tech companies (cnbc.com). We note that on September 19, Bezos unveiled Amazon's Climate Pledge and personally pledged $10 billion to fight climate change on February 17 while Satya Nadella, Microsoft's CEO, declared sustainability as an "existential priority" on January 16.

University of Cambridge sets precedent – its next academic year will be online

On May 20, the University of Cambridge set precedent as the first university to announce that the next academic year will be conducted online. Although students at the prestigious U.K. university will be able to attend small seminars, there will be no face-to-face lectures.

Ola lays off 1,400 employees after ridesharing revenue plummets 95%

Ola, the **SoftBank**-backed ridesharing leader in India, is laying off 1,400 employees, equal to 35% of its workforce. Ola is trying to stem losses after seeing its revenue plummet 95% the past two months (reuters.com).

U.K. looks to recruit 80,000 workers for "Pick for Britain" campaign

"If we are to harvest British fruit and vegetables this year, we need an army of people to help." This call for duty comes from Prince Charles as the U.K. looks to recruit 80,000 students and newly unemployed workers for its newly launched "Pick for Britain" campaign. The U.K. is facing a shortfall of migrant labour as border closures have blocked seasonal workers from Eastern Europe, with only one-third currently in the U.K. (forbes.com). Speaking of preventing food waste, Imperfect Foods, the discount grocery subscription box service, has seen a 40% increase in its user base since the start of the pandemic. To meet this

new demand, Imperfect Foods, which was founded in San Francisco in 2015, has raised a $72 million Series C round. Imperfect Foods has been able to capitalize on its sustainability-driven mission *"to reduce food waste and build a better food system for everyone"* during the pandemic by rescuing food like cheese plates from **JetBlue** and popcorn kernels meant for movie theatres (techcrunch.com).

Chapter 17: The Twilight Zone Economy

June 2, 2020

With the physical world re-opening, we are exiting the "Ghost Town Economy" and entering a new way of life that I call the "Twilight Zone Economy" — the area where society's physical and digital states of existence meet.

Looking back, it's hard to believe it was less than three months ago, on March 10, when I came up with the concept of "The Ghost Town Economy", as per the title of my research note, in which I shared the scathing email I had just sent to my son's elementary school:

> *"I just wanted to let you know that Brady will not be participating in tomorrow's spring concert and I sincerely wish the school would consider postponing the event in light of the escalating risk of the coronavirus."*

Thank goodness the school ended up cancelling the concert as across the border in Washington, 53 of 61 people that attended a choir practice that night ended up contacting coronavirus and two died. Although schools here re-opened yesterday, we are keeping Brady and Adam at home and continuing with their digital learning — welcome to the twilight zone of education.

189

As the physical world starts to re-open, we are once again witnessing a new shift in both societal and corporate behaviour, which is leading to further transformation of the corporate landscape and distortion of all three sides of the value pyramid.

Agricultural products supply at risk as migrant farm workers see early outbreaks

As we head into the summer produce season, we are starting to see early outbreaks among migrant farm workers like we saw with the meat processing plant workers in April. In Canada, there has been an outbreak of 85 cases at a farm in Norfolk County, Ontario which grows sweet corn, watermelon, asparagus and pumpkins. In the U.S., outbreaks are starting to develop across the country with all 200 workers testing positive at a farm in Tennessee, 60 cases at a farm in Washington and over 50 cases at a farm in New Jersey. Although most grain crops can be machine harvested, fruits and vegetables require manual labour and there is a short harvesting window of only a few weeks. According to the Migrant Clinicians Network, there are 2.7 million hired farm workers in the U.S., with three-quarters being immigrants. Like with the meat packers, the farm workers work shoulder-to-shoulder, are transported to work in crowded buses and vans, and are likely to show up sick to work as they're afraid of losing their jobs. Although farm workers work outside, they are even more vulnerable to community spread as they live in cramped communal housing and travel from farm to farm (fortune.com).

Hotel industry comes back to life but economy rebounds faster than luxury

The hotel industry is starting to come back to life as lockdowns ease. According to STA, hotel occupancy rebounded from the trough of 21% reached during the week ending April 11 to 32.4% for the week ending May 16. However, this is still far below the 61.8% rate in early March prior to the lockdown. In addition, we are seeing a huge bifurcation in the hotel segments with average occupancy for economy hotels at 44.2%, more than double the 18.8% rate for luxury hotels. And the luxury hotel segment is likely to remain under pressure given its high exposure to business travel, conventions and international travelers, which will be much slower to return (wsj.com).

Could Zoom be the next big app platform?

"Zoom will be the next big platform for start-ups to build billion-dollar businesses." This comment from Jim Scheinman, a founder partner of Maven Ventures and early investor in Zoom, comes as he shares how **Zoom** was able to attract 600 entrepreneurs earlier this month for its first Zoom app marketplace contest. The ten finalists, which were invited to participate in a virtual Shark Tank pitch event, highlight Zoom's potential to expand its market through building an app ecosystem as it includes Pledging (pledging donations), iScribeHealth (virtual physician consultations), Bloom (specialized online classes for kids) and the winner, Docket (tools to make meetings more efficient) (cnbc.com).

NEW GHOST TOWN ECONOMY VICTIMS

Although the physical world is starting to re-open, the coronavirus continues to claim the lives of companies that were too fragile to survive the ghost town economy. This past week's victims include another rental car company, a discount home goods retailer, a restaurant chain, a laser eye centre chain and potentially another fitness chain.

Advantage Rent A Car, Tuesday Morning and Vision Group Holdings file for bankruptcy

On May 27, Advantage Rent A Car, the fourth-largest rental car company in North America, filed for bankruptcy (wsj.com). It's interesting as this comes just five days after Hertz filed for bankruptcy, which bought Advantage out of bankruptcy for $33 million in 2009 and then sold it to Macquarie Capital in 2012. But then Advantage filed for bankruptcy a second time in 2013 and was acquired in 2014 by its present owner, Catalyst Capital Group in Toronto. The same day, **Tuesday Morning**, the discount home goods retailer, filed for Chapter 11 bankruptcy protection. Tuesday Morning plans to permanently shut 230 stores, or one-third of its retail base of nearly 700 stores, and attempt to negotiate a significant number of its existing leases (cnbc.com). The big takeaway is the coronavirus pandemic attacked Tuesday Morning's key weakness — its lack of an e-commerce distribution channel. We also saw the U.S. division for Belgium-based Le Pain Quotidien file for bankruptcy protection. To avoid liquidation, Le Pain Quotidien is selling its 98 locations for $3 million to Aurify Brands LLC, a fast casual restaurant operator. Le Pain Quotidien, which derives over half of its sales from the hard-hit NYC metro area, could not make enough money to survive by keeping its locations open for takeout and delivery only (wsj.com).

On May 29, Vision Group Holdings filed for bankruptcy. The banning of elective surgery forced the privately held operator of Lasik Vision Institute and TLC Laser Eye Center chain to close its 120 Lasik eye centres and terminate over 800 employees, or two-thirds of its staff. But it wasn't able to survive as it was in a financially fragile state prior to the pandemic with $160 million in debt (wsj.com). And we could soon see another victim: 24 Hour Fitness, which was forced to shut down all its 430 clubs in the U.S. two-and-a-half months ago, is preparing to file for bankruptcy (usatoday.com). 24 Hour Fitness is the second-largest fitness chain in the U.S. with over 4 million members and 22,000 employees. It was struggling even prior to the pandemic as it has been weighed down by $1.3 billion in debt as a result of its $1.85 billion buyout by AEA Investors and Ontario Teachers' Pension Plan back in May 2014. On March 24, it had fully drawn the entirety of its $120 million revolving credit line. **Macy's** seems to have escaped death as it was able to raise $1.3 billion in 5-year bonds at an 8.375% interest rate. But in order to attract investors, Macy's had to offer significant collateral as these senior secured notes are backed by three properties in NYC, San Francisco and Chicago, 35 stores in select malls and 10 distribution centres (wsj.com).

TECH GIANTS ARE THRIVING IN DIGITAL WORLD

The tech giants are capitalizing on the pandemic to add structural capital and continue to innovate, positioning them to thrive in the digital world during and after the new twilight zone economy.

Amazon hires 125,000 workers as FTE; Facebook launches live event app; Instagram's IGTV introduces ads

Amazon intends to bring on 125,000, or 70%, of the 175,000 temporary workers it has hired in the U.S. since the pandemic started as full-time employees (wsj.com). **Facebook** is launching a new app called Venue to enable fans to engage digitally around live events. This is timely as although sports leagues are preparing to return to the physical world, they will be doing so in ghost stadiums. Venue will service as a digital companion for live events, offering fans the opportunity to engage in interactive questions, polls and short chats. Facebook debuted Venue at Sunday's NASCAR race (cnbc.com). Facebook is also introducing ads on Instagram's IGTV to enable video creators to generate money. The ads, which will run up to 15 seconds, will appear right before the content and Facebook plans to give at least 55% of the ad revenue to the creator. Instagram will also allow viewers to directly support their favourite creators through buying heart badges. The badges, which cost $0.99 for one heart, $1.99 for twos and $4.99 for three, will appear next to a viewer's name through the live video when they comment so creators can easily see who is supporting them (techcrunch.com).

Google Maps embraces twilight zone economy; Google Assistant

tests Voice Match feature

Google (**Alphabet**) has added new features to Google Maps to reflect the new twilight zone economy. On the physical layer, Google Maps will let shops list special hours like "seniors' hour" and restaurants list options like curbside pick-up. On the digital layer, businesses can offer virtual appointment booking and ask for donations via **PayPal** or GoFundMe and ghost kitchens can finally appear on the listings (cnet.com). We note Google Maps is following the move made by **Yelp** on May 4 to add virtual service offerings to its platform and enable restaurants to identify their curbside pick-up option. And Google Assistant is testing a new Voice Match feature that uses your voice as verification for purchases you make using a smart speaker (theverge.com). This could eliminate friction from the v-commerce process and, interestingly, follows Google's announcement a few weeks ago that merchants can list products in Google Shopping for free.

Quibi and HBO Max's new streaming services fail to take off

It looks like Quibi will fall far short of its target of 7 million sub-scribers in the first year as it has only managed to sign up 1.5 million users for its free 90-day trial since it launched its "quick bite" new video-streaming service on April 6. Although livestreaming hours have doubled during the lockdown, it seems like people have been looking to watch long-form content on their big screen TVs while they they're sheltering at home, not short-form content on their smartphone. As a result of the low viewership, Quibi's strong base of advertisers, which includes **Procter & Gamble, T-Mobile, PepsiCo, Anheuser-Busch InBev**, Walmart, **Progressive**, Google, Taco Bell (**Yum! Brands**) and **General Mills**, are looking to defer payments to Quibi and seek new deal terms, jeopardizing Quibi's $150 million in ad deals (wsj.com).

Warner Media's (**AT&T**) debut of its new HBO Max streaming service has also not gone well as only 90,000 people downloaded the app on its May 27 launch day. HBO Max is trying to compete against Netflix and Disney+ in the intensely competitive streaming wars but it is charging a premium price of $15 per month versus $9 for Netflix and $7 for Disney. Although HBO Max offers a wide variety of choice with over 10,000 hours of movies and TV, the content seems to be mostly dated and a jumbled assortment ranging from *Friends* to *Sesame Street* to *Casablanca* to *Wizard of Oz*. And HBO Max is also lacking in terms of convenience as it did not secure distribution deals with **Roku** or Amazon (cnbc.com).

WELCOME TO THE TWILIGHT ZONE ECONOMY

In the past week, we have seen evidence of how the workplace, auction houses, restaurants and the sharing economy are entering the twilight zone economy as the physical and digital states meet.

Google's gives $1,000 to 'ees for WFH supplies; Walmart's 10,000 tech 'ees can keep WFH

On May 26, Sundar Pichai, Google's CEO, sent an e-mail to employees titled *"Working from home and the office"*. Although Google will start to re-open its offices on July 6, it won't start building to 30% capacity until September. In keeping with Google's decision on May 7 to extend its work-from-home policy until the end of the year, Google will reimburse employees up to $1,000 for equipment and furniture to improve their productivity and comfort while working from home (blog.google). On May 28, Walmart sent an internal memo to its 10,000 tech employees to advise them that like Twitter employees, they will be able to keep working remotely, perhaps forever. As Walmart states: *"We believe the way of working in the future, particularly in tech, will be fundamentally different than it was before. We believe it will be one in which working virtually will be the new normal, at least for most of the work we lead...We will have physical office space and it will be used primarily for*

195

collaboration, to sync up and strengthen camaraderie" (cnbc.com).

Auction houses re-think centuries-old auction practices as embrace digital world

To survive the new ghost town economy, auction houses like **Sotheby's**, Christie's and Phillips had to leave behind the physical world and move up to the digital world. This transition was pretty successful as $1.96 billion of art was sold at auction since the lockdown, down only 16% from the $2.33 billion a year ago. Sotheby's itself held over 50 online auctions, generating over $100 million in sales. As a result, the industry is re-thinking centuries-old auction practices like replacing print catalogs with digital versions and holding weekly online sales versus live physical auctions every six months (wsj.com). When I read about this, I remembered how back in June 2018, Sotheby's acquired Thread Genius, which was founded in late 2015 in NYC by one of the founding members of **Spotify**. Thread Genius uses visual search and image recognition AI to deploy complex algorithms to predict what art or luxury items people might want to purchase based on previous purchases and searches. At the time, Sotheby's said it intended to use Thread Genius to expand its total addressable market beyond the high end by creating a middle-market marketplace through unlocking supply in private homes and attracting a new tier of middle market customers. In addition, Thread Genius would help Sotheby's customers determine the right time to put items up for auction, essentially shifting the annual auction calendar to more of an on-demand marketplace.

DoorDash launches Storefront for restaurants to bridge digital abyss

DoorDash is launching a new initiative called Storefront to help restaurants create their own websites so they can directly manage their online pick-up and delivery orders. This could be a savior for the estimated 40% of DoorDash's restaurant partners who are stranded on the wrong side of the digital abyss as they don't have any online ordering system (cnbc.com). Although restaurants are starting to re-open, their survival during the twilight zone economy will still likely depend on their ability to offer online pick-up and delivery as safety and physical distancing requirements reduce their dining capacity and erode the experience.

Criticism over Uber's scrapping of e-bikes foreshadows rebounding demand for shared assets

As the physical world re-opens, we are starting to see a rebound in demand for the sharing economy as shared assets like electric bikes and scooters are emerging as an attractive safer alternative to mass transit. As a result of its integration with Lime, **Uber** is handing over its fleet of tens of thousands of its new model Jump electric bikes and scooters to Lime. But it is coming under criticism for scrapping thousands of its older models as so many people could use them right now as a safer form of commuting as they return to the workplace. According to Uber, it was too complicated to give them away due to maintenance, liability, technology and safety issues (cnbc.com). Although ridesharing is slowly starting to rebound, people are still fearful of catching coronavirus from the driver. In this new twilight zone economy, robo-taxis would be a much more attractive alternative. To this point, Didi Chuxing just raised over $500 million for its autonomous driving division in a round led by **SoftBank**'s Vision Fund. Didi plans to roll out its "robo-taxi" soon in Shanghai and has licenses to test its autonomous cars in also Beijing and Suzhou in China and in California (cnbc.com).

BIG TECH GIANTS ARE STARTING TO ACQUIRE AI COMPANIES

Although AI investments have slowed down a bit as venture capital has dried up and unicorns will continue to crash into the coronavirus valley, this is creating an opportunity for the big tech giants to make acquisitions in AI companies. We are also seeing companies embrace AI on the healthcare front to fight the coronavirus.

Apple buys Inductive, Amazon in talks to buy Zoox, Bezos invests in Beacon

Apple has bought Inductive, a Waterloo-based AI machine learning start-up, to improve Siri's data (engadget.com). Amazon is in advanced talks to buy Zoox, an autonomous driving technology company (wsj.com). We note that Zoox has raised $955 million since launching in San Francisco in 2014. It's interesting as back in May Amazon was in talks to acquire TuSimple, another autonomous driving technology company, but that never materialized. But Amazon has been moving deeper into the auto space — in September, it ordered 100,000 electric delivery vehicles from Rivian, in which it made a $440 million strategic investment in February. On the logistics front, Jeff Bezos is investing in the $15 million Series A round for Beacon, which is looking to disrupt the $1 trillion freight forwarding industry. Beacon, which describes itself as the "next generation freight forwarding and supply chain finance company", was founded in London in 2018 by two former Uber executives. Beacon seems to have the support of Uber's founders: in April 2019, Travis Kalanick and Garrett Camp participated in Beacon's $3.5 million seed round, alongside former Google CEO, Eric Schmidt. Beacon has also attracted talent from Amazon as its CTO is the former head of software engineering for transportation technology at Amazon (cnbc.com).

CVS delivers prescriptions via self-driving robots; Novant Health launches America's first emergency drone

CVS Health is piloting a program at one of its drugstores in Houston to deliver prescriptions to customers at home using Nuro's self-driving robots (theverge.com). This is a shift in strategy for Nuro who has been partnering on grocery delivery with **Kroger** and pizza delivery with **Domino's Pizza**. We note Nuro raised a massive $940 million Series B round from SoftBank's Vision Fund in February 2019. We are also seeing drones deployed in the fight against coronavirus. On May 27, Novant Health launched America's first emergency drone operation after the FAA granted it an emergency wavier to deliver PPE and critical medical supplies to frontline medical teams in North Carolina. Novant Health is partnering with Zipline, which has deployed its unmanned aerial vehicles in parts of Africa and has raised $233 million since launching in San Francisco in 2013. Zipline's drones will be deployed on two initial routes ranging between 20 and 30 miles and can carry up to four pounds and fly at speeds up to 80 mph (cnbc.com).

China's health tracking system raises digital surveillance concerns; Wuhan tests 9 million people in 10 days

One reason why China has been so successful in controlling the coronavirus is its use of AI health tracking systems. But now privacy concerns over digital surveillance are escalating in China after the city of Hangzhou announced it was looking to introduce a new permanent version of the health tracking system it developed to fight the coronavirus. Hangzhou is currently using a QR-code health-rating app run by **Alibaba**'s Alipay. The new version would assign individuals a coloured health badge and a health score ranging from 0 to 100 based on data from electronic medical records and physical examinations results as well as lifestyle choices like exercise, sleep, drinking and smoking. This would enable the government to use big data to rate group health in different physical settings, such as apartment buildings, residential communities and businesses (wsj.com).

China's other weapon against the coronavirus is testing. For example, on May 25, Wuhan announced it successfully conducted a mass scale testing of 9 million of its 11 million residents over the past 10 days. Wuhan took this proactive measure over concerns of the emergence of a second wave following an outbreak of 6 new coronavirus cases, ending its record of 35 days without a new case. Wuhan's citizens were able to check their results on apps within days of testing and the good news is that only 218 asymptomatic carriers were identified. Wuhan was able to achieve mass scale testing by adopting an approach known as "sample pooling", in which it bundles together 5–10 samples into a single nucleic-acid test. But this process only works as a preventative measure when the results of pools are largely negative (wsj.com).

RED FLAGS FOR ESSENTIAL RETAILERS

Although essential retailers like Walmart and Costco could continue to benefit from the structural tailwind created by the coronavirus as we enter the twilight zone economy, we are concerned by these two new developments, which we view as potential red flags.

Walmart's thredUP partnership is a red flag of despair

We have mixed views on **Walmart**'s new partnership with thredUP. On the positive side, thredUP will provide Walmart with valuable supplier capital (i.e., Walmart is featuring thredUP's second-hand apparel items on its website) at a time when so many of Walmart's customers are more cost-conscious than ever. But we see a big red flag as Walmart is following in the footsteps of the desperate retailers that previously partnered with thredUP, like now-bankrupt department stores **Stage Stores** and **JC Penney**, and struggling apparel retailers Macy's and **Gap** (cnbc.com). And as we've previously cautioned, we expect these partnerships to only accelerate the awareness and adoption of apparel resale online platforms, leading to a rising rival threat of substitutes for department stores and apparel retailers.

Costco's SSS rose 4.3% in Q3 2020

Costco's same-store-sales rose 4.8% in Q3 2020, as the 9.3% increase in average ticket more than offset the 4.1% decline in traffic, and its e-commerce sales rose 65% (cnbc.com).

Chapter 18: The Virtual Life

June 9, 2020

Hiking up a majestic mountain...traveling in a mining car along a golden path...riding a horse though a desert...shooting arrows at an archery range...taking a group selfie in front of a birthday cake at twilight.

This is how we celebrated Adam's 7th birthday last week — but his party didn't take place at the newly re-opened Disney World Resort — it took place in a virtual birthday party world that Brady built in Minecraft. And Minecraft isn't just for kids — two Boston University seniors just held a Quaranteen University graduation ceremony in Minecraft for 500 students graduating from universities all over the world.

As we enter the twilight zone economy, we are seeing new developments pointing to the rising of the virtual world. Alibaba is launching virtual tradeshows for merchants in the U.S. on its B2B platform. Fashion is going virtual as Chanel debuts its new Resort Collection on Instagram, Gucci offers virtual personalized shopping and luxury brands prepare for upcoming virtual fashion shows in Paris and Milan. Luxury multi-residential rental buildings in NYC are also embracing the virtual world, offering a wide range of Zoom experiences, including yoga classes, puppet shows and cooking classes. As Eric Yuan, founder of Zoom, just stated: "I truly believe video is

a new voice...The way for us to work, live and play is completely changed."
Welcome to the Virtual Life.

Structural tailwind is emerging for off-price retailers like TJX

Although **TJX Companies** was shut out of the market during the ghost town economy, it is positioned to thrive in the new twilight zone economy. On the demand side, we expect to see the emergence of a structural tailwind for discount retailers from a new class of cost-conscious consumers that lost their jobs or businesses to the pandemic. On the supply side, the 89% drop in clothing sales in the U.S. in April created a mountain of apparel stock that has built up in stores, warehouses and even shipping containers. Although basic apparel inventory can stay in storage, this is not the case for seasonal or fashion apparel items, which have a much shorter shelf life. To quickly offload their unsold inventory, companies are offering in-store discounts and turning to off-price retailers like **TJX Companies**, who is seeing "incredible availability", and Parker Lane Group, who is processing double its usual volume of up to 1.5 million apparel items a month. However, physical off-price retailers will not have a monopoly on this bounty as Amazon is planning to host a "Fashion Summer Sale Event" on June 22 to help retailers unload their unsold inventory. The event, which is expected to run for 7–10 days, is invitation only and Amazon is asking sellers to offer a discount of at least 30% (cnbc.com).

Adoption skyrockets for TikTok, Instagram & Snapchat for kids during lockdown

"We don't expect a 'reset' to pre-COVID-19 screen times now that more children and parents have become used to increased screen-time." This statement comes from Qustodio, a digital safety app maker, in its newly published report, *Connected More than Ever — Apps and digital natives: the new normal.* The report, based on data gathered on the online habits of 60,000 families with kids aged 4–15 in the U.S., U.K.

and Spain, provides evidence on how kids have embraced the digital world during lockdown by escaping to social media, gaming and video apps:

- **Social Media Adoption Soared During the Lockdown, Especially with TikTok:** The percentage of kids using TikTok rose from 17% to 48%, Instagram (**Facebook**) from 20% to 47% and Snapchat (**Snap**) from 16% to 36%. The time spent on the apps also increased with TikTok up 16% (from 82 to 95 minutes), Instagram up 20% (from 50 to 60 minutes) and Snapchat up 14% (from 57 to 65 minutes).
- **Time Spent Playing Games Increased 23% Since Lockdown:** The time spent playing games rose 23% since lockdown, from 66 to 81 minutes, and the two most popular gaming apps are Roblox (54%) and Minecraft (**Microsoft**) (31%).
- **Time Spent Playing YouTube Increased 13% Since Lockdown:** Time spent on YouTube (**Alphabet**) has increased 13% since the lockdown (86 to 97 minutes). Twice as many kids watch videos on YouTube versus **Netflix** (69% versus 33%) and Twitch (**Amazon**) is emerging as a new platform with 9% of kids using it.

Speaking of TikTok, it has expanded in the past few months beyond dancing and lip-synching videos to enable people to create and share short-form content (both on-demand and livestreamed) on sports, gaming, cooking, fashion, beauty and educational topics (cnet.com). And Minecraft is acting as a substitute for physical venues as the first graduation ceremony was just held inside Minecraft (**Microsoft**). On May 22, over 500 students graduating from universities all over the world attended the Quaranteen University graduation ceremony, the inspiration of two Boston University seniors (rollingstone.com).

Alibaba offers livestreamed industry trade shows on its B2B plat-

form

On June 2, **Alibaba** launched Online Trade Shows USA, which will offer livestreamed industry-specific trade shows for merchants on its B2B platform in the U.S., with 20 shows already scheduled for the next 120 days. As John Caplan, Alibaba.com's president for North America and Europe stated, this will create a *"pivot in how small businesses connect and engage"* as with digital options they won't have to *"invest three days and thousands of dollars to travel"'*. Alibaba also introduced two other digital features for merchants on its B2B platform in the U.S., which has become Alibaba's fastest-growing marketplace with the number of buyers up 70% and transactions up 100% in the past year. On the payments front, Alibaba is partnering with MSTS, a B2B credit company, to offer Alibaba.com Payment Terms which allows buyers to wait up to 60 days before paying for goods. On the logistics side, Alibaba is partnering with Freightos, a digital freight marketplace, to offer Alibaba.com Freight which allows businesses to compare, book and track ocean and air freight (marketwatch.com). Ironically, at a time when the world is going virtual, one of the world's largest tech events that showcases the latest digital and virtual technology is sticking to the traditional physical venue. Despite the threat of a second wave of coronavirus, the Consumer Technology Association is defiantly planning to go ahead with its annual Consumer Electronics Show (CES) in Las Vegas in January. The event is one of the largest conventions in Las Vegas, attracting 175,000 attendees (theverge.com).

UPS & FedEx add B2C delivery surcharges as Amazon Prime Air leases 12 more planes

UPS and **FedEx** are adding delivery surcharges to some residential shipments in the U.S. to help offset the increased costs as a result of the surge in volume of B2C shipments. They are both adding a 30¢ surcharge to residential packages from large customers, with UPS qualifying this as those that have increased their monthly volumes by over 25,000 packages since the pandemic started and FedEx charging this to all customers that send over 40,000 packages a week or those whose volume is up over 120%. They are also adding an oversize surcharge, $31.45 for UPS and $30.00 for FedEx. And FedEx is adding a 40¢ surcharge for its SmartPost packages (wsj.com). Meanwhile, as further evidence that Amazon will be reducing its reliance on third-party air carriers, it is leasing 12 **Boeing** 767-300 converted cargo planes from **Air Transport Services Group** (ATS Group). One of the cargo planes joined Amazon's Prime Air fleet in May and the rest will be delivered next year, bringing its total fleet to over 80 aircraft. Amazon Prime Air is also expanding its structural capital on the ground as it will soon be opening two regional air hubs (one in Florida later this summer and one in California next year) and its new $1.5 billion central air hub in Kentucky next year (cnbc.com). We note that back in December 2018, ATS Group secured 20 used Boeing 767s from American Airlines that it would be acquiring over the next 3 years and leased the first 10 to Amazon.

Amazon is developing an AI-driven virtual try-on apparel shopping service

At the upcoming Conference on Computer Vision and Pattern Recognition, which will be held virtually from June 14 to 19, Amazon researchers from its Lab126 will present a series of papers on Outfit-VITON. The image-based virtual try-on system will let you visualize how clothing items will look on you. In addition, Amazon is developing image search with text feedback that will allow you to ask for "something more formal" or "change the neck style". Amazon is also developing technology to retrieve complementary items by predicting compatibility with other clothing and accessory items (venturebeat.com). Meanwhile, **Pinterest** is copying Amazon and Google as it has added a "Shop" tab in its smart Lens camera so you can take a picture of something and it will show you its in-stock merchandise matches (techcrunch.com).

Reitmans closes stores as Ascena Retail and Brooks Brothers explore filing for bankruptcy

Reitmans, who filed for bankruptcy on May 19, will be cutting 1,400 jobs as it permanently closes all of its 77 Addition Elle and 54 Thyme Maternity stores. This represents just over a 20% reduction in its base of 6,800 employees and 576 stores. Reitmans has not announced its plans for its remaining three brands, which encompass 259 Reitmans, 106 Penningtons and 80 RW & Co stores (financialpost.com). Meanwhile, **Ascena Retail Group** is exploring filing for Chapter 11 bankruptcy protection and selling three of its seven apparel brands while keeping Ann Taylor and Loft. This comes a year after Ascena closed down its Dress Barn women's value fashion brand and sold its majority interest in Maurices to a London-based private equity firm. Although Ascena started to re-open some of its stores in early May, it is seeing significantly reduced customer traffic (pymnts.com). And Brooks Brothers is in talks with banks about debtor-in-possession financing for a potential bankruptcy as early as July (cnbc.com). And in Canada, **Walmart** is permanently closing all its 106 in-store Tire & Lube auto express service centres to focus on accelerating its online growth (ctvnews.ca).

AMC Entertainment warns it has "substantial doubt" it can remain in business

On June 3, **AMC Entertainment Holdings** warned that it has "substantial doubt" it can remain in business as it is generating effectively no revenue. Although it is starting to re-open its movie theatres as lockdowns ease in some areas, it faces serious challenges on the supply side as distributors may choose to delay the release of new movies until operating restrictions are eased more broadly (cnn.com).

CBL warns of ability to continue as a going concern as SPG sues Gap for not paying rent

206

On June 5, **CBL & Associates**, which operates 108 shopping malls in the Southeast U.S., warned that its ability to continue as a going concern is in doubt. It did not pay its $11.8 million interest payment that was due on June 1 and it has violated a covenant in its senior secured credit facility. CBL was only able to collect 27% of rents due from tenants in April and expects May will be the same. In addition, CBL has high exposure to newly bankrupt **JC Penney**, which has 47 stores in CBL's 108 malls, or 44%, with 8 of them expected to close permanently (cnbc.com). We note that Mall of America, the largest shopping mall in the U.S, is delinquent on its $1.4 billion mortgage as it missed its April and May interest payments. As a red flag, on June 2, **Simon Property Group** sued **Gap** for failing to pay over $66 million in rent and other charges during the pandemic (cnbc.com). We note that in April, Gap stopped paying rent on its shuttered stores, which totals $115 million per month, and was in negotiations to defer rent payments or agree on an abatement with its landlords, of which the largest is Simon Property Group who has 412 Gap stores in its malls. But, as David Simon, Chairman, CEO & President, commented a few weeks later on May 11 during Simon Property Group's Q1 2020 conference call: *"the reality is, we have a lease and they have to pay..."*

Banks looking to accelerate closure of physical branches

As we enter the new twilight zone economy, banks are seeing this as an opportunity to accelerate the closure of physical branches. As the lockdown forced people to rapidly adopt digital banking, this shift in consumer behaviour is expected to endure, reducing the importance of the physical footprint of banks (wsj.com).

Gucci offers remote personalized shopping as fashion shows go virtual

Gucci (**Kering**) is bringing the experience of having an in-store personal shopper to the digital layer with the launch of Gucci Live. Gucci has created a faux luxury store/studio in Florence from which its sales staff can deliver one-on-one remote personalized shopping services via videoconferencing for its elite clientele (voguebusiness.com). Fashion is also going virtual in the new twilight zone economy. Chanel unveiled its new Resort Collection via video on Instagram and Chanel's website. Chanel will also be participating in Paris' digital couture show on July 7 (footwearnews.com). At the upcoming Milano Digital Fashion Week being held from July 14 to 17, luxury brands are coming up with creative ways to showcase their latest fashions without an audience. For example, Italian luxury fashion house, Ermenegildo Zegna is coming up with a "phygital" show which combines live models, digital technology and cinematography supplemented by additional online content on its website and social media. And it's not just the format of fashion shows that is changing, but their frequency. Gucci's creative director, Alessando Michele, declared the fashion calendar obsolete as he announced Gucci will scale back its number of fashion shows from five to two and go seasonless (wsj.com).

Article's DTC furniture sales soar 200% in April

Article, a Vancouver-based e-commerce mid-century modern furniture company, is thriving during the pandemic as its monthly sales hit an all-time high in April, up 200% from a year ago, as it saw a 2x increase in both existing and new customers (forbes.com).

"Video is a new voice" proclaims Zoom's founder

"*I truly believe video is a new voice. Video is going to change everything about the communication. The way for us to work, live and play is completely changed.*" This proclamation comes from Eric Yuan, founder & CEO of Zoom, during Zoom's Q1 2020 conference call on June 3. A perfect example of this is found at luxury multi-residential buildings in NYC which have embraced the digital layer to try to fill the void caused by the closure on the physical level of on-site amenities like fitness centres, swimming pools, theatre rooms and lounges, and activities like fitness classes, book clubs and social mixers. To maintain the sense of community and keep their tenants entertained, they are offering a wide range of virtual experiences on Zoom, including yoga classes, puppet shows, comedy shows and cooking classes (wsj.com).

Amazon deepens its partnership with Slack

Amazon and **Slack** are deepening their partnership as they join forces to compete against Microsoft. Under the new deal, all Amazon employees will now have access to Slack's workplace collaboration tools and Slack is deepening its reliance on AWS, using its Chime infrastructure to deliver its voice and video-calling service and will pay Amazon at least $425 million over the next five years. Slack's CEO, Stuart Butterfield, announced this new partnership during Slack's Q1 2020 conference call. Although Slack added 90,000 total and 12,000 paid customers during the quarter, this quarter-over-quarter growth rate of 14% and 11%, respectively, paled in comparison to Zoom, which saw its number of daily participants increase by 30-fold from 10 million to 300 million. In defense, Butterfield stated that Slack isn't a "digital substitute" like Zoom and *"You just can't adapt Slack that quickly. You can't move from e-mail to channel-based messaging in that short amount of time, which I wish that call cultures could change overnight."*

Peloton launches Apple TV app

Peloton is looking to improve the experience of working out at home with the launch of its new **Apple TV** app. This will provide Peloton with a valuable new customer acquisition channel for its Digital Membership, which it first introduced two years ago, as new members can access the app on Apple TV for a free 30-day trial (techcrunch.com). More importantly, it will further advance Peloton's accessibility-focused social mission *"to use technology and design to connect the world through fitness, empowering people to be the best version of themselves anywhere, anytime"*.

Tovala raises $20 million to grow its smart oven/meal kit delivery

service

Tovala, a Chicago-based food tech company that offers a smart oven with a companion meal delivery service, just raised a $20 million Series B round. Like many meal kit companies, Tovala has thrived during lockdown, with its subscriber base increasing 20% since mid-March (techcrunch.com). The countertop oven, which costs $299 (down from $399 when it launched in July 2017), foreshadows the future of cooking: all you need to do is scan the meal sleeve and then it cooks the chef-prepared healthy meal in 10–30 minutes at temperatures up to 550° Fahrenheit, automatically switching between baking, boiling and steaming cooking methods.

Facebook and PayPal invest in Indonesian super app, Go-jek

Facebook and **PayPal** just invested in Go-jek, the Indonesian Super app that is building an on-demand empire of payments, food delivery, transportation and logistics. Although the investment amount for this Series F round was not disclosed, we note that Go-jek has raised $4.5 billion since launching in Jakarta in 2010. This investment is strategic for Facebook as it is looking to help bring small businesses online, similar to the $5.7 billion investment it made in late April for Indian telecom operator Jio Platforms Ltd. (**Reliance Industries**) to enable people to buy products via WhatsApp. PayPal's investment is also strategic as it is looking to connect Go-jek's GoPay users with its network of over 25 million merchants worldwide (cnbc.com).

Tembici raises $47 million to expand rollout of docked electric bikes in Latin America

Tembici, the leading micro-mobility player in Latin America, has raised a $47 million Series B round to double down on the rollout of more of its docked electric bikes. Tembici has seen its market bifurcate during the lockdown with increased demand from delivery drivers but plummeting demand from commuters. But as offices re-open, Tembici expects demand to surge for its e-bikes which will provide commuters with a safer alternative than mass transit (techcrunch.com).

Travelodge seeks rent reduction for its shuttered budget motels through CVA in U.K.

Travelodge, which was forced to close its 564 budget motels in March, is seeking rent reduction through filing a CVA (Company Voluntary Arrangement). As Travelodge won't be able to open its motels until July 4 at the earliest, it is proposing to landlords that they cut its rent in half for the rest of this year and next year, with the return to full rent in 2022. Travelodge says its 10,000 jobs are at stake (uk.finance.yahoo.com).

Dunkin' looks to hire 25,000 employees

On June 8, **Dunkin' Brands Group** announced that its Dunkin' franchisees are looking to hire 25,000 employees. Although its coffee and donut shops located on college campuses and in transportation hubs remain closed, over 90% of its 8,500+ locations are open with modified operations (finance.yahoo.com).

WeWork's co-founder steps down

Miguel McKelvey, the co-founder of WeWork, is leaving the company at the end of June. The old guard is being wiped out as Artie Minson and Sebastian Gunningham, who were appointed co-CEOs on September 24 after Adam Neumann was ousted as CEO, have also left WeWork (reuters.com).

Seattle legislates gig economy companies to provide sick pay for workers

Seattle City Council just passed an emergency ordinance that re-quires gig economy companies like **Uber**, **Lyft**, DoorDash and Instacart to provide sick pay to their workers. Under the new legislation, companies will have the choice to provide workers with one day of paid sick leave for every 30 days they have worked since October 2019 or to give everyone a base of five sick days and then one day for each 30 days going forward. This legislation, which will be in place until at least the end of 2023, could set a precedent for other cities to follow, leading to the ultimate reclassification of independent contractors to employees (wired.com). We note that even prior to the pandemic, back in September, Seattle was considering legislation to set a minimum pay for Uber and Lyft drivers.

Google Maps rolls out COVID-19 safety features

Google is rolling out new features on Google. Google Maps will alert travelers of COVID-19 checkpoints or border restrictions, like the still closed U.S./Canada border. For commuters, Google Maps will now display transit alerts and indicate how crowded the bus or subway will likely be, although this feature is not yet available in Canada. And if you need to visit a COVID-19 testing facility, Google Maps will alert you whether you need an appointment or not (techcrunch.com).

Chapter 19: The Ghost Castle

June 23, 2020

Cruise ships are grounded until September 15...AMC reverses its controversial stance on the optional wearing of masks...Live Nation debuts first-ever drive-in concert series...Canada reaches agreement with Mexico to improve safety conditions for migrant farm workers...Amazon uses AI cameras in warehouses to enforce physical distancing...

What is the underlying theme behind these latest developments? SAFETY. As I explored in my June 16 research report, "The Three Ghosts Haunting the New Twilight Zone Economy", the safety ghost, which I symbolize as the Ghost Castle, is one of three ghosts lurking in the twilight that has arisen from the coronavirus pandemic. And it is the Ghost Castle that is acting as a catalyst to fast-forward the capsizing of the Ghost Ship while giving wings to the Ghost Unicorn.

The retail REITs continue to take on water as Brookfield Property Partners has apparently requested forbearance from some of its lenders while three-quarters of its tenants have requested changes to their lease agreements. At the same time, safety constraints barring customers from trying on beauty products in the store are giving wings to L'Oreal, Ulta Beauty and Sephora which invested in their own virtual try-on apps. Likewise, although the upcoming Premier League soccer matches will be played in ghost stadiums, Amazon will be able to offer interactive virtual engagement for fans through its Twitch platform. And Empire's launch of its new Ocado-powered online grocery service is timely for customers that want to avoid the risk of going to the grocery store.

Beauty goes virtual as trying on of beauty products is no longer allowed

"In e-commerce, we achieved in eight weeks what it would have otherwise taken us three years to do." This statement comes from **L'Oreal**'s Chief Digital Officer, Lubomira Rochet, in discussing how the pandemic has accelerated the digital transformation of the beauty industry. The acquisition that L'Oreal made back in March 2018 of ModiFace is paying off as the average time customers spend using the virtual try-on app to test hair colour or foundation has more than quadrupled since the pandemic, from two minutes to nine minutes. Fifteen companies, including **Amazon** and Boots (**Walgreens**), have added ModiFace to their websites and apps, and L'Oreal is setting itself up for a world where half of its business is e-commerce and 80% of customer interactions are online (ft.com). Even though stores are starting to re-open, they will no longer be able to offer the experience of physically trying on products or in-person consultations. Although drug retailers like Boots can offer virtual try-on of L'Oreal products, it is still at a disadvantage to beauty retailers Ulta Beauty and Sephora who offer virtual try-on for a much wider range of brands. For example, **Ulta Beauty**'s GLAMLab virtual try-on app, which it first launched in 2016, has seen its usage increase over five times during the pandemic, with 19 million different shades of makeup tried on (cnn.com). **Sephora** launched its virtual try-on app, Sephora Virtual Artist, in 2017. The two companies are also offering virtual beauty advisors, with Sephora launching virtual services via **Zoom** in mid-May (theverge.com).

Empire launches Ocado-powered online grocery delivery service

Empire is launching Voila by Sobeys, its new online grocery delivery service powered by Ocado. Empire is rolling out the service first in Vaughan, the location of its new 250,000-square-foot automated warehouse, and to the rest of the GTA in the coming weeks, with its fleet of delivery vans increasing from 100 to 400–500 vans. When Ocado partnered with Empire back in January 2018 to provide an end-to-end grocery e-commerce solution and design and construct an automated warehouse, the two companies never imagined the catalyst for adoption would be a pandemic. But as Michael Medline, Empire's CEO, stated: *"It's probably going to be three times as fast as we had expected. ... We're looking at how quickly we can expand to other markets in Canada as well."* (theglobeandmail.com). And all the pieces of the puzzle are coming together as Voila by Sobeys will also offer food from Farm Boy, which Empire acquired in September 2018 for $800 million. In Europe, **Carrefour** has launched a voice-based grocery shopping service in France powered by Google Assistant (pymnts.com). We note that Carrefour partnered with Google (**Alphabet**) back in June 2018 to gain access to its Google Assistant v-commerce platform as part of its then announced €2.8 billion investment over the next five years in online shopping to fend off Amazon.

BPP requests forbearance as three-quarters of mall tenants request changes to lease agreements

Brookfield Property Partners (BPP) has apparently requested forbearance from lenders who are owed payments on a dozen of its malls. BPP has also requested 12-month extensions on mall loans coming due this year but creditors of four of these malls have not yet decided whether to grant this request. BPP is starting to play hardball with its tenants as it has refused to waive payments, giving them until the end of 2021 to pay and sued Gap last week for failing to pay rent, following in the footsteps of **Simon Property Group** (SPG) who sued Gap on June 2. And BPP faces further challenges as three-quarters of its tenants have requested changes to their lease agreements (ft.com). In addition, BPP and SPG are in discussions to acquire **JC Penney** to ensure the survival of one of their biggest anchor tenants. JC Penney, which filed for Chapter 11 bankruptcy protection on May 15, is planning to shrink its fleet of department stores by nearly 30%, from 846 to 604, by next year. Authentic Brands, which joined SPG and BPP in paying $81 million for Forever 21 back in February, may also team up with them. Authentic Brands and SPG are also currently in discussions with Brooks Brothers, which is exploring bankruptcy as early as July (financialpost.com). The risk for SPG and BPP is that as JC Penney is an anchor tenant, when it vacates a mall, this could trigger a co-tenancy clause which would allow the remaining mall tenants to exercise their right to terminate their lease or renegotiate terms with lower rents until another retailer occupies the vacated anchor space.

DavidsTea may pursue formal restructuring as Valentino sues to exit Fifth Avenue lease

On June 16, **DavidsTea** announced it may pursue formal restructuring if it is not successful in negotiating with its landlords to close some of its unprofitable locations. DavidsTea has not paid rent on any of its 231 stores for April, May or June and they have sat empty since it closed them on March 17 (bnnbloomberg.ca). Meanwhile, Valentino is suing to terminate the lease for its four-storey boutique on Fifth Avenue in NYC. The Italian luxury clothing company alleges in the complaint it filed with the Supreme Court of the State of New York: *"In the current social and economic climate, filled with COVID-19-related restrictions, social distancing measures, a lack of consumer confidence and a prevailing fear of patronizing, in-person, 'non-essential' luxury retail boutiques, Valentino's business at the premises has been substantially hindered and rendered impractical, unfeasible and no longer workable"* (wsj.com). **AT&T** is fast-forwarding the closure of 250 retail locations in the U.S. as a result of the pandemic. However, this is not a significant reduction in AT&T's retail footprint as it only represents 4% of its base of 5,785 stores in the U.S. (theverge.com). And the vultures are starting to feast as Amazon is leasing a former **Macy's** store at Redmond Town Centre to convert into office space to house 600 AWS employees. Macy's closed the 111,000-square-foot store early last year (seattletimes.com).

Walmart acquires tech and IP assets of digital health company for $200 million

Walmart is investing in its healthcare business with the acquisition of the technology and IP assets of CareZone for an estimated $200 million. CareZone will provide Walmart with valuable structural capital as its app helps manage medications, organize health information and access health services (pymnts.com).

Amazon will livestream Premier League soccer matches for first time on Twitch

Amazon will be livestreaming Premier League soccer matches on Twitch for the first time. This is brilliant as although the games will be played in ghost stadiums, fans will be able to engage interactively by shouting out virtually from the sidelines via text and emojis on Twitch. The upcoming four soccer matches will also be available for anyone to watch on Amazon Prime, even non-Amazon Prime members (cnbc.com). It's interesting as Twitch's interactive virtual platform will provide Amazon with a unique advantage for broadcasting sports and we believe Amazon will use this playbook for upcoming NFL games, which are likely to be played in ghost stadiums when they return. We note that last month Amazon renewed its exclusive streaming partnership with the NFL for "Thursday Night Football" games for another three years.

Spotify announces exclusive podcast partnership with DC as Twitter rolls out audio tweets

On June 18, **Spotify** announced a new partnership with DC Entertainment (**Warner Bros.**) to exclusively produce and distribute a new slate of narrative scripted podcasts. The deal involves the intellectual property of the entire DC universe, including Spiderman, Wonder Woman and Batman (cnbc.com). The previous day, Spotify announced that it had reached an exclusive deal with Kim Kardashian West for a criminal-justice podcast (wsj.com). Spotify seems to be on a spending spree to tie up exclusive content to reach its aspiration to become the "Netflix of Audio" as this deal follows a month after Spotify announced that it has signed an exclusive multi-year podcast licensing deal with Joe Rogan that is reported to be worth more than $100 million. Even Twitter is joining the audio movement. **Twitter** is starting to roll out audio tweets — letting you tweet with your voice. Each voice tweet is limited to 140 seconds but if your audio recording is longer than that, Twitter will create a thread and add a new voice tweet. Although this is a great new feature, it may create challenges in terms of content moderation (techcrunch.com).

Facebook acquires Mapillary and debuts WhatsApp payments in Brazil

Facebook's buying spree continues as it is acquiring Mapillary, a crowdsourced street-level imagery platform. Mapillary has raised $24.5 million since it was launched in Sweden in 2013, with **BMW** iVentures leading its $15 million Series B round in April 2018. Mapillary will provide Facebook with valuable structural capital to enhance its open mapping efforts, which are important for services like Facebook Marketplace (cnbc.com). Meanwhile, Facebook is debuting WhatsApp payments in Brazil. Facebook users will be able to send and receive money on WhatsApp using Facebook Pay. The service is free for consumers but businesses will have to pay a 3.99% processing fee. To use it, people and businesses in Brazil will need to link up their WhatsApp account to their **Visa** or **Mastercard** and transactions will be verified via a fingerprint or 6-digit PIN (techcrunch.com).

Google integrates Google Meet into Gmail and launches AI-powered Pinterest rival

Google is aggressively going after the videoconferencing market, integrating Google Meet, which it opened up to everyone for free at the end of April, into Gmail and Google Calendar. Google will now let you join a Google Meet event right from your inbox by clicking on a link in Gmail to a Meet event. In a few weeks, the Gmail app will feature a tab at the bottom of the screen which will show all your upcoming Google Meet meetings and enable you to schedule a Meet in Google Calendar, as well as get a link to share and start a meeting (techcrunch.com). Google has also quietly launched Keen, an AI-powered rival to **Pinterest**. Keen lets users create a "keen" such as baking and then curate content, share the collection and find new content based on what you saved and follow other keens (theverge.com). We note that back in February, Facebook also launched a competitor to Pinterest called Hobbi. The photo and video-sharing app lets you organize and document your personal projects and hobbies into themed collections.

Cruise ships now grounded until September 15

On June 19, the Cruise Lines International Association announced that the cruise lines have agreed to voluntarily extend suspension of operations out of U.S. ports until September 15 (cnbc.com). Cruise ships have been sitting empty since the CDC issued a no-sail order for all cruise ships on March 14 and this extends the ban by nearly two months as it was supposed to end on July 24. This also means that **Carnival** will not able to resume cruise service that it had announced back on May 5 for eight of its ships to set sail from the ports of Galveston, Miami and Port Canaveral starting August 1.

AMC's initial mask optional stance is a red flag

On June 18, **AMC Entertainment** faced heavy criticism by public health experts and a social media backlash after declaring it will not mandate guests to wear masks in its movie theatres when it re-opens next month as it *"didn't want to be drawn into the political controversy"*. However, the next day, AMC reversed its decision, stating that all customers will be required to wear masks. AMC is planning to re-open 450 of its 600 theatres on July 15 and the rest by the end of July. It will also be reducing seating capacity initially to 30% and then increase to 40% and 50% (wsj.com). We believe AMC's initial stance to make masks optional is a red flag of its desperation to ignore public safety to bring people back to its theatres. We note that on June 3, AMC warned that it had "substantial doubt" it could remain in business as it was generating no revenue.

Live Nation announces first ever drive-in concert series in the U.S.

Live Nation, the live entertainment company which has been shut down since mid-March, has announced the first ever drive-in concert series in the U.S. The nine "Live from the Drive-In" concert series will take place in three cities, featuring artists like Brad Paisley, Darius Rucker, Jon Pardi and Nelly (marketwatch.com). We note that a month ago the first drive-in concert took place in Denmark, where Mads Langer played to a crowd of 2,000 fans that sat socially distanced inside their cars. However, Live Nation's drive-in concert will be more of an outdoor tailgate event as there will be two empty parking lot spaces between cars and people will be allowed to bring in their own pre-cooked food and drinks, including alcohol.

Amazon uses AI cameras in warehouse to enforce physical distancing

Amazon is using AI cameras in its warehouses to monitor social distancing. Amazon's "Distance Assistants" use machine learning models to measure the approximate distance between workers to alert employees if they come closer than six feet from one another. Amazon is rolling out the AI cameras in high-traffic areas and is making the technology open source so other companies can use it in their facilities (cnbc.com).

Canada reaches agreement with Mexico over improved safety conditions for farm workers

On June 16, Mexico temporarily banned workers from traveling to Canada to work on the farms following the recent infection of hundreds and the death of two migrant farm workers (cnn.com). This would have created a shortage of 5,000 workers, but five days later Canada reached an agreement with Mexico over improved safety conditions for migrant farmworkers coming from Mexico (cbc.ca).

DoorDash raises $400 million a week after Just Eat Takeaway.com acquires Grubhub for $7.3 billion

DoorDash raised a $400 million Series H round from existing investors at a valuation of just under $16 billion. This represents a premium of over 20% to the $13 billion valuation from its last funding round in November 2019 (techcrunch.com). Competition is intensifying in the restaurant delivery space as on June 10 **Just Eat Takeaway.com** acquired **Grubhub** for $7.3 billion.

Chapter 20: Secrets Behind the Mask

June 30, 2020

When we wear a mask out in public, it is a sign of respect that we care about protecting each other. So when we see companies putting social values ahead of profits, it is a sign of respect that they care about protecting society — essentially, they're wearing a mask.

The strategic moves that companies are taking during the pandemic are providing us with valuable insights into who are the "Anti-Maskers" and the "Maskers". Anti-Maskers was actually the name of the league formed in San Francisco in January 1919 to protest the mandated wearing of masks. This week exposed two Anti-Maskers in Canada: Cineplex, which is standing firm on its highly controversial mask optional policy, and Sienna Senior Living, which owns 5 of Ontario's 20 worst hit nursing homes and has, to date, been responsible for 758 patient infections and 292 deaths. In contrast, lululemon is a true Masker as it just acquired Mirror for $500 million to keep its guests safe by bringing its ambassador community to them on the digital layer, which I believe will be a huge growth catalyst. And lululemon also just joined the #StopHateforProfit advertising boycott of Facebook, signalling that it puts humanity before profits as one of its values.

The bottom line is the coronavirus pandemic and the Black Lives Matter movement are together unmasking the social values of companies —

uncovering the S in ESG.

lululemon's $500 million acquisition of Mirror will be a significant growth catalyst

On June 29, **lululemon** announced it was acquiring Mirror, a DTC at-home digital connected fitness competitor to **Peloton**, for $500 million (investor.lululemon.com). I was excited back in early November when I learned that lululemon participated as a strategic investor in Mirror's $34 million Series B round as I believed it could be a big growth catalyst for lululemon because it could *"foreshadow a new way for lululemon to expand its TAM as it could potentially leverage its ambassador network to create content for Mirror's platform (i.e., classes like yoga, barre and meditation)."* The two things that stood out to me back then were that this was lululemon's first investment in a tech company and, more importantly, its founder, Brynn Putnam, is a former NYC ballet dancer, and a former lululemon ambassador. Ms. Putnam will be continuing on as CEO of Mirror.

On the conference call discussing the Mirror acquisition, lululemon's CEO, Calvin McDonald, observed that *"covid brought the future closer to the present"* and shared how the pandemic has accelerated the emerging trends of digital content changing how and where its guests sweat, grow and connect. With 75% of luluemon's guests now using digital fitness tools, up from 64% pre-Covid, Mirror will be a key component of lululemon's new membership strategy. Digital content is also changing the studio and trainer models for its ambassadors, and Mirror will be the key to bringing its ambassador community to guests on the digital layer.

Cineplex's masks optional policy is a red flag

We are concerned that **Cineplex**'s decision to stand firm on its policy to make masks optional is a red flag of its desperation to ignore public safety to bring people back to its theatres (cbc.ca). Its decision is especially disconcerting given **AMC Entertainment**'s decision last week to quickly reverse course on its mask optional policy. We note that Cineplex is in a very fragile state as on June 12, Cineworld Group backed out of its $2.1 billion acquisition of Cineplex that it announced back on December 15, just months prior to the pandemic.

Amazon Prime Video is expanding into live TV: could Twitch be part of the strategy?

Amazon is looking to differentiate itself from **Netflix** and **Disney** by expanding from on-demand video to disrupting traditional live TV. In a recent job listing for a *"Prime Video Linear TV - Principal Product Manager, Technical"*, Amazon states: *"We in Prime Video Catalog are building next gen linear catalog systems to provide best-in-class Linear TV experience to Prime Video customers. It is Day 1 for the linear TV experience on Prime Video."* In another recent listing for a *"Senior Software Development Engineer - Prime Video"*, Amazon states that *"Linear TV enables customers to watch 24/7 streams of their favorite TV stations airing programs including sports, news, movies, award shows, special events and TV shows"*. It's interesting as last week, Amazon announced it will be livestreaming Premier League soccer matches on Twitch for the first time. Connecting the dots, we believe there could be the exciting potential for Amazon Prime Video to integrate Twitch into its live TV programming.

#StopHateforProfit advertising boycott of Facebook provides valuable insights for S in ESG

Facebook is coming under intensifying pressure for its refusal to deal with hate speech and racism on its platform as iconic companies start to pull their ad dollars (cnn.com). This #StopHateforProfit advertising boycott actually gives us valuable insight (especially for ESG investors who care about the S factor – social) as those who were the most proactive to join are those who truly put humanity before profits as one of their values. In terms of timing, the first publicly traded company to commit was The North Face (**VF Corp**) on June 20, followed by **Verizon** on June 25. On June 26, the boycott gained momentum with CPG companies (**Coca-Cola, Unilever, Hershey**), apparel retailer **Levi Strauss & Co.** and auto manufacturer **Honda.** The two beverage giants, **Diageo** and **PepsiCo**, joined on June 28 and the next day they were joined by restaurants **Starbucks** and **Denny's**, and lululemon. On June 29, Amazon took direct action against hate on its Twitch platform by temporarily banning President Donald Trump for posting "hateful content". Trump joined Twitch last year to stream his rallies and events (cnbc.com).

Facebook's WhatsApp payments suspended by Brazilian government

Facebook's challenges continue as the Brazilian government suspended Facebook's WhatsApp payments only a week after its launch. Brazil's central government stated the suspension was made to *"preserve an adequate competitive environment"* and to ensure *"functioning of a payment system that's interchangeable, fast, secure, transparent, open and cheap"* (techcrunch.com). This is a setback for Facebook as it was the debut of WhatsApp payments, which let users send and receive money on WhatsApp using Facebook Pay. On the positive side, Instagram is expanding access to Instagram Shopping to more businesses, including creators who want to sell their own merchandise (pymnts.com).

Target finally launches curbside pick-up of groceries

Target has sped up its plans to offer curbside pick-up of groceries. Target is adding 750 fresh and frozen grocery items to in-store and curbside pick-up at 400 stores by the end of this month and 1,500 by the holidays, representing 80% of its 1,871 locations (cnbc.com). Target had paused this plan back on March 26 as it was struggling to meet the surge in demand and didn't have time to train employees on new processes. But it decided to push forward which is a smart move given its customers are rapidly adopting online shopping, as evidenced by the nearly 150% and 600% increase in in-store and curbside pick-up last quarter.

Retail bankruptcies continue with GNC, Chuck E. Cheese and Intu Properties

On June 23, **GNC Holdings** filed a "pre-packaged" bankruptcy plan, having an offer to sell the company for $760 million and backing from 90% of its creditors. As part of the plan, GNC plans to accelerate the closing of 800–1,200 stores, or between 11% and 16% of its existing base of 7,300 stores. GNC plans to keep the remaining stores open as it has secured $130 million in liquidity, including $100 million in debtor-in-possession financing and $30 million from a modification to its existing credit facility (pymnts.com). On June 25, CEC Entertainment, the parent of Chuck E. Cheese, filed for Chapter 11 bankruptcy protection. Chuck E. Cheese is the restaurant entertainment venue known for hosting kids' pizza parties. CEC Entertainment is owned by Apollo Global Management, which took it private in 2014 for $948 million (wsj.com). On June 29, Seafolly, an Australian swimsuit maker partly owned by **LVMH**, filed for administration. Seafolly is sold in 1,200 stores in 46 countries around the world (reuters.com). And the flight from bricks to clicks continues as **Microsoft** will permanently close all its 83 Microsoft Store locations and re-focus on investing in its digital storefronts on Microsoft.com (cnbc.com).

TikTok launches "TikTok for Business", Snap will debut first shoppable show this year

TikTok is officially entering the advertising space with the launch of "TikTok for Business", its new brand and advertising platform. "TikTok for Business" offers advertisers a variety of options, including Brand Takeovers (a 3–5-second ad), In-Feed Videos (up to 60 seconds), Hashtag Challenges (brands engage in the user community by inviting TikTok users to create content around a specific hashtag) and

Branded Effects (brands or products can be added to the foreground or background of a video in 2D, 3D or AR). This places TikTok in direct competition with Facebook, Instagram, **Twitter** and Snap (techcrunch.com). Speaking of **Snap**, it announced that Snapchat will debut its first shoppable show this year. "The Drop" will focus on exclusive streetwear collaborations, with each episode exploring the relationship between the designer and the celebrity (variety.com). This seems similar to *Making the Cut*, the shoppable fashion design competition series that Amazon Prime Video debuted on March 27, in which the winning designs are available to buy after each episode on Amazon's new "Making the Cut" store. But the big difference is that Snapchat is focusing on the 13–24 age group, of which it commands a 90% share. Gucci (**Kering)** has also partnered with Snap to let you virtually try on Gucci sneakers and purchase them on its app. This is the first branded use of Snapchat's shoppable augmented reality filter technology. In addition to helping Gucci increase conversion rates and reduce return rates, this offers a valuable safety proposition for its customers that don't want to set foot in a physical store (footwearnews.com).

We question the efficiency and economics of Tanger's new Virtual Shopper concierge service

Tanger Factory Outlet Centers has launched Virtual Shopper, a new personal shopping concierge service for customers that want a safer shopping option than physically visiting the outlet mall. Virtual Shopper offers a superior value proposition in terms of variety of choice (shoppers can access Tanger's total portfolio of products across its 39 outlet centres) and convenience (a personal shopper will shop for them in the stores and then offer curbside pick-up or delivery of the items). This is a great concept but we question its efficiency and economics as it is a very low-tech service as customers need to fill out a shopping form online, state what items they are interested in, preferred brands, size and colour, and upload photos if they want and then the personal shopper needs to take this info and go shopping for them (tangeroutlet.com). While Tanger has the advantage of valuable supplier capital, we believe the future of shopping is more along the lines of **Stitch Fix**, the AI-powered personal styling subscription service.

Coronavirus exposes structural cracks of Canada's nursing homes

The coronavirus pandemic has exposed the structural cracks of Canada's long-term facilities. As a result of nursing homes being understaffed, poorly equipped, run down and densely populated (with 2–4 beds per room commonplace), over 80% of coronavirus deaths in Canada have taken place in nursing homes. According to the International Long-Term Care Policy Network, the next closest countries are Ireland (62%) and France (50%), with the U.S. at only 40%. According to the OCED, Canadian government spending on long-term care facilities is 25% below average among developed countries (wsj.com). One of the biggest victims is **Sienna Senior Living**, which owns 5 of Ontario's 20 worst hit nursing homes and has, to date, has been responsible for 758 patient infections and 292 deaths, which led to the recent resignation of Lois Cormack, the company's President & CEO (thestar.com). As I warned in my April 1 research report, *The Survival Guide to the Ghost Town Economy*, Senior REITs will face permanent fragility as *"we believe the fear being created by the outbreak of the coronavirus in seniors' homes could be long-lasting, accelerating the "aging-in-place" movement and negatively impacting Senior REITs"*.

Amazon acquires Zoox for over $1.2 billion as Volvo partners with Waymo

On June 26, Amazon acquired Zoox, an autonomous driving technology company at a purchase price of reportedly over $1.2 billion (venturebeat.com). We note that Zoox has raised $955 million since

CHAPTER 20: SECRETS BEHIND THE MASK

launching in San Francisco in 2014. It's interesting as back in May, Amazon was in talks to acquire TuSimple, another autonomous driving technology company, but that never materialized. But Amazon has been moving deeper into the auto space: in September, it ordered 100,000 electric delivery vehicles from Rivian, from which it made a $440 million strategic investment in February. Meanwhile, **Volvo** Cars Group has entered into a new global partnership with Waymo to develop autonomous electric vehicles for ride-hailing. Waymo will be the exclusive global partner for Volvo Cars. Volvo Cars will provide the physical layer (i.e., design and manufacture vehicles) while Waymo will provide the AI layer (i.e., focus on AI, including hardware such as cameras, radar and lidar) (reuters.com). We note that in early March, Waymo raised $3 billion in a venture round from its first set of outside investors to fund the expansion of its autonomous driving operations. Alphabet itself invested in the round and remains the majority owner and brought in strategic investors such as **Magna International** and **AutoNation** and even the Canadian Pension Plan Investment Board. On the delivery front, Amazon is looking to speed up deliveries for customers in New York as it just signed a lease for a 1 million-square-foot delivery station in Queens (nypost.com).

Amazon launches $2 billion Climate Pledge Fund, AWS rolls out no-code development tool

On June 23, Amazon announced it is launching a $2 billion Climate Pledge Fund to invest in clean energy. There is no time horizon for the venture capital fund, which will invest in a range of industries such as transportation, energy, battery storage, manufacturing, food and agriculture, and the $2 billion is said to be an initial investment (wsj.com). We note the fund is named after the "Climate Pledge" that Bezos announced back on September 19 as he pledged to achieve net zero carbon commissions by 2040, a decade ahead of the Paris Accord's climate agreement. Meanwhile, AWS is rolling out Amazon

Honeycode, a new no-code development tool. Amazon Honeycode, a web-based drag-and-drop interface builder, makes it easy for anybody in a company to build their own web and mobile application. Amazon Honeycode is free for up to 20 users and then charges per user and for storage (techcrunch.com).

WFH trend could provide structural tailwind for Musk's plan to beam high-speed Internet to rural Canadians via SpaceX's satellites

SpaceX has applied to the CRTC for a Basic International Telecommunications Services license. Elon Musk wants to beam high-speed Internet via SpaceX's Starlink satellites to offer high-speed Internet to Canadians living in remote areas (cbc.ca). This could be timely given the rising work-from-home movement is starting to make people rethink where they live and could start to spur an exodus from cities to remote areas. Amazon could also benefit from this trend as last April, Bezos announced "Project Kuiper", his plan to launch a constellation of 3,236 low Earth orbit satellites to *"provide low-latency, high-speed broadband connectivity to unserved and underserved communities around the world"*.

7-Eleven rolls out voice payment at the gas pump via Apple's Siri

Soon you'll be able to pay for gas at the pump at 7-Eleven (**Seven & I Holdings**) gas stations using **Apple**'s Siri. But Apple is not an active partner in this new service as 7-Eleven just built this voice commerce capability using the new updates to Apple's Siri Shortcuts (voicebot.ai). It's interesting as when **ExxonMobil** partnered with **Fiserv** and Amazon to enable them to pay for gas at the pump using Alexa it was all about enhancing the convenience value proposition for its customers. Now, in the age of coronavirus, this service is of even more value as it increases the safety proposition by reducing the number of surfaces customers need to touch.

Nike looks to shift to digital layer as it accelerates its Consumer Direct strategy

Nike's sales declined 38% in Q420 as the 79% increase in its digital sales was not enough to offset the sales lost from its stores being closed. This, combined with the 50% reduction of shipments to its wholesale partners during the quarter, led to Nike's inventory being up 31% versus a year ago. However, Nike is taking steps to reduce its inventory as it: *"proactively cancelled pre-COVID-19 factory purchase orders for the fallen holiday seasons by roughly 30% on a unit basis... seasonless flow of inventory by shifting product to offer dates, so we can use relevant summer and fall product to meet near-term demand...we've invested in targeted promotions and markdowns to accelerate the liquidation of excess inventory."*

Looking forward, based on the following new insights we gained from Nike's Q420 conference call on June 25, we believe the company is uniquely positioned to thrive after the coronavirus pandemic as it announces an acceleration in its Consumer Direct strategy:

- **Shifting sales from physical to digital layer**: *"Nike digital represented nearly 30% of our total business... looking ahead, we now expect our overall business to reach 50% digital penetration... increased digital fulfillment capacity by more than 3x in North America and EMEA."*
- **Generating higher margins on digital sales**: *"sale of an incremental unit via digital generates double the revenue versus a sale to wholesale, with a higher gross margin, translating into 2x the operating income dollars."*
- **Building community on the digital layer**: *"in March and April, China's monthly active users on the Nike training app increased over 350% since the beginning of the calendar year...workouts on the Nike training club app more than tripled, peaking in April at nearly 5-million workouts per week during the month. 25-million new members registered that's up over 100%."*
- **Gaining share through digital engagement**: *"NTC weekly active*

231

users which is a really important metric, because someone may only buy footwear and apparel a few times a year, but engaging with us each week maybe even each day brings Nike into their lives and so we grew weekly active users triple digits in the quarter, 25-million workouts with women alone in Q4 and that which is — and so we think the activity levels and the engagement's growing. And then it's really clear that increased engagement leads to increased purchases."

Chapter 21: Masked Superheroes

July 7, 2020

"Promotion focus is about maximizing gains and avoiding missed opportunities. Prevention focus, on the other hand, is about minimizing losses." — Heidi Grant Halvorson and E. Tory Higgins, *Focus: Use Different Ways of Seeing the World for Success and Influence*

In the early days of the pandemic, we saw companies take war-like measures to produce much-needed medical supplies and services to help us survive. In the new twilight zone economy, it is even more imperative for companies to have a prevention focus to keep us safe as we re-enter the physical world. And now we are starting to see companies like Microsoft, Walmart and Amazon come up with creative ways to leverage their assets to help us cross the safety abyss and thrive — in essence, balancing prevention with promotion.

    Microsoft is coming to the rescue of those that lost their jobs to the coronavirus with its global skills initiative, advancing its accessibility-based social mission "to empower every person and every organization on the planet to achieve more". Likewise, Walmart is coming to the rescue of families struggling to find ways to keep their kids safely entertained while they are stuck at home this summer. Not only is Walmart transforming 160 Walmart Supercentre parking lots into drive-in movie theatres, but it also created Camp by Walmart, a virtual interactive summer camp for kids. And Amazon is coming to the rescue of those people who desire the experience of watching a movie with friends — but safely from the comfort of their own homes — with the roll out of its new "Watch Party" co-viewing feature.

As I wrote last week: "when we see companies putting social values ahead of profits it is a sign of respect that they care about protecting society — essentially, they're wearing a mask." So a big thank you to all our masked corporate superheroes.

Microsoft comes to the rescue of newly unemployed with its global skills initiative

Microsoft has launched a global skills initiative to bring digital skills to people who have lost their job to the coronavirus pandemic. Microsoft is bringing together its assets from LinkedIn, GitHub and Microsoft to help 25 million people identify the most in-demand jobs, acquire digital skills for free and connect skills to opportunities. Microsoft has seen a huge spike in demand for digital learning, with hours spent on LinkedIn Learning, which offers over 16,000 courses, up 382% in May versus a year ago, and usage of GitHub Learning Lab, which has over 50 million developers on its platform, rising over 900%. Microsoft sees 149 million new tech jobs being created over the next five years in software development, cloud and data roles, data analysis/machine learning/AI, cyber security and privacy protection (blogs.microsoft.com). We believe this ambitious initiative will advance Microsoft's accessibility-based social mission *"to empower every person and every organization on the planet to achieve more"*, which will enhance the psychological attachment with its stakeholders, leading to increased brand equity.

Walmart comes to the rescue of families with drive-in movie theatres and Camp by Walmart

Walmart's creative proactive initiatives to provide safe and free entertainment for families during the pandemic will enhance its emotional connection with customers, enhance customer loyalty and increase its brand equity. Walmart is transforming 160 Walmart Supercentre parking lots into drive-in movie theaters. It is partnering with Tribeca Enterprises and plans to offer over 300 showtimes between August and October (cnn.com). This is a brilliant idea as it enables Walmart to capitalize on its structural capital (its empty parking lots) and supplier capital (will offer curbside pick-up of food and snacks) to offer its customers a safer entertainment option during the pandemic than going to a traditional movie theatre. The drive-in movie theatre is making a comeback but there is a lack of supply as the number of drive-in movie theatres in the U.S. has fallen from a peak of 4,062 in 1958 to only 305. By adding 160 drive-ins, Walmart will actually increase the number of drive-in movie theatres by over 50%, from 305 to 465, but this still represents just over 1% of the over 40,000 movie theater screens.

To entertain kids stuck at home this summer, Walmart has created a virtual interactive camp. Camp by Walmart, which starts on July 8, can be accessed through the Walmart app and will feature more than 200 activities over the summer. The morning kick-off will be led by Head Camp Counselor Neil Patrick Harris and there will also be a "Skills" talent show teaching new skills and a "Smarts & Crafts" session teaching kids about creativity through arts, crafts and fashion. Walmart is also bringing in star talent with its "Great Family Challenge" with Drew Barrymore doing make-up tutorials and LeBron James leading mental and physical activities (corporate.walmart.com). Camp by Walmart will be powered by Eko, a media and technology start-up founded in NYC in 2010 that provides platforms for the creation and delivery of interactive video entertainment. We note Walmart actually partnered with Eko in 2018 to create interactive shows for Vudu, and then last October to build KidHQ, a virtual online toy store for the Christmas season.

Uber will be #2 player in U.S. food delivery market with $2.65 billion acquisition of Postmates

On July 6, **Uber** announced it is acquiring Postmates for $2.65 billion in stock (wsj.com). This comes less than a month after **Just Eat Takeway.com** swooped in from under Uber and acquired **Grubhub** for $7.3 billion. The acquisition of Postmates, which had an 8% share of the U.S. food delivery market as of May according to Second Measure, will increase Uber Eat's share to 30%, putting it in second place, ahead of Grubhub (23%) but still behind DoorDash (45%). The deal is unlikely to raise anti-trust concerns as the only two cities where Uber Eats would have over 50% share are LA and Miami. Competition is intensifying though as DoorDash raised $400 million just a few weeks ago.

Although Postmates confidentially filed to IPO back in February 2019, it started working with Qatalyst Partners last July to explore selling the company and had discussions with a number of companies, including Uber, DoorDash and Walmart. Last September, it raised a $225 million round at a valuation of $2.4 billion and said its IPO was back on, but in October it announced it was delaying its IPO owing to market conditions, closing its office in Mexico City and laying off dozens of employees as it looked to find a possible buyer. Uber and Postmates have recently been working together, filing suit against the state of California on December 30 alleging that AB-5 was unconstitutional.

FedEx is positioned to thrive during the twilight zone economy

FedEx is positioned to thrive during the twilight zone economy as the pandemic is creating a structural tailwind for e-commerce, which is expanding to both higher-value items and older demographics. It is also creating a temporary tailwind from the reduction in cargo shipping capacity from passenger airlines. We gained the following insights from FedEx's Q4 2020 conference call on June 30:

- **Quantum Leap to E-commerce**: *"e-commerce as a percentage of U.S. retail increasing from 16% in calendar year 2019 to 27% in April 2020"*
- **E-commerce Expanding to Higher-value Items**: *"We have seen a huge uptick in the categories that people are willing to purchase online, certainly moved into a higher value. We saw this trend obviously pre-COVID, but it has accelerated when you think about things like furniture, large packages, high-value electronics."*
- **E-commerce Finally Expanding to Older Demographics**: *"we saw a huge change in who is buying online, over 65 finally moved to online."*
- **Quantum Shift to B2C Deliveries**: *"total U.S. domestic residential volume was 72% versus 56% a year ago"*
- **Tailwind from Reduction in Passenger Airline Capacity**: *"demand for FedEx capacity continued to soar as we maintained essential services amid the pandemic. As a result, our flight hours were up 2.6%... almost 70% of the commercial cargo that moves between the U.S. and Europe moves in the bellies of the passenger airlines...We expect that the passenger airline capacity is going to be down for some time to come and a significant portion of air cargo intercontinental goes on passenger aircraft and that traffic is now going to flow on FedEx capacity, which is a premium. It's both on the transatlantic and transpacific."*

Fujitsu will allow its 80,000 workers in Japan to permanently work remotely

Fujitsu will allow its 80,000 workers in Japan to now permanently work remotely. Under its new "Work Life Shift" plan, employees will be able to work from anywhere: home, hub or satellite office. As a result, Fujitsu will reduce its office space by 50% and switch to an entire flexible hot desk system by the end of 2022 (zdnet.com).

AWS establish a new space unit

Amazon's AWS is establishing a new space unit called Aerospace and Satellite Solutions. It will provide services for nearly every space subsector, including satellite networks, space stations, rocket launches, mission control operations, human spaceflight support and robotics systems (cnbc.com). Last April, Amazon announced "Project Kuiper", its plan to launch a constellation of 3,236 low Earth orbit satellites to *"provide low-latency, high-speed broadband connectivity to unserved and underserved communities around the world"*. What's interesting is that AWS Ground Station was said back then to be the vital link for transmitting data to and from satellites in orbit.

Amazon announces a new distribution centre in Ottawa, its 14th in Canada

Amazon is building a second distribution centre in Ottawa, its 14th in Canada. The 450,000-square-foot warehouse will handle smaller goods, like books, electronics and toys (globalnews.ca). Amazon has also set a new tentative date for Prime Day, which it usually holds in mid-July, for October 5. (cnbc.com). We note last year, Amazon sold 175 million items over the 48-hour period.

CB&L misses another interest payment as BPP brings virtual fitting rooms to its malls

CBL & Associates, which operates 108 shopping malls in the Southeast U.S, has entered into a forbearance agreement with its lenders over its missed $11.8 million interest payment on June 1. But it is not out of the danger zone as it missed an $18.6 million interest payment on its unsecured notes due in 2026 on June 16, which has triggered another one-month grace period (cnbc.com). We note that on June 5, CBL warned that its ability to continue as a going concern was in doubt. Although the dominoes are falling for retail REITs, **Brookfield Property Partners** (BPP) remains in denial about the obsolescence of the mall as it is now bringing virtual fitting rooms to its malls. BPP is partnering with Fit:Match, a 3D AI-powered apparel shopping match platform, to roll out its kiosks in its malls. Through a contactless 10-second body scan, Fit:Match uses 3D combined with AI to generate over 150 points of biometric data and over 12 measurements which it synchs with inventory from BPP's retailers to show you items offering a 90% fit match (cnbc.com). Fit:Match actually opened its first concept store in one of BPP's malls last November but the pandemic has increased the attractiveness of this service for shoppers who are afraid to try on clothes and for retailers who are looking to increase their conversion rates and reduce returns. However, we note that last month Amazon shared that it is developing Outfit-VITON, an image-based virtual try-on system, which lets you visualize how clothing items will look on you — and the big takeaway is you won't have to visit a mall to do this.

Frank and Oak, Lucky Brand & G-Star Raw file for bankruptcy

The retail tsunami builds... On June 29, the parent of Frank and Oak, a Montreal-based apparel company with 16 stores across Canada, filed for bankruptcy protection (globalnews.ca). Frank and Oak was actually founded as a DTC apparel company in 2012 but then shifted to omnichannel in 2013 when it opened its first physical store in Montreal. On July 3, Lucky Brand filed for Chapter 11 bankruptcy protection. Lucky Brand is only planning to close 13 of its +200 North American stores as it is looking to be bought by SPARC. SPARC is the retail consortium comprising Simon Property Group and Authentic Brands which has been stepping in to buy bankrupt apparel retailers such as Aeropostale and Forever 21 and is currently in talks with JCP and Brooks Brothers. Simon Property Group is one of Lucky Brand's biggest unsecured creditors, being owed over $4.6 million (wsj.com). On July 6, G-Star Raw filed for Chapter 11 bankruptcy protection in the U.S. The Dutch denim brand had already filed for voluntary administration in Australia on May 15 (fashionunited.uk). G-Star Raw operates 27 brand stores across the U.S. and is sold in 116 other stores, including **Macy's**.

One of largest restaurant franchisees in U.S. files for bankruptcy

On July 1, NPC International, one of the largest restaurant franchisees in the U.S. with 1,200 Pizza Huts (**Yum! Brands**) and 385 **Wendy's**, filed for bankruptcy protection (wsj.com). Although Pizza Hut itself has benefited from increased demand for pizza delivery during the pandemic, NPC was already struggling before the pandemic. On January 31, it missed interest payments on nearly $800 million in loans and on February 20 it disclosed it was considering filing for bankruptcy.

Tesla delivers 90,650 vehicles in Q2; Mercedes shuts down vehicle subscription service

On July 2, **Tesla** announced that it delivered 90,650 vehicles during Q2, beating Wall Street's expectation of 70,000 vehicles by 30%. Tesla's new Model 3 model accounted for 88% of the vehicles delivered and 93% of the 82,000 vehicles produced during the quarter (cnbc.com). Tesla is also contributing to the wartime efforts against the coronavirus. On July 1, Elon Musk tweeted *"Tesla, as a side project, is building RNA microfactories for CureVac & possibly others"*. Tesla is building mobile molecule printers to help CureVac, a clinical-stage biopharmaceutical company, develop a vaccine for coronavirus (reuters.com). We note CureVac has raised $722 million since it was launched in Germany in 2000, including funding from the Bill & Melinda Gates Foundation. Meanwhile, Mercedes-Benz (**Daimler**) is shutting down its "Mercedes-Benz Collection" subscription service as of July 31 (theverge.com). Last June, Mercedes-Benz expanded the program to Atlanta based on the success of its year-long pilot in Nashville and Philadelphia, where 82% of its subscribers were new customers. But it was only able to attract a few hundred customers for its luxury vehicle subscription service, which was available with three tiers of pricing, ranging from $1,095 to $2,995 per month.

AMC delays reopening by two weeks as Amazon Prime Video rolls out "Watch Party"

On June 29, **AMC Entertainment** pushed back its movie theatre re-opening plans by two weeks. This came after **Disney** and Warner Bros. (**AT&T**) announced late the prior week that, owing to the surging coronavirus cases, they will be delaying the release of two high-profile movies (apnews.com). Disney is delaying the release of Mulan from July 24 to August 21 and Warner Bros. is delaying the release of Tenet from July 31 to August 12 (apnews.com). But why risk your life going to a movie theatre when you can just watch a movie safely virtually with friends from the comfort of your own home? Amazon Prime Video is rolling out a new "Watch Party" co-viewing feature for U.S. Prime members. "Watch Party" enables up to 100 Amazon Prime members to watch video content together at the same time and socialize through the built-in chat feature which supports text and emojis. The screen is controlled by the host and synched to the participants' devices (techcrunch.com). It's interesting as in early April Twitch introduced Watch Parties, which enables the host to livestream Amazon Prime Video titles, appearing as a thumbnail picture-in-picture in the corner of the screen, with viewers allowed to submit chats.

Microsoft shuts down Mixer livestreaming service; Amazon Game's first PC game fails

Microsoft is shutting down Mixer, its struggling livestreaming service. As part of a broader strategy between Microsoft's Xbox and **Facebook** Gaming, Microsoft is moving its Mixer community over to Facebook Gaming. Microsoft failed to build a community for Mixer, as evidenced by its inability to attract viewers during the pandemic (up only 0.2% versus a 99% gain for the industry) and less than 1% share of the livestreaming market (37.1 million of 3.9 billion total hours in April). But Amazon's Twitch will remain the dominant player with 38% viewing share versus only 7% for Facebook Gaming. On the positive side, Microsoft plans to bring Mixer's structural capital (ultra-low latency video streaming, real-time interactivity and video distribution technology) to its enterprise-focused Microsoft Teams platform (blog.mixer.com). But Amazon hasn't been able to capitalize on its Twitch community in the game space as Amazon Games' first PC game is a failure. Amazon is putting Crucible, which it launched for free on May 20, back into closed beta after receiving poor feedback from players (bbc.com).

Cirque de Soleil goes bankrupt as Las Vegas casinos face Covid-19 lawsuits from workers

On June 29, Cirque de Soleil filed for bankruptcy protection. It also cut 3,500 employees that it had furloughed back in March when it was forced to close down all its shows. Cirque has entered into a "stalking horse" agreement with its existing investors (La Caisse, TPG Capital, **Fosun International**), who will be taking over its liabilities and investing $300 million. Cirque hopes to re-open its shows in Las Vegas by the start of next year but it will face a lot more challenges with its touring shows (cnbc.com). But Las Vegas casinos themselves are facing lawsuits for failing to protect their employees from COVID-19 following the deaths of 19 union workers and dependents. On June 29, the Culinary Union Local 226 and Bartenders Union Local 165, which represent 60,000 hospitality workers, filed a lawsuit against Harrah's (**Caesars Entertainment**) and **MGM Resorts International's** MGM Grand and Bellagio casinos. The unions accuse the casinos of failing to immediately shut down food and beverage outlets and other areas after learning of positive cases, for not immediately informing employees after their co-workers tested positive and for not adequately contract-tracing before allowing employees to return to work. Although masks were voluntary when Las Vegas casinos re-opened on June 4, they have been made mandatory since June 26 (wsj.com). As a former casino owner himself, Trump is not likely to be sympathetic to these unions.

We note that on April 28, he invoked the Defense Production Act to order meat processing plants to stay open, but, more importantly, it provided liability protections for big employers like Smithfield Foods (**WH Group**), **Tyson Foods** and JBS USA Holdings (**JBS SA**).

Instacart raises an additional $100 million

On July 3, Instacart raised $100 million, on top of the $225 million funding round it raised last month as it continues to experience an un-precedented surge in demand for grocery delivery (siliconangle.com).

Sotheby's sets new auction records at its virtual auctions

Sotheby's set eight new auction records at the three virtual auctions it held on June 29, which generated $363 million in total sales (news.yahoo.com). This success will definitely make the auction industry re-think centuries-old auction practices like replacing print catalogs with digital versions and holding weekly online sales versus live physical auctions every six months.

Spotify launches real-time lyrics feature

Spotify is launching a real-time lyrics feature in 26 markets across Southeast Asia, India and Latin America. The lyrics, which are provided by Musixmatch, are displayed at the bottom of the screen in the song's language (techcrunch.com). We note that Musixmatch, which has raised €13.1 million since launching in Bologna in 2010, describes itself as a *"music AI company that develops algorithms and tools for music discovery, recommendations and search through the power of lyrics"*.

Google acquires smart glasses maker North for $180 million

Google (**Alphabet**) is opportunistically acquiring North for $180 million. This is less than the $200 million the smart glasses company has raised since it launched in Kitchener, Ontario in 2012. Google doesn't seem to be acquiring North for its products, as it will not be shipping the updated version of North's smart glasses which were supposed to hit the market this year, but moreso for its ambient com-puting technology (cnbc.com). We note that in December 2018, North acquired **Intel**'s technology portfolio for its cancelled Vaunt glasses, which included 230 patents or applications covering *"everything from new techniques, user interfaces, to ways to interact with the glasses"*. North introduced its first generation of Focals smart glasses with Alexa functionality in January 2019 for $1,000, but ended up dropping the price within a month to $600. The Amazon Alexa Fund is also an investor in North, having participated in its $120 million Series B round in September 2016.

Smart bins provide insights into economic activity during pandemic

Although the initial objective of smart bins, which compact up to five times more waste than traditional bins, was to increase efficiency of waste collection, the data is providing valuable insight into how cities move during a pandemic. The speed at which the smart bins fill up is a good proxy of economic activity around them. For example, the smart bins at train stations in Leeds are still not filling up, showing that people are still avoiding public transit (zdnet.com).

Facebook shuts down Hobbi

Facebook is shutting down Hobbi, its **Pinterest**-like competitor app, after being downloaded only 7,000 times since it was launched in February. Its photo and video-sharing app, which was developed by Facebook's New Production Experimentation team, let you organize and document your personal projects and hobbies into themed collections (techcrunch.com). It's interesting as last month Google quietly launched Keen, its AI-powered rival to Pinterest, to let users create a "keen" and then curate content, share the collection and find new content based on what you saved and follow other keens.

Chapter 22: The Imagineers

July 14, 2020

In 1940, Alcoa created an internal "Imagineering" program to encourage the innovative use of aluminum in order to keep up with demand. And just as World War II was the catalyst for Alcoa to introduce Imagineering (i.e., blending imagination with engineering), the coronavirus pandemic is emerging as a catalyst for many companies to be Imagineers — merging technology with humanity. For example, what if you didn't have to touch the vending machine? What if auctioneers could host livestreamed auctions across different cities? What if videoconferencing could be more fun? Thanks to the Imagineers from Coca-Cola, Christie's and Microsoft these things are coming true.

The word "Imagineering" was actually registered by Disney in 1990 and is defined as the implementation of creative ideas in practical form. Personally, I love Disney and like many of you, have fond memories: visiting Disneyland for the first time at age 3, watching "The Wonderful World of Disney" on TV every Sunday night, exploring Disney World with my fiancé and reliving the magic of "the happiest place on Earth" with my young boys. And when I learned a few weeks ago that Walmart was launching Camp by Walmart, a virtual summer camp for kids, I thought to myself, "Why didn't Disney re-imagine summer camp and launch Camp Mickey?" But now, given Disney's decision to re-open Disney World as the number of new daily coronavirus cases in Florida hits an all-time high of 15,299, I'm starting to think Disney itself is an "Anti-Masker" and more like Scrooge McDuck — caring more about its money bin than the health and safety of its employees, customers and the community.

Walmart makes strategic moves with launch of Walmart+ and hiring of Medicare insurance agents

In the past week, **Walmart** made a number of strategic moves, positioning it to capitalize on the customer equity it is building by transforming 160 Walmart Supercentre parking lots into drive-in movie theatres and launching Camp by Walmart:

- **Launching Walmart+:** Walmart is launching Walmart+, its competitor to Amazon Prime, in July. Walmart has been testing Walmart+ publicly since March and the membership service will apparently cost $98 per year and include same-day grocery delivery and fuel discounts (cnbc.com). We note this is the same price as its Delivery Unlimited grocery delivery membership program it rolled out in September and is nearly 20% less than **Amazon** Prime's annual membership of $119. Although Walmart+ does not include media benefits like Amazon Prime Video and ad-supported Amazon Music, the launch of Walmart+ is timely given the rapid adoption of online shopping as a result of the pandemic.
- **Hiring Medicare Insurance Agents:** Walmart is also moving deeper into healthcare with the creation of "Walmart Insurance Services LLC". In a job posting, Walmart is looking to hire several Licensed Medicare Insurance Agents in the Dallas area to sell supplemental Medicare insurance starting the first week of August (cnbc.com). We note that last month Walmart acquired the technology and IP assets of CareZone for an estimated $200 million. CareZone will provide Walmart with valuable structural

capital as its app helps manage medications, organize health information and access health services.

Meanwhile, Flipkart, which is 81% owned by Walmart, has made two strategic moves:

- **Launching 2GUD**: Flipkart launched 2GUD, an influencer-based video shopping social platform. Influencers will be able to curate their favourite products into a collection on their own virtual store and then promote them through creating video content in which they share fashion trends, beauty tips and gadget reviews. Customers can then buy products which are part of the video (cnbctv18.com). We note that a month ago Flipkart moved into v-commerce, with the launch of its own voice assistant.
- **Investing in Arvind Youth Brands**: Flipkart is strengthening its fashion portfolio, investing $35 million for a 27% stake in Arvind Youth Brands, a subsidiary of Arvind Fashion (economictimes.indiatimes.com).

Twitter's new subscription platform could be a significant catalyst

Twitter is looking to build a subscription platform. In a job posting, Twitter discloses that it is looking for someone to work with its Payments and Twitter.com teams to help launch its subscription platform codenamed Gryphon (cnbc.com). This could be a significant catalyst as it would enable Twitter to monetize its social network of 166 million monthly active users beyond just advertising.

Why is Disney opening Disney World as daily new cases in Florida hit over 15,000?

This weekend, the number of new daily coronavirus cases in Florida hit an all-time staggering high of 15,299 — what better time than for **Disney** to re-open Disney World. But on Monday, Disney announced that it is being forced by the government to shut down Hong Kong Disneyland, which it just re-opened on June 18. The Hong Kong government is taking draconian measures and once again limiting the number of group gatherings from 50 to 4 people in response to a new spike in the number of coronavirus cases (cnbc.com). But the number of new daily coronavirus cases in Hong Kong is not 15,299, but 52, which makes Disney's lack of judgement and social consciousness in deciding to re-open Disney World even more glaring.

Coronavirus pandemic and 5G are catalysts for accelerating factory automation

The coronavirus pandemic could act as a catalyst for the $213 billion U.S. meat industry to accelerate investment in automation. Since meat processing plants started to emerge as coronavirus outbreak hotspots in mid-April, there have been 29 deaths and 17,300 infections, or 3% of the 585,000 total workforce. The meat processing industry is ripe for automation in the age of coronavirus as it:

1. has the highest density of all manufacturing industries (3.2 workers per 1,000 square feet versus average of 1.0)
2. was already one of the most hazardous industries pre-pandemic (rate of 4.3 injuries/illnesses per 1,000 workers is nearly 40% higher than the national average)
3. has high worker turnover (40–70% versus average of 31% for all manufacturers)

Although European meat plants have shown that higher automation can lead to increased productivity (1 worker in Europe can do the job of 8–9 workers in the U.S.), the U.S. meat industry has not invested much capital yet in automation as companies have been able to get away with paying workers an average of less than $16 per hour (wsj.com). However, these costs are likely to rise as the coronavirus has exposed how big employers like Smithfield Foods **(WH Group)**, **Tyson Foods** and JBS USA Holdings **(JBS SA)**, who accounted for the majority of the plant closures, exploit their workers. And the prospects of higher labour and operating costs will likely lead to investment in automation. Furthermore, 5G is expected to be a catalyst for smart factories as in addition to greater speed and bandwidth, 5G offers lower latency, enabling real-time communications, combined with improved network security. As Erik Simonsson, head of the **Ericsson** USA 5G Smart Factory, states: *"Our fast and secure 5G connectivity enables the smart factory with agile operations and flexible production, utilizing industrial solutions such as automated warehouses, automated assembly, packing, product handling and autonomous carts"* (cnbc.com).

Digital world is thriving as mobile usage rose 40% in Q2

The digital world is thriving during the pandemic as global mobile usage rose 40% year-over-year in Q2, hitting a record of 200 billion hours in April. According to App Annie, this increase in usage, combined with the increase in app downloads (**Apple**'s iOS up 20% to 10 billion and **Alphabet**'s Google Play up 10% to 25 billion) led to increased consumer spending on apps (Apple's iOS up 15% to $17 billion and Google Play up 25% to $10 billion). People escaped during the lockdown to gaming apps, which accounted for 30% of total downloads on iOS and 45% on Google Play (appannie.com). As evidence of our thesis that the digital world is thriving, people downloaded apps to find new ways to:

- **Work**: Business up 115% on Google Play
- **Meet Health and Fitness Needs**: Health & Fitness up 75% on Google Play; Health and Fitness up 30% on iOS and Medical up 20% on iOS
- **Learn**: Education up 50% on Google Play
- **Shop**: Shopping up 25% on iOS

Microsoft Team introduces "Together Mode" as Zoom launches Hardware as a Service

Microsoft is looking to improve the experience of Microsoft Team video meetings with the introduction of its new "Together Mode" feature. By placing virtual live avatars of participants against a shared virtual background, instead of individual box backgrounds, this should help people see each other's body language and better engage. It's interesting as Microsoft uses AI to segment your face and shoulders to create a virtual avatar of yourself. Although it is starting with a virtual auditorium, it plans to expand to other backdrops such as coffee shops and classrooms. Microsoft continues to make the platform better as it will soon support 1,000 active participants, up from 250, and will be adding live transcripts later this year (theverge.com). Meanwhile, **Zoom**, which was the #2 most downloaded app in Q2 worldwide, is expanding its ecosystem from software into hardware with the launch of Zoom Hardware as a Service (HAAS). Zoom is partnering with hardware manufacturers DTEN, Neat, Poly and Yealink to offer its customers hardware for both Zoom Rooms and Zoom Phone at a monthly fixed price. Zoom is also partnering with **ServiceNow**, which will run Zoom HAAS on its platform to manage service requests. This is a timely offering as companies are starting to seek scalable, low-capital and supported hardware solutions to enable their employees to keep working remotely (techcrunch.com).

We are also seeing the emergence of start-ups looking to improve the videoconferencing experience. For example, Mmhmm, a new virtual camera for videoconferencing platforms such as Zoom, Google Meet and Youtube, has raised $4.5 million. Mmhmm is looking to improve the videoconferencing experience by giving you greater control over your screen. In addition to providing you with a selection of virtual backgrounds, Mmhmm gives you a screen that you can use to share content such as Powerpoint presentations, websites, live videos, as well as Airplay from your phone. And even better, Mmhmm allows you to adjust the size of yourself as well as your screen and move each around your virtual background. Mmhmm was founded by Phil Libin, the former CEO of Evernote, and received angel funding from the founders of Instagram (Kevin Systrom & Mike Krieger), Twitter (Biz Stone) and Eventbrite (Julia & Kevin Hartz) (theverge.com).

Nike opens Nike Rise concept store in China

Nike just opened a new concept store in Guangzhou called Nike Rise. Like its Nike Live store concept, which it piloted in LA in July 2018, Nike Rise offers a digitally enabled journey by creating a seamless connection between tech and human interaction. It has added a new local app feature called Nike Experiences which turns the city of Guangzhou into a digitally enabled playground for Nike Members by connecting them to weekly sport-minded activations and giving them access to in-store workshops and events hosted by Nike's network of athletes, experts and sports influencers. It also offers the Nike by You personalization bar which enables you to personalize items with design elements inspired by the city's sport culture, such as jerseys representing the city's sport teams. It also offers the in-store experience of Nike Fit, the technology that Nike launched last May to enable you to use your smartphone to scan your feet to determine the right shoe size. Nike plans to add more Nike Rise stores to its global fleet next year (news.nike.com).

Brooks Brothers, DavidsTea, Sur Le Table, Muji USA & New York & Co. file for bankruptcy

The past week we saw two bankruptcies in the apparel retail space. On July 6, Brooks Brothers, the men's business suit maker founded in 1818, filed for bankruptcy. Brooks Brothers operates over 200 stores in North America, having already closed 50 permanently during the pandemic, and 500 worldwide. To support its operations in bankruptcy, it has secured $75 million in debtor-in-possession financing from

WHP Global. Although Brooks Brothers will continue its offshore manufacturing, it is closing down its U.S. facilities which make suits, ties and some shirts and account for 7% of its total goods produced (cnbc.com). Brooks Brothers is seeking to find a buyer and has been in discussions with SPARC, the retail consortium comprising **Simon Property Group** and Authentic Brands. On July 13, **RTW Retailwinds**, the parent company of apparel retailer New York & Co., filed for Chapter 11 bankruptcy protection. RTW Retailwinds plans to permanently close all of its 378 retail and outlet stores and is evaluating selling its e-commerce operations and related intellectual property in bankruptcy proceedings (cnbc.com).

The dominoes are also falling for experiential retailers. On July 8, **DavidsTea** filed for bankruptcy. DavidsTea did not pay rent on any of its stores for April, May or June which have sat empty since they were closed on March 17. DavidsTea plans to close 82 of its 182 stores in Canada and all of its 42 stores in the U.S. and warned it may close additional stores if it is not able to negotiate more favourable lease terms (ctvnews.ca). On July 8, Sur Le Table filed for Chapter 11 bankruptcy protection. The upscale kitchenware retailer plans to close half of its 120 stores and has arranged a stalking horse bid with Fortress (cnn.com). Although a structural tailwind is building for kitchenware retailers as the lockdown has led to the formation of new habits such as cooking, baking and eating at home, the challenge for Sur Le Table will be to shift to the digital layer as due to safety constraints, it is no longer able to offer its experiential in-store cooking classes. On July 10, Muji USA (**Ryohin Keikaku Co.**) filed for bankruptcy protection. The minimalist Japanese experiential retailer with a philosophy of "No Brand Quality Goods" operates 18 stores across the U.S., having opened its first store in the U.S. over a decade ago. Muji USA was unprofitable even before the pandemic but it only accounts for 2.5% of Ryohin Keikaku Co.'s total sales (japantimes.co.jp).

Google launches $10 billion Google for India Digitization Fund

Google is launching a $10 billion Google for India Digitization Fund, which will invest in a combination of partnerships, infrastructure and equities over the next 5–7 years, capitalizing on the opportunity of bringing technology to the half of India's 1.3 billion population that is not yet online. Google will focus on the following four areas: 1) help businesses get online; 2) introduce new products and services; 3) provide affordable local access; and 4) use technology to promote social issues, including health and education (wsj.com). On the education front, in response to the pandemic, Google has partnered with CBSE, the Indian government body overseeing education, to deliver a "blended learning experience" across 22,000 schools by the end of this year. As part of this initiative, Google will look to train over 1 million teachers and capitalize on its structural capital to offer G Suite for Education, Google Classroom and YouTube. However, Google will face three difficult challenges: 1) quality of digital content in Indian languages; 2) teacher readiness; and 3) access to devices and the Internet (techcrunch.com).

U.S. online grocery orders soar 500% year-over-year as Uber introduces grocery delivery

Online grocery orders in the U.S. reached $7.2 billion in June, up 500% from $1.2 billion last August, according to a new research report from Brick Meets Click and Mercatus. The exponential growth was driven by three factors: 1) increase base of customers (up 183%, from 16.1 million to 45.6 million); 2) increase in order frequency (up 68%, from 1.2 to 1.9 orders per month); and 3) increase in average order value (up 17%, from $72 to $84). Online grocery shopping has risen each month of the pandemic, from $4.0 billion in March to $5.3 billion in April to $6.6 billion in May (techcrunch.com). This comes as **Uber** officially introduces its grocery delivery service in partnership with Cornershop, which it acquired a majority stake in back in October. You can now order groceries through the Uber and Uber Eats apps in Toronto and Montreal as well as select cities in Latin America, and it will be available in Miami and Dallas later this month (uber.com/newsroom). We note that Uber's newly announced $2.65 billion acquisition of Postmates will enable it to further accelerate its expansion into grocery delivery.

Amazon rolls out 2,200 heavy-duty delivery trucks as Rivian raises $2.5 billion

Amazon is rolling out 2,200 Amazon-branded delivery trucks that it quietly acquired last year from **Shyft Group**. The heavy-duty Ultimaster "walk-in" delivery trucks are more like the bigger and boxier delivery trucks used by **UPS** and **FedEx** (reuters.com). We note that on June 26, Amazon acquired Zoox, an autonomous driving technology company, and in September it ordered 100,000 electric delivery vehicles from Rivian. Speaking of Rivian, it just raised a massive $2.5 billion funding round. The round was led by T. Rowe Price and included existing strategic investors, Amazon, which made a $440 million strategic investment in Rivian last February, and **Ford**, which made a $500 million strategic investment in Rivian last April but cancelled its planned new Lincoln-branded electric vehicle in May as a result of the pandemic. Although pandemic-related supply chain interruptions delayed Rivian's production schedule, it is still going ahead with plans to launch three new electric models next year: its R1T pick-up, R1S SUV and Amazon delivery van. The pick-up and SUV will be priced at $70,000 before EV tax credits (wsj.com).

Twilio moves deeper into IoT with acquisition of Electric Imp

Twilio has acquired Electric Imp, which provides a secure IoT platform to connect devices to cloud services. Although Twilio quietly made the acquisition a few months ago, it just disclosed it now. Electric Imp will provide Twilio with valuable structural capital and enable it to accelerate its IoT business, which it launched in 2016 (

techcrunch.com). We note Electric Imp has raised $44 million since it launched in LA in 2011.

Coca-Cola's touch screen soda fountain is now contactless

Coca-Cola Freestyle, the touch screen soda foundation it introduced in 2009, will soon be contactless. In late March, at the beginning of the pandemic, Coca-Cola decided to fast track the Freestyle app it had been developing and add software code to create a much safer contactless experience. The process is frictionless as you don't need to download an app, you just need to autoscan the QR code by holding your camera up to the display and this will pull up the machine user's interface on your smartphone. Coca-Cola plans to roll out this feature at all of its Freestyle soda fountain machines this year, including at fast-food restaurants like **Wendy's** and **McDonald's** (finance.yahoo.com).

Cadillac Fairview transforms mall parking lots into drive-ins as Amazon Prime Video adds user profiles

In Canada, Cadillac Fairview (CF) is transforming some of its mall parking lots into drive-in movie theatres. Cadillac Fairview did a pilot of CF Drive In at its mall in Markville the last weekend of June and now plans to expand the concept to some of its other nineteen shopping malls across Canada (retail-insider.com). Although this enables CF to capitalize on its structural capital (its empty parking lots) to offer customers a safe entertainment option during the pandemic, it seems like a controversial move as it poses a direct competitive threat to CF's own tenants, **Cineplex** and Landmark Cinemas (**Kinepolis Group NV**). I don't know about you, but I'd rather watch a movie on a boat than in a mall parking lot. Paris is debuting "Cinema sur l'Eau" — a floating movie theatre on the Seine River that people can watch from 38 socially distanced boats. In addition, there will be 150 socially distanced deckchairs on land that people can watch the movie from (nypost.com). Although movie theatres in France opened late last month at 50% capacity, this seems to be a much safer and fun way to watch a movie.

But as you know, the new movie theaters are **Netflix** and Amazon. And Amazon is finally adding user profiles to Amazon Prime Video. Like with Netflix, you will now be able to access your own Watchlist and personalized recommendations, as well as track your viewing process. Amazon will allow up to six user profiles per household, including kids, who will have their own "Kids" profile, which will restrict access to age-appropriate content and restrict them from making any purchases (techcrunch.com).

Sirius XM buys Stitcher for $325 million as Spotify launches "Soundtrack Your Workout"

Sirius XM Holdings is moving deeper into the podcasting space with the $325 million acquisition of Stitcher from **E.W. Scripps**. This follows only a month after Sirius XM's acquisition of Simplecast, a podcast management platform. Stitcher will provide Sirius XM with valuable structural capital in the form of its podcasting platform (to create, distribute and monetize platforms) and podcasting app ($4.99 per month with an ad-supported free version) as well as valuable supplier content as it owns podcast networks (techcrunch.com). But Sirius XM faces intense competition from Spotify who has made a number of aggressive moves as it aspires to become the "Netflix of Audio". And now **Spotify** lets you create a personalized workout playlist. This is timely as we are all looking for creative ways to stay active and healthy, as evidenced by Spotify users having created over 1 million workout-themed playlists over the past two months alone. You just have to go to "Soundtrack Your Workout" and answer a short quiz, answering questions such as the type of exercises you do, your workout length, who you work out with, your intensity level and your mood. Spotify then synchs this data with your musical tastes to create a workout playlist and you can even add in podcasts (techcrunch.com).

Sony makes $250 million strategic investment in Epic Games,

maker of Fortnite

Sony is making a $250 million strategic investment in Epic Games, the maker of Fortnite which passed 350 million players in May and is emerging as a virtual social venue. Under the deal, the two companies are looking to broaden their collaboration to create unique experiences for customers and creators by leveraging Sony's portfolio of entertainment assets and technology with Epic's social entertainment platform and digital ecosystem. As Tim Sweeney, Founder and CEO of Epic, stated: "*Sony and Epic have both built businesses at the intersection of creativity and technology, and we share a vision of real-time 3D social experiences leading to a convergence of gaming, film, and music*" (businesswire.com). Although the collaboration is meaningful, as Epic is valued at nearly $18 billion, this only provides Sony with a 1.4% minority stake in the company. On the healthcare front, according to the Australian Medical Association, telehealth accounts for 20% of all doctor consultations funded by the Medicare Benefits Schedule and should be become a permanent fixture of the health system (zdnet.com). And Amazon is adding "hands-free" Alexa to its mobile Alexa app so you will no longer need to tap the blue Alexa button at the bottom of the screen (techcrunch.com).

Christie's hosts livestreamed omnichannel auction in four cities

On July 10, Christie's generated $421 million in sales from its omnichannel auction that was hosted by auctioneers in Hong Kong, London, Paris and NYC. A total of 210 bidders attended the auction on the physical layer while 80,000 attended the livestreamed auction on the digital layer. The auction was successful as it generated $421 million in total sales and all but 5 of 79 offerings found buyers (wsj.com). We note this follows the success of Sotheby's which set eight new auction records at the three virtual auctions it held on June 29, which generated $363 million in total sales.

Seeing emergence of livestreaming shopping marketplaces

Popshop Live, a mobile livestreaming shopping marketplace founded in LA in 2016, just raised a $3 million seed round. Popshop Live lets individuals create and host their own shopping channel, providing them with access to gamification features, show templates, real-time performance statistics and metric reports. In addition, sellers can manage their inventory through its integration with **Shopify** (techcrunch.com). We note this is a direct competitive threat to **Qurate Retail**'s HSN and QVC.

You can now use Uber to book a boat trip in London

Uber has entered into a multi-year partnership with Thames Clippers to let you book boat journeys in London. The existing fleet of 20 boats and 23 piers will be branded as "Uber Boats by Thames Clippers" and you can book them using Uber's app which will generate a QR code for passengers to board. But unlike Uber's ridesharing service, the boats will not be on-demand as they will operate on set routes and payment is not done through the Uber app but existing payment methods, such as contactless and Oyster cards (theverge.com).

Chapter 23: Halloween is Not Over

July 21, 2020

"Covid is a fraud". I couldn't believe my eyes as I read the sign carried by a guy marching in downtown Vancouver with a crowd of 100+ anti-mask protestors in front of St. Paul's Hospital, which just reported a coronavirus outbreak in its neonatal unit. I don't understand what these people were protesting as masks have not yet been mandated here, although I think it could be coming given we have seen a stampede of U.S. retailers jumping on the mask bandwagon pioneered by Costco, Apple and Starbucks. And we are going to see a lot of innovation in masks as Marc Benioff and Jim Cramer just launched the $1 million Next-Gen Mask Challenge.

It is the digital layer — where we don't need to wear a mask — where the twilight zone economy is still thriving. For we continue to see innovation with Zoom introducing a Zoom for Home purpose-built tablet, AWS leveraging Twitch's technology to offer "livestreaming as a service" and Google announcing a global digital jobs program.

Although we have exited the ghost town economy, Halloween is not over as we have learned we need to wear a mask to survive outside the safe haven of our home.

AWS brilliantly leverages Twitch's technology to offer "livestreaming as a service"

On July 15, **Amazon** quietly launched AWS Interactive Video Service (IVS). This is a brilliant move as livestreaming has exploded during the pandemic and it essentially enables Amazon to leverage the technology that powers Twitch to offer "livestreaming as a service" to companies. AWS IVS is an attractive solution for companies looking to set up livestreaming as it removes the cost, complexity and time of building their own video infrastructure. Customers just need to send the live video to AWS IVS which will transcode and optimize it, offering a latency of less than three seconds (businesswire.com).

Amazon Live, Amazon's livestreaming home shopping channel powered by AWS IVS, is now open to Amazon Influencers. They can now use the Amazon Live Creator app which enables them to livestream for free directly to Amazon.com and the Amazon app. Fans can also chat with the host and each other in a Twitch-like side panel next to the live video (techcrunch.com). We note Amazon launched Amazon Live in February 2019 for U.S. Professional Sellers enrolled in Amazon's Brand Registry. This move further increases Amazon's direct competitive threat to **Qurate Retail Group**'s HSN and QVC.

Domino's Pizza and Chipotle Mexican Grill are positioned to thrive during and after the pandemic

Domino's Pizza is thriving during the pandemic as its same-store sales for the U.S. grew 16.1% in Q2 and it opened up 84 net new global stores. On Domino's Q2 2020 conference call on July 16, we gained further insights into how Domino's is proactively enhancing all four layers of the functional value proposition to position itself to continue to gain market share:

- **Safety**: *"we expect that customer expectations around safety and contactless experiences will remain heightened for the foreseeable future...moved very aggressively to implement our Domino's car side delivery - contactless in that our store team members will bring the* pizza out of the store and will put it in the customer's trunk or backseat wherever they want to put it."

- **Convenience:** "Nearly 75% of our sales in the US are coming through digital channels...When you think about a digital adoption, when you think about the migration from on-premise to off-premise through delivery and carryout, those things have just accelerated and leapt forward by a year or two or three years."

- **Pricing:** "we've got to have great value with our national offers, great value on our menus and we've got to have great value with respect to what we charge customers to deliver that food... One of the things that we have heard over the quarter is that customers are actively putting more food in the basket to have leftovers the next day."

- **Variety of choice:** "Just last Monday we began rolling out a new product. Our new chicken wings with a greatly improved wing and terrific new sauces. We've added these to our $7.99 platform offering a 10-piece wing option...we're looking to other opportunities around menu innovation as well to take advantage of the fact that the customers are just choosing to order delivery more often and across a much wider variety of food."

Most importantly, it seems like Domino's Pizza will be looking to capitalize on the retail and restaurant apocalypse to aggressively expand its restaurant base: "I also think that we are going to have in the near and medium term a fairly unprecedented opportunity in terms of the availability and affordability of real estate out there...I think also we may see a more favorable market in terms of rents."

Chipotle Mexican Grill is also positioned to thrive during and after the pandemic as it is adding new stores with Chipotlanes and staff. Chipotle is adding a Chipotlane, a drive-thru lane that lets people pick up online orders, to over 60% of its new stores, which require 50% more workers. To staff the new stores, Chipotle is hiring 10,000 workers, representing a 12% increase in its employee base. It is a good time to be hiring as Chipotle has hired 8,000 new workers since May out of the 700,000 job applications it has received, and is looking to hire another 2,000 (wsj.com).

Masks: A good way to determine which companies care about protecting society

A good way to determine which companies care about protecting society (i.e., the S factor in ESG) are those that have been the most proactive to mandate their customers to wear masks. On July 15, **Walmart** announced it is now requiring customers to wear masks at all of its Walmart and Sam's Club stores. To enforce the requirement, Walmart has created a new employee role of health ambassador, who will be stationed at the door (cnbc.com). Shortly after, **Best Buy** announced it will now require customers to wear masks at all of its stores. Best Buy will even provide face coverings for customers that don't have one (cnn.com). Hours later, **Kroger** and then **Kohl's** followed suit and they were joined the next day by **Target, CVS Health** and Publix Super Markets (apnews.com). However, we note Walmart's move comes 2 1/2 months after **Costco** set precedent on May 1 as the first retailer to make the controversial move to require customers to wear a mask in its stores. This was followed by **Apple**'s announcement on May 17 and **Starbucks**' on July 7.

On July 13, the XPRIZE Pandemic Alliance announced the launch of the $1 million Next-Gen Mask Challenge in sponsorship with Marc Benioff, founder of **Salesforce.com**, and CNBC's Jim Cramer. The eight-month challenge is open to young adults aged 15 −24 to develop the next generation of surgical-grade consumer face mask. The masks will be judged based on the following three criteria: 1) filtration efficiency on par with surgical masks; 2) style that will promote positive mask-wearing behaviour; and 3) must address at least 5 of the following top 10 barriers to wearing masks: fogging of glasses, get too hot, are uncomfortable, cause breathing difficulties, make conversations challenging, can't exercise while wearing, cause pain or don't fit properly, block facial expressions, can't eat or drink, aren't eco-friendly, are ugly or boring, and are difficult to acquire (prnewswire.com). It's interesting as back in October, Benioff published his book, *Trailblazer: The Power of Business as the Greatest Platform for Change*, in which he stated: *"In the future, innovation cannot advance in a positive direction unless it's grounded in genuine and continued efforts to lift up all of humanity."*

New insights into consumer spending from Census Bureau, CIRP & NRF

Over the past week, we gained insight into how the pandemic is continuing to impact consumer spending patterns from new data from the Census Bureau, CIRP and NRF:

1. Census Bureau: U.S. retail sales rise 1% in June but pandemic continues to impact what & how we buy

According to the Census Bureau of the U.S. Department of Commerce, total retail and food services sales in June were up from 1.1% a year ago and rose 7.5% from May (census.gov). We gained the following insights into consumer spending behaviour from the year-over-year numbers:

- **Spending Continues to Shift Online**: Non-store retail sales were up 24%.
- **Commuting Is Still Not Back**: Gasoline station sales are down 19.1%.
- **Non-essential Spending Is Still Down**: Sales are still down for: clothing (-23%), electronics and appliance (-13%), department stores (-11%), health and personal care (-6%) and furniture (-4%).
- **People Are Buying Goods to Keep Them Entertained**: Sporting

goods/hobby stores was up 21%.

- **People Are Investing in Home and Garden Improvement**: Material & garden stores was up 17%.
- **People Are Still Eating at Home**: Food and beverage stores was up 12% while food services and drinking services was down 26%.

As people head to material and garden stores like **Lowe's**, it is looking to give back and support its rural communities by turning a few of its parking lots into drive-in movie theatres. The movie is free but Lowe's is encouraging donations for its Local Initiatives Support Corporation national non-profit which is giving out $25 million in small business grants in rural locations. Each car will also receive a complimentary "pandemic" movie bucket which includes masks, hand sanitizer, sanitizing wipes, bottled water and snacks (cnbc.com).

2. CIRP: Pandemic changes the way we shop and what we buy on Amazon

We gained the following insights from Consumer Intelligence Research Partners' analysis of buyer shopping patterns on Amazon for Q2 (cultofmac.com):

- **People Are Avoiding the Grocery Store and Buying Groceries on Amazon**. 35% of Amazon's customers are buying groceries on the platform, up from 22% a year ago. This is likely the reason for the increase in the frequency of purchases (from 2.1 to 2.5 times per month) and number of items in each order (from 1.9 to 2.2).
- **People Are Avoiding the Mall and Buying Clothes on Amazon**. 24% of Amazon's customers are buying clothes on the platform, up from 18% a year ago.
- **The Pandemic Has Led to a Reduction in Discretionary Spending for the Have-nots**. Amazon customers are shopping less for electronics (from 25% to 20%) and home goods (from 20% to

16%).

3. NRF: Expects back-to-school spending to jump 13% as parents invest in tech for at-home learning

Back-to-school spending is expected to increase this year as parents invest in technology hardware to turn their homes into classrooms in an anticipation of schools remaining closed or only partly open. According to the National Retail Federation, average spending per household for K-12 is expected to rise 13% this year to $787.49, a big jump from last year's increase of only 2%. The increase comes as the number of households buying electronic items shifts upward from 54% to 63%, with spending going toward laptops (36%), headphones and speakers (22%) and accessories (21%). In addition, the percentage of households shopping online is expected to rise from 49% to 55% as back-to-school shopping shifts away from physical stores like department stores (53% to 37%), discount stores (50% to 36%), clothing stores (45% to 30%) and office supply stores (31% to 23%) (nrf.com).

Walmart investing $3.5 billion in Canada, $1.2 billion in Flipkart in India & selling Asda Group in U.K.

Over the past week, **Walmart** made a number of strategic moves in its global operations:

- **Canada**: Walmart will invest $3.5 billion over the next five years in Canada. Walmart plans to spend $1.1 billion to build two new distribution centres in Vaughan and Surrey, as well as renovate its existing one in Cornwall. In addition to expanding full pick-up service to 270 of its 400 stores by the end of this year, Walmart plans to renovate 150 stores, adding cashierless features such as self-checkout and mobile payment technology (financialpost.com).
- **India**: Walmart led a $1.2 billion funding round in Flipkart, slightly

increasing its existing 81% majority equity stake in Flipkart (techcrunch.com).

- **U.K.**: Walmart is relaunching its planned sale of its majority stake in Asda Group, capitalizing on the strength in food retail resulting from the pandemic (wsj.com). We note that in May 2018, Walmart announced it was selling Asda to **J Sainsbury** in a deal that would value it at $10.1 billion at the time, but in April 2019, the U.K. competition watchdog blocked the sale. The problem was that if the deal went through, J Sainsbury would be the largest U.K. grocery retailer, with 2,800 stores and 330,000 employees, with over a 31% share, surpassing **Tesco**, which was the leader at nearly 28% share.

Google invests $4.5 billion in Jio in India as it announces its global digital jobs program

On July 15, Google (**Alphabet**) announced it is investing $4.5 billion for a 7.73% stake in Indian telecom operator Jio Platforms Ltd. (**Reliance Industries**). Google's investment is strategic as it will be working on a customized version of its Android operating system to develop low-cost entry-level smartphones which will support Google Play and the future wireless standard 5G (techcrunch.com). We note this is Google's first investment for its newly launched $10 billion Google for India Digitization Fund, which it announced two days prior. Interestingly, it represents nearly half of the fund, which Google said it will invest in a combination of partnerships, infrastructure and equities over the next 5–7 years. We note that in April **Facebook** invested $5.7 billion for a 9.99% stake in Jio Platforms at the same $58 billion valuation.On a global basis, Google is looking to come to the rescue of people who have lost their jobs to the coronavirus pandemic. On July 13, Google announced its digital jobs program as part of its Grow with Google Initiative. Google is offering a new suite of three

Google Career Certificates to train people for high-paying and high-growth careers in the fields of Data Analytics, Project Management and UX Design. The career programs are designed and taught by Google's employees. In addition, Google will be awarding 100,000 need-based scholarships to enable people to obtain this training (blog.google.com). We note Google's digital jobs program comes two weeks after **Microsoft** launched its global skills initiative.

Amazon is opening health clinics for its warehouse workers

Amazon is opening neighbourhood health clinics for warehouse workers and their families. Amazon will be piloting the project with the opening of 20 health clinics over the next few months near its fulfillment centres, sort centres and delivery stations in Dallas, Phoenix, Louisville, Detroit and San Bernardino. The health clinics will be operated and staffed by Crossover Health (cnbc.com). We note that back in May, Amazon expanded Amazon Care, its private healthcare offering, from its office employees to its warehouse workers in Seattle. Speaking of warehouses, Amazon is preparing for the holiday season by imposing inventory quantity limits on third-party sellers and waiving inventory removal fees. Although Amazon is on track to open 33 new fulfillment centres in the U.S. this year, this pre-emptive move shows that it is concerned about running out of storage space in its warehouses (cnbc.com).

Amazon will debut smart shopping carts at its first new grocery store

Amazon's first new grocery store in LA will feature Dash Carts, smart shopping carts built on its Amazon Go cashierless technology. When you enter the store you need to scan the QR code in your Amazon app which will sign you into a Dash Cart and load up your Alexa shopping list. The smart cart is equipped with cameras and scanners that use computer vision to identify items and a built-in scale to weigh them as well as a coupon scanner. Once you're ready to check out, you just exit via the Dash Cart Lane, and like with Amazon Go your purchases are charged to your Amazon account and you receive an e-mail copy of your receipt (cnbc.com). This smart shopping cart sounds very similar to that developed by Caper, a Brooklyn-based start-up that raised a $10 million Series A round in September to help grocery retailers compete against Amazon Go.

Meanwhile, **Kroger** will stop giving change in coins to customers as the pandemic has led to a significant coin shortage. In addition to a reduced coin production rate at the U.S. Mint, the circulation of coins in the economy has dropped as people stay home. Kroger is giving customers the option of using exact change, loading the change onto their loyalty card or donating the change to Kroger's Zero Hunger | Zero Waste foundation (finance.yahoo.com).

SPG plays hardball against tenants while it starts to add micro-distribution hubs to its malls

Simon Property Group (SPG) is starting to play hardball against more of it tenants. On July 14, SPG filed a lawsuit against Eddie Bauer, which hasn't paid rent since April, to recover $6.2 million in rent payments. According to records, SPG also sued Brooks Brothers for $8.7 million in missed rent last month, just before Brooks Brothers declared bankruptcy on July 6 (therealdeal.com). We note that SPG sued **Gap** on June 2 for failing to pay over $66 million in rent and other charges. As David Simon, Chairman, CEO & President, foreshadowed during Simon Property Group's Q1 2020 conference call: *"the reality is, we have a lease and they have to pay... obviously if they decide they are in bankruptcy, then that's when they get the right to reject a lease..."* While SPG publicly fights against its mall tenants, it is taking the first step of repurposing its malls into fulfillment centres as it is partnering with Fillogic to launch tech-enabled micro distribution hubs at select malls (finance.yahoo.com). We note Fillogic was launched in NYC in 2018 to provide retail and logistics services. And as retail REITs struggle to collect rent from boxes inside the mall, they are looking to monetize real estate outside the mall. For example, **Brookfield Property Partners** is turning its mall parking lots into drive-in theatres. BPP is renting its parking lots to Kilburn Live, the live events division of Kilburn Media, an LA entertainment agency. Kilburn Live has opened up drive-in theaters at five BPP malls and more are on the way (cnbc.com).

Zoom introduces Zoom for Home purpose-built tablet

Zoom is introducing Zoom for Home — DTEN ME — a purpose-built tablet for Zoom calls. The tablet, which comes preloaded with Zoom software, features a 27" stand-alone screen with eight microphones and three wide-angle cameras designed for high-resolution video. Zoom for Home costs $599 and will start shipping next month (techcrunch.com). We note Zoom is also partnering with DTEN for its new Zoom Hardware as a Service (HAAS), which it just launched a week ago. The work-from-home movement accelerates as **Siemens** is empowering over one-third of its global workforce to permanently work from anywhere a few days a week. Siemens will now allow over 140,000 employees at over 125 locations in 43 countries to work 2–3 days a week away from the office (citynews1130.com).

Spotify introduces podcast charts as it launches exclusive Michelle Obama podcast

Spotify is introducing two new podcast charts to help listeners discover new podcasts. The Trending chart will show the top 50 shows with the highest growth in listener numbers and the Top chart will show the 200 most popular overall podcasts localized by region and separated into categories. Both charts will be updated daily (theverge.com). On the content front, Spotify announced it will be launching its exclusive Michelle Obama podcast on July 29. This is part of the multi-year deal that Spotify signed last June with Higher Ground, the production company owned by Michelle Obama and former President Barack Obama (cnbc.com).

269

Cruise ships now grounded until end of September

On July 16, the CDC extended the no-sail order for all cruise ships from July 24 to the end of September. This isn't a surprise as on June 19 the Cruise Lines International Association announced that the cruise lines agreed to voluntarily extend suspension of operations out of U.S. ports until September 15. Cruise ships have been sitting empty since the CDC issued a no-sail order for all cruise ships on March 14 (wsj.com). It's interesting as **Carnival** announced back on May 5 that eight of its ships would set sail starting August 1 from the ports of Galveston, Miami and Port Canaveral, which have since all become coronavirus hotspots.

Navistar partners with TuSimple to develop self-driving semi-trucks

Navistar International is partnering with TuSimple, an autonomous driving technology company, to work with it over the next four years to develop a self-driving Class 8 semi-truck. As part of the deal, Navistar is also investing an undisclosed amount in TuSimple (cnbc.com). We note that last May, Amazon was in talks to acquire TuSimple and last August, **UPS'** venture arm took a minority stake in TuSimple.

Uber acquires Routematch, renews Google Maps, & helps with contract tracing

In the past week, **Uber** made a number of strategic moves on the structural capital side of the value pyramid:

- **Acquiring Routematch**: Uber is advancing its efforts to become a SaaS provider to public transit agencies with the acquisition of Routematch. Routematch provides software to over 500 transit agencies to help them with trip planning, vehicle tracking, pay-ments and tools. It is an established company as it was founded in Georgia in 1999 and has 170 employees, which will join Uber along with the CEO (techcrunch.com). We note that a year ago

Uber integrated real-time public transport data from the cities of Denver and London into its app. This move could also be part of Uber's bigger play to take a more collaborative approach with cities and build a multi-modal transportation network. It's interesting timing though as I'm thinking we will see a societal shift from mass transit to ridesharing as those with the means seek a safer option as they return to the workplace.

- **Renewing Google Maps agreement**: Uber has entered into a four-year agreement with Google for access to Google Maps. This replaces Uber's previous agreement with Google and although the financial terms were not disclosed, we do know that Uber paid Google $58 million for using Maps from 2016 to 2018. This time the pricing model is based on billable trips versus requests and includes tiered volume-based discounts (finance.yahoo.com).

- **·Leveraging Data to Help with Contact Tracing**: Uber is offering health departments free access to its ridesharing data to help them with contact tracing. Uber is able to provide health departments with quick access to data on drivers and/or riders that have come into contact with someone infected with COVID-19. In addition, Uber is automatically blocking customers with confirmed infections from using its service for 14 days (reuters.com).

Uber sued by Massachusetts for driver misclassification

On July 14, Massachusetts filed a lawsuit against Uber and Lyft for misclassifying drivers as independent contractors instead of employees (theverge.com). We note that less than a month ago, on June 11, California set precedent as the first state to rule Uber and Lyft drivers will be considered employees under AB5. Meanwhile, Uber's restructuring continues as it is looking to raise $500 million in funding for Uber Freight which would give it an implied valuation of $4 billion (freightwaves.com).

Chapter 24: The Hydra

July 28, 2020

"the last five months have made it very clear that digital tech intensity is key to business resilience"

This statement by Satya Nadella, Microsoft's CEO, during its earnings call last week clearly underlines how the pandemic has acted as a catalyst to accelerate structural disruption. But companies shouldn't just look to be resilient, they should look to become antifragile. As Nassim Nicholas Taleb writes in his book, "Antifragile: Things that Gain from Disorder": "Antifragility is beyond resilience or robustness. The resilient resists shocks and stays the same; the antifragile gets better." As Taleb illustrates in his book, the Phoenix bird from Greek mythology is resilient as it is reborn from its own ashes when it is destroyed but the serpent-like Hydra monster is antifragile as each time one of its heads is cut off, two grow back.

The digital platforms of the tech giants are positioning them to not just rise from the ashes of the pandemic, but to grow new heads by expanding their total addressable market through fulfilling more and more of our basic needs and desires. The market is recognizing their magical power as the combined weight of Apple, Microsoft, Amazon, Alphabet and Facebook in the S&P 500 Index has risen from 17% at the beginning of this year to 22%, which is double their 11% weighting from when I started researching *structural disruption in 2017. But instead of just classifying companies as value or growth based on quantitative metrics, investors should research companies from a qualitative perspective to discover which ones are looking to not just survive the pandemic like a Phoenix but making strategic moves to develop Hydra-like powers.*

Walmart partners with Yahoo Mail!, expands Health clinics & creates Flipkart Wholesale

On July 21, **Walmart** broke with tradition and announced that its stores will be closed on Thanksgiving so its employees can spend the holiday with their family. Once again, Walmart is setting precedent as on July 27, **Target** and **Dicks Sporting Goods** followed suit and announced they will also close their stores for Thanksgiving (usatoday.com). In the past week, Walmart has continued to make strategic moves, positioning it to capitalize on the goodwill that it is building with employees and customers:

- **Grocery Delivery**: Walmart is partnering with Yahoo! Mail (**Verizon**) to enable people to shop for groceries from their inbox. By using "Groceries from Walmart", Yahoo Mail users can now browse and fill their shopping cart from their inbox (globalnewswire.com). With this move, Walmart is clearly going for the older less digitally savvy demographic which still uses Yahoo Mail.
- **Healthcare**: Walmart is opening at least six Walmart Health clinics in greater Atlanta. This will bring the number of Walmart Health clinics to 13 by the end of this year, which is quite aggressive given it only opened its first concept store in Georgia in September and its second in March (cnbc.com). Walmart Health is Walmart's standalone supercentre for healthcare services that offers primary care, dental, optometry, auditory and behavioural health services, as

well as laboratory tests and X-rays and wellness education. It's interesting as just a few weeks ago I spoke with Brittain Ladd, a former Amazon employee and supply chain expert, who told me he thinks Walmart's strategy could be to shrink the inventory in its stores, move it online to Walmart+ and then turn this space into health clinics.

- **India**: Walmart is consolidating its retail operations in India, selling its 28 wholesale stores in India to Flipkart with the intention of creating Flipkart Wholesale later this summer. Walmart's stores in India, which are named Best Price Modern Wholesale, are warehouse-club-style member-only stores that serve independent retailers and other small businesses (wsj.com). We note this strategic move comes only a week after Walmart led a $1.2 billion funding round in Flipkart, slightly increasing its 81% equity stake.

Empire is positioned to gain grocery share by accelerating its Ocado-powered grocery delivery service

On July 24, **Empire** unveiled Project Horizon, its new $2.1 billion three-year strategy to accelerate online grocery and gain market share. The exciting news is that Empire plans to accelerate Voila by Sobeys, its new online grocery delivery service powered by **Ocado** that it launched a month ago in Vaughan, the location of its new 250,000-square-foot automated warehouse. Empire plans to open a new Ocado warehouse in Montreal in early 2022, which will support Ottawa and Quebec, and then two more warehouses in Western Canada, providing it with coverage of 75% of Canadian households and 90% of grocery spending. In addition, Empire plans to invest capital to improve store productivity, expand its private label and use analytics and technology to improve personalization (supermarketnews.com).

Microsoft CEO states digital tech intensity is key to business resilience

"the last five months have made it very clear that digital tech intensity is key to business resilience. Organizations that build their own digital capability will recover faster and emerge from this crisis stronger. We are seeing businesses accelerate the digitization of every part of their operations from manufacturing to sales and customer service to reimagine how they meet customer needs from curbside pickup and contactless shopping in retail to telemedicine in healthcare."

This statement by Satya Nadella, CEO of **Microsoft**, highlights how the pandemic is forcing all companies to quickly leap up to the digital layer. He sees secular tailwinds as companies *"re-adjust to what is going to be an increased e-commerce, contactless re-imagined world, re-configured supply chain."* During Microsoft's Q4 2020 conference call on July 22 we gained new insights into how the pandemic has led to rapid digital adoption in the way we:

- **Network**: Content shared on LinkedIn is up nearly 50% year-over-year.
- **Learn (Professionals)**: LinkedIn Live streams are up 89% since March and professionals watched nearly four times the amount of LinkedIn learning content in June than a year ago.
- **Work**: *"We are seeing increased usage intensity across the platform as people communicate, collaborate and co-author content in Teams."* Peak meeting minutes in a single day from Teams users increased during the quarter from 4.1 billion to 5.0 billion. The number of organizations with more than 100,000 employees using Teams increased during the quarter from 20 to 69. There are now 1,800 organizations with more than 10,000 users.
- **Learn (Students)**: *"More than 150 million students and teachers around the world now rely on our tools, including Teams, Stream, OneNote as well as Flipgrid to prioritize student engagement and learning outcomes."*

Microsoft comes to rescue of NBA as it opens up Teams to third-party apps

Microsoft is coming to the rescue of the NBA with its new "Together Mode" feature it just introduced for Microsoft Teams. Starting July 30, the NBA will outfit each basketball court with 17-foot tall LED screens which will wrap around three sides of the arena. These virtual stands will be populated with over 300 cheering fans which will give them the feeling of sitting next to one another at a live game and provide players with the energy and support of these fans. And viewers watching the game will also get to feel the energy of the crowd (microsoft.com). It's interesting as the pandemic fast-forwarded NBA's playbook for creating next-gen experiences for basketball fans envisioned when it signed a multi-year alliance with Microsoft only back in April.

Microsoft is looking to further innovate Microsoft Teams as it is opening it up to third-party apps for the first time, which will be able to integrate into the platform before, during and after video meetings (theverge.com). It seems like Microsoft is following **Zoom**'s playbook, as in early May Zoom attracted 600 entrepreneurs for its first Zoom app marketplace contest. And **Facebook** continues to innovate as it is mashing together Messenger Rooms with Facebook Live livestreaming to roll out a new feature that will enable you to live broadcast video calls with up to 50 participants. This is a brilliant idea as it can be used to broadcast events like speaker panels and networking events (cnbc.com). We note Facebook launched Messenger Rooms on April 26 and Workplace Rooms on May 21.

Chipotle's investments in digital layer payoff as its digital sales rise 216% in Q2

Chipotle Mexican Grill's Q2 comparable sales were only down 9.8% as its digital sales rose 216%. Unlike most restaurants, Chipotle continues to have a high level of financial flexibility as it ended Q2 with $935 million in cash and equivalents and no debt. From

Chipotle's Q2 2020 conference call on July 22, we gained further insights into how the investments it has been making on the digital layer are starting to pay off. Although in-store ordering is still down 37% from pre-COVID, delivery is up 125% and order ahead is up 140%, with digital now accounting for over 60% of its sales. Chipotle fulfills its digital orders through its dedicated in-store make lines and outsources deliveries to all the third-party food delivery platforms, with 60% of orders coming through their platforms and 40% through Chipotle's white-label delivery with DoorDash. Chipotle opened 37 new restaurants in Q2, with 21 of them having a Chipotlane, bringing the total of Chipotlanes to just over 100. The value of Chipotle's digital loyalty program is also increasing as Chipotle added over 3 million members over the quarter to its Rewards program, bringing the total to 15 million. And it is starting to target these customers, who account for 70% of its digital orders, with personalized promotions.

Nike shakes up executive leadership team to accelerate its DTC strategy

Nike is shaking up its executive leadership team to accelerate its DTC strategy (cnbc.com). With its new Consumer Direct strategy, which it announced during its Q4 2020 conference call on June 25, Nike is looking to increase Nike digital from nearly 30% to 50% of total sales and increase its digital fulfillment capacity by more than three times in North America and EMEA.

Spotify signs licensing agreement with Universal Music as it announces launch of video podcasts

On July 22, **Spotify** signed a new global, multi-year licensing agreement with Universal Music Group **(Vivendi SA)**. This is a major achievement for Spotify as Universal Music Group is the world's largest record company with 40% share in the U.S. Universal Music Group will provide Spotify with massive supplier capital for its two-sided marketplace and, more importantly, serve as an early adopter testing and development partner for Spotify's tools, services and marketing products (wsj.com). The day prior, Spotify announced the global launch of video podcasts. To enable listeners to multi-task, Spotify will switch seamlessly between video and audio (techcrunch.com). This is a brilliant strategic move as adding visuals will let podcasters create a deeper connection with their listeners. It also makes us wonder whether Spotify is looking at moving next into livestreaming, both for podcasting and music. Meanwhile, Pandora (**Sirius XM Holdings**) is rolling out interactive voice ads in beta testing as it tries to figure out how to connect advertisers with consumers when they're not looking at their phone. Based on Pandora's tests, 72% of people found the new audio ad format easy to engage with and just under half liked or loved the concept of responding to an ad with their voice (techcrunch.com).

Google's move to extend WFH policy to next July could fuel WFH revolution

On July 27, Google (**Alphabet**) announced it will allow its 200,000 full-time and contract employees to work from home until at least next July (wsj.com). We note that on May 7, Google extended its work-from-home policy from June 1 to the end of this year. We believe Google's move could set a new precedent for others to follow, especially given the increased uncertainty over the coming school year caused by the rising COVID-19 cases. According to Gallup, more than 100 million Americans were working from home at the peak of lockdown in early May. Although the percentage of employed Americans working from home has since declined from 70% to 53%, the reality is we are in the early stages of the Work from Home revolution as the pandemic has changed "work" from a noun (from a place we go to) to a verb (to what we do) (wsj.com). And although WeWork management claims it is turning the company around, the reality is that WeWork's vacancy rate in Manhattan is expected to reach over 20% in the next few months, with 1.9 million square feet of office space sitting empty.

This is nearly double Manhattan's current 12.1% office vacancy rate (therealdeal.com).

Safety trumps sustainability as offices run HVAC systems 24/7 & bring in outside air

Safety is trumping sustainability when it comes to office real estate. Unlike hospitals and labs, office buildings have no air filtration requirements. This is a problem for landlords as they could face potential lawsuits if they are found negligent for tenants becoming infected in their building. As a result, at the recommendation in April of the American Society of Heating, Refrigerating and Air-Conditioning Engineers, many property managers are running their HVAC systems 24/7 and bringing in outside air, which uses more energy than re-circulating indoor air. This could create greater carbon emissions as according to the UN Environment Programme buildings and constructions account for 39% of all energy-related carbon emissions (wsj.com).

Amazon offers auto insurance for the first time

Amazon is moving deeper into financial services, offering auto insurance for the first time. Amazon is partnering with Acko General Insurance in India to offer auto insurance through Amazon Pay. It is looking to provide an attractive value proposition in terms of convenience (the process is all digital and takes under two minutes), pricing (Amazon Prime members receive extra benefits, including exclusive discounts) and variety of choice (the insurance covers both cars and motorbikes) (techcrunch.com). We note that Amazon has been innovating in India with Amazon Pay, introducing the ability in October to use Alexa to pay for utility, Internet, mobile and satellite cable TV bills, and the ability to buy a movie ticket on Amazon.

Hertz reaches settlement with ABS debtors; Fiat Chrysler partners with Waymo

Hertz is taking advantage of the new demand for used vehicles coming from those seeking a safer option than mass transit as they return to the workplace in the middle of the pandemic. Hertz has reached an interim $650 million settlement with debtors of its $14.4 billion ABS to enable it repay them by offloading part of its leased vehicle fleet by the end of this year. Under the deal, Hertz will be doing a fire sale of 182,521 leased vehicles, representing over one-third of its current leased fleet of nearly 500,00 vehicles. Hertz expects to receive $3.9 billion in proceeds from the sale of 182,521 sales, implying an average vehicle sales price of just over $21,000 (finance.yahoo.com). This is a victory for Hertz as when a company with an ABS files for bankruptcy, like it did on May 22, its ABS holders only had to wait until 60 days to do a forced liquidation and foreclose on and sell these vehicles. On the autonomous driving front, **Fiat Chrysler** is entering into an exclusive deal with Waymo (Alphabet) to develop light commercial self-driving vehicles to deliver goods. Fiat Chrysler will start with integrating the "Waymo Driver" autonomous driving system into its full-size Ram ProMaster van. Fiat Chrysler has been working with Waymo since 2016 to integrate Waymo Driver into its Chrysler Pacific minivan and now it is expanding its partnership to cover ride-hailing, commercial delivery and personal vehicles. As a result, Fiat Chrysler will be ending the work it has been doing with Aurora since last June to integrate Aurora's technology into its Ram Truck commercial vehicles, including its cargo vans and trucks (reuters.com).

Apparel retailer bankruptcies continue with Ascena Retail Group and Mendocino

On July 23, **Ascena Retail Group** filed for Chapter 11 bankruptcy protection. Ascena plans to permanently close 1,100 stores, representing nearly 40% of its base of 2,800 stores. Ascena will be closing a significant number of its 1,000 Justice tween girls' apparel stores as well as all its 300 Catherine plus-size fashion stores while selling Catherine's IP and e-commerce business out of bankruptcy to Australian retailer **City Chic Collective**. Ascena will also close a select number of stores from its three core brands: Ann Taylor, Loft and Lane Bryant. As Ascena's stores are mainly mall-based, its three largest unsecured creditors include **Simon Property Group, Brookfield Property Partners** and **Boston Properties** (wsj.com). Ascena Retail will be closing all its 45 apparel stores in Canada, which includes 37 Justice, 7 Loft and 4 Ann Taylor stores (ctvnews.ca). The Canadian retail apocalypse continues as on July 20 Mendocino Clothing Company, a Toronto-based apparel retailer, filed for bankruptcy. Mendocino will shift its operations online and close all, or nearly all, of its 28 Mendocino and M Boutique stores in the GTA (ctvnews.ca).

Gap counter-sues SPG while SPG & Authentic Brands bid $305 million for newly bankrupt Brooks Brothers

In a twist of fate, **Gap** is counter-suing Simon Property Group (SPG), arguing that its leases should be modified or terminated as coronavirus-related restrictions made the core purpose of its leases *"illegal, impossible, and impracticable"*. Gap is also asking for a refund of the rent and expenses paid in advance for March 2020, alleging *"breach of contract, declaratory relief and unjust enrichment"* (therealdeal.com). We note that SPG sued Gap on June 2 for failing to pay over $66 million in rent and other charges during the pandemic. Meanwhile, SPARC Group, the retail consortium comprising SPG and Authentic Brands, is bidding $305 million for Brooks Brothers with plans to keep at least 125 of the +200 stores in North America open (cnbc.com). It's interesting as SPG actually also sued Brooks Brothers last month for $8.7 million in missed rent, just weeks before it filed for bankruptcy on July 6. The other bidder is WHP Global, who is providing $75 million in debtor-in-possession financing to support Brooks Brothers' operations in bankruptcy.

Manhattan rents decline 30% on Lower Fifth Avenue while

Neiman Marcus closes new flagship store in Hudson Yards

According to Cushman & Wakefield, asking rents declined 7% in Q2 on the luxury retail shopping corridor of Upper Fifth Avenue (49th to Central Park) and 30% on the mid-market shopping corridor of Lower Fifth Avenue (42nd to 49th Street). The only neighbourhood to see an increase in rents was Lower Manhattan, where rents rose 9% (bnnbloomberg.ca). Speaking of Manhattan, Neiman Marcus, who filed for bankruptcy on May 7, is closing its new flagship department store in Hudson Yards that it opened only 16 months ago (cnbc.com). I remember how disillusioned I was when I visited Hudson Yards in NYC last April, just a month after its grand opening, as I confided in my May 2, 2019 research note, *The Experience: "The five-storey mall — albeit new and shiny — was really just a mall and walking through it paled in comparison to the rich experience of strolling down Madison Avenue or browsing through Soho. The mall itself offered nothing really new in terms of experiences and seems a bit risky with Neiman Marcus as its anchor department store tenant."* Perhaps Neiman Marcus will be transformed into office space as in London, **Unibail-Rodamco-Westfield** has received permission from city council to turn two-thirds of its 104,000-square-foot House of Fraser department store at its Westfield London mall into flex office space (retailgazetteco.uk).

AMC delays opening to mid-August as Disney & Warner Bros. delay release of Mulan & Tenet

Last week, **Disney** and Warner Bros. (**AT&T**) announced they will once again be delaying the release of their two high-profile movies (cnbc.com). We note Disney's *Mulan*, which had already been pushed back from July 24 to August 21, is being delayed infinitely. Warner Bros.' *Tenet*, which had already been delayed from July 31 to August 12, will open internationally before debuting in the U.S. in early September. Disney will also be pushing back the debut of its future Star Wars and Avatar movies by a year. Paramount Pictures (**ViacomCBS**) also announced that it will be pushing back its two biggest upcoming films — *A Quiet Place Part II* and *Top Gun: Maverick* — to 2021 (cnbc.com). As a result of these release delays and the spiking coronavirus cases, **AMC Entertainment** will delay the opening its movie theatres by a month to mid-August. AMC had planned to re-open 450 of its 600 theatres on July 15 and the rest by the end of July (cnbc.com).

Cineplex's request for Ontario government to loosen occupancy restrictions is another red flag

Cineplex is asking the Ontario government to loosen its restrictions on theatre occupancy limits. Under the current Stage 3 re-opening guidelines, only a maximum of 50 people are allowed to be in indoor venues, like movie theatres (toronto.ctvnews.ca). This, combined with Cineplex's decision to stand firm on its policy a few weeks ago to make masks optional, is a red flag of its desperation to ignore public safety to bring people back to its theatres.

AWS' Contact Lens solution could be a timely WFH solution for call centres

Amazon is looking to transform call centres through Contact Lens. By leveraging AWS' storage, transcription, natural language processing and search capabilities, Amazon has created an easy-to-use contact analysis tool to help companies reduce the costs, improve the experience and scale their call centres. Contact Lens is currently being used by a wide range of companies, including John Hancock (**Manulife Financial**), **Capital One Financial**, **Intuit**, **GE** Appliances, **Square**, **Fujitsu**, Mutual of Omaha, and Dow Jones (**News Corp.**) (businesswire.com). We believe Contact Lens could be a timely solution for companies looking to empower their call centre employees to continue working from home.

Amazon expands Scout delivery robot service pilot

Amazon continues to advance its own last-mile delivery efforts as it is expanding its Scout delivery robot service pilot to Atlanta, Georgia and Franklin, Tennessee (techcrunch.com). We note Amazon first piloted Scout in Snohomish County, Washington in January 2019 and then expanded the service last August to Irvine, California. The six-wheeled blue delivery robot, which Amazon developed in-house, is the size of a beach cooler and cruises along at walking pace. And Amazon has a new fun sustainability initiative for kids stuck at home this summer that will solve the problem of what to do with all the empty Amazon boxes that are piling up at home. Its "less packaging, more smiles" page provides instructions on how to re-use Amazon boxes to build structures such as a fort box, cat condo, mini-golf windmill, box car, rocket and a robot costume (aboutamazon.com).

Amazon in discussions to acquire 9.9% stake in India's largest retail chain

Amazon is in discussions to acquire a 9.9% stake in Reliance Retail, the largest retail chain in India with nearly 10,000 stores (techcrunch.com). It's interesting as in January Amazon entered a long-term strategic relationship with Future Retail, India's second-largest retail chain with over 1,500 stores across the country to become its authorized online sales channel and list their items on Prime Now. We also note that Reliance Retail is owned by **Reliance Industries**, the same parent of Indian telecom operator Jio Platforms Ltd. who received a $4.5 billion investment from Facebook in April and $5.7 billion from Google in mid-July.

Amazon's Alexa now works on 100,000 smart home devices, up from 85,000 in October

Amazon's Alexa now works on 100,000 smart home devices, up from over 85,000 in October. The number of unique brands still remains at 9,500 (developer.amazon.com). At its Alexa Live conference, Amazon unveiled new features for its community of 700,000 developers who have built skills on the Alexa platform. Most of the new 31 features were minor but there were two big ones: Alexa Conversations and

Alexa for Apps. Alexa Conversations, which is still in beta, makes it easier for you to have a natural conversation with Alexa. For example, when you ask your smart vacuum to turn on, it could then ask you if you want it to focus on or avoid certain rooms. Alexa for Apps which is in preview, will let you ask Alexa to search for something on an app, like Twitter (techcrunch.com). In addition, Amazon is starting to roll out a totally redesigned Alexa app which is personalized to showcase your most-used features (cnbc.com).

Amazon's Twitch's livestreaming hours reach 1.6 billion in June, up 60% year-over-year

According to a new report from StreamElements and Arsenal, Twitch's livestreaming hours reached 1.8 billion hours in April at the peak of the lockdown and have since fallen to 1.5 billion in June, but this is still up 60% year-over-year. Facebook Gaming is gaining momentum as it reached 334 million hours in June, up 200% year-over-year, but it is still only one-fifth the size of Twitch. Although gaming continues to dominate livestreaming, the pandemic is giving rise to new-use cases such as Music, Just Chatting, Art and Travel & Outdoors (blog.streamelements.com). We note that Amazon is looking to further capitalize on the livestreaming movement as on July 15 AWS quietly launched its "Twitch-as-a-service" to companies.

TikTok launches $200 million Creator Fund as it looks to save itself from being banned in U.S.

TikTok is launching a $200 million TikTok Creator Fund to help U.S.-based content creators earn a livelihood and is looking to hire 10,000 staff in the U.S. TikTok is making these aggressive moves just weeks after it was banned in India as it looks to save itself from next being banned in the U.S. by President Trump over security concerns (techcrunch.com).

Carrefour expands Uber Eats grocery delivery partnership to rest of France & Belgium

On July 27, **Carrefour** announced it is rolling out its grocery delivery partnership with **Uber** Eats, which it launched in Paris on April 6, to the rest of France and to Belgium. As of July 20, Carrefour had expanded Uber Eats' 30-minute grocery delivery service from 16 stores at launch to 330 stores, reaching 25% of the French population. Carrefour has also expanded variety of choice from 130 products at launch to 250 products with plans to double to 500 by early September (carrefour.com). Meanwhile, Misfits Market just raised an $85 million Series B round to expand its ugly produce subscription box service. Misfits Markets, which sells misshaped fruits and vegetables at a 20–25% discount to retail, was founded in Philadelphia in 2018 (techcrunch.com). It is now in a sweet spot to expand its sustainability-focused mission as the pandemic has led to the convergence of the following three new forces: economic (increased cost-consciousness among have-nots), societal (formation of new habits such as cooking and eating at home) and technological (accelerated adoption of online grocery shopping). We note Imperfect Foods raised a $72 million Series C round in May.

Tesla is eligible for inclusion in S&P 500 after reporting fourth consecutive profitable quarter

On July 22, Elon Musk once again defied skeptics, reporting **Tesla**'s fourth consecutive profitable quarter and making it eligible for inclusion in the S&P 500 Index. He is changing the rules of the game for the auto industry, even in the midst of a global pandemic, as evidenced by his strong assertion: *"Demand is not a problem. Definitely not."* During Tesla's Q2 2020 conference call, we gained the following other new insights into how he is positioning Tesla to thrive well after the pandemic:

- **Opening a new Gigafactory in Austin**: *"we're going to be building our next Gigafactory in Texas. It's going to be right near Austin. We'll* be doing *Cybertruck there, the Tesla Semi. And we'll be doing Model 3 and Y for the eastern half of North America."*

- **Aggressively pricing Tesla Solar to gain share**: *"recently adjusted the pricing of our retrofit solar. So Tesla Solar is the lowest cost solar in the United States. Solar is now 30% cheaper than the U.S. average"*
- **Focusing on Energy**: *"Tesla Energy will be roughly the same size as Tesla Automotive"*
- **Unlocking value through upgrading fleet to full self-driving**: *"you have like at least a few million cars, suddenly becoming five times more valuable or something like that. Certainly five times higher utility. They go from like 12 hours a week of utility to 60 hours...is probably worth at least $100,000 per car."*
- **Rising demand for nickel**: *"any mining companies out there, please mine more nickel. Tesla will give you a giant contract for a long period of time if you mine nickel efficiently and in an environmentally-sensitive way."*
- **Disrupting auto insurance with Tesla Insurance**: *"We're building a great, like a major insurance company. If you're interested in revolutionary insurance, please join Tesla...able to use the data that's captured in the car, in the driving profile of the person in the car, to be able to assess correlations and probabilities of crash and be able then to assess a premium on a monthly basis for that customer."*

Big Six tech giants account for 41% of NASDAQ & 22% of S&P 500

The market is becoming dominated by the Big Six tech giants: Apple, Microsoft, Amazon, Alphabet, Facebook and Tesla. As of July 22, the Big Six accounted for 48% of the value of the NASDAQ 100, 41% of the 2,700 companies in the NASDAQ and 22% of the S&P 500 (which at this point, still excluded Tesla). The Big Three alone accounted for over one-third of the value of the NASDAQ 100, with Apple at 12% and Microsoft and Amazon at 11% (cnbc.com).

Chapter 25: Corona Lemonade

August 5, 2020

"When life gives you lemons, make lemonade."

This proverbial phrase provides sound wisdom as we all struggle to deal with the never-ending lemons in our life sprouting from the ongoing coronavirus pandemic. Last week my anxiety skyrocketed when I found out that my boys, who have been in relative isolation since I pulled them out of school two days early back in March, will be forced to return to school in September with no mask mandate for teachers or students. In the search to quell my anxiety, I came across Dale Carnegie's classic 1948 self-help book, aptly titled, "How to Stop Worrying and Start Living". And in it, I came across this nugget of advice for investors:

"The most important thing in life is not to capitalise on your gains. Any fool can do that. The really important thing is to profit from your losses. That requires intelligence; and it makes the difference between a man of sense and a fool."

We're starting to see companies make lemonade out of the corona lemons, positioning them to profit from their initial losses. Although Zillow paused Zillow Offers at the start of the pandemic, it has fully resumed it and is looking to make lemonade through its newly launched self-tours which will enable it to cost effectively scale its home buying platform while providing a safer experience. Universal is capitalizing on the forced closure of movie theatres to get AMC to agree to shorten the "theatrical window" from 75 to 17 days. And Chipotle is looking to make lemonade from the restaurant apocalypse by capitalizing on its cult-like following to launch an online Chipotle Goods store.

Zillow launches self-tours for Zillow-owned homes as it fully resumes Zillow Offers

Zillow has launched self-tours for its inventory of Zillow-owned homes. This is a brilliant idea as it will enable the company to cost effectively scale its Zillow Offers home-buying platform while providing a safer and more convenient experience for homebuyers (zdnet.com). And, ultimately, it could accelerate the obsolescence of the real estate agent by showing the unnecessity of a real estate agent's role in the home-buying process. This comes as Zillow Offers, which Zillow paused back on March 23, is now back up running in all 24 markets as it just resumed home buying in Las Vegas, South Florida, Tampa Bay and Houston (investors.zillowgroup.com). Zillow is also confident in the ability of its employees to work remotely; on July 30, it announced that 90% of its employees will now have the flexibility to work from home indefinitely (zillowgroup.com). Zillow was actually one of the first companies to announce in late April that it would allow its employees to work from home until the end of this year. And now it is following the lead of Twitter, which set precedent on May 12 as the first company to allow employees to work from home forever.

AMC's agrees to shorten the "theatrical window" for Universal from 75 to 17 days

The pandemic is leading to the disruption of the "theatrical window" for movie theatres. On July 28, **AMC Entertainment Holdings** agreed to shorten the "theatrical window" from 75 to 17 days for Universal (**Comcast**) in return for an undisclosed share of the revenue from digital channels (wsj.com). It's interesting as back on April 28, Adam Aron, CEO of AMC, threatened to not book any of NBCUniversal's movies in theatres and published an open letter stating: "*AMC believes that with this proposed action to go to the home and theatres simultaneously, Universal is breaking the business model and dealings between our two companies...It assumes that we will meekly accept a reshaped view of how studios and exhibitors should interact, with zero concern on Universal's part as to how its actions affect us...It also presumes that Universal in fact can have its cake and eat it too*". Meanwhile, **Netflix** continues to innovate as it is introducing new playbook controls for phones and tablets to let people watch videos slower or faster. This feature is especially of value for deaf people as it will let them slow down the speed of captions on the screen, and to blind people as it will let them speed up the shows (theverge.com).

Chipotle is capitalizing on its cult-like following to launch an online Chipotle Goods store

Chipotle Mexican Grill is capitalizing on its cult-like following to expand into merchandise with the launch of its online Chipotle Goods store. Chipotle Goods is aligned with Chipotle's sustainability-focused mission as it is upcycling the nearly 300 million avocado pits it uses each year in its restaurants to make a plant-based dye for its new Avocado Dye collection of t-shirts, sweatshirts and tote bags. In addition, its **Shopify**-powered online store offers a range of apparel and accessories along with bags, luggage and water bottles (chipotlegoods.com). This is a brilliant idea from a marketing perspective as it will turn Chipotle fans into walking billboards, positioning it to gain share from the restaurant apocalypse.

Trump tries to broker a deal for TikTok to Microsoft after threatening to ban it

In the middle of the pandemic, President Trump has turned his focus to becoming an investment banker, trying to broker a deal for TikTok to **Microsoft**. The shocking turn of events unfolded this weekend:

- **August 1**: President Trump announces he will ban TikTok from the U.S. with an Executive Order as early as August 2.
- **August 2**: Microsoft confirms it has had discussions with Byte Dance and President Trump to acquire TikTok's operations in the U.S., Canada, Australia and New Zealand.
- **August 3**: President Trump sets September 15 as a deadline for TikTok to find a U.S. buyer, after which he will shut it down.
- **August 4:** China accuses President Trump of doing a "smash and grab" and a mafia deal following his statement that the U.S. Treasury would get "a very large percentage" of the deal, equating to a "substantial amount of money".

TikTok is exploding during the pandemic as people migrate to this short-form video-sharing app to connect with others as they escape the physical world, reaching 2 billion downloads at the end of April, just 5 months after it passed 1.5 billion downloads. It has proven especially popular with kids, with the percentage of kids in the U.S. using it rising from 17% to 48%. Although TikTok would provide Microsoft with the hottest social network and 100 million users in the U.S. alone, we question whether it would be a good fit for Microsoft, who is more focused on enterprises and professionals. In addition, Microsoft would only be acquiring the operations of TikTok in four countries, which would create challenges as it is a global social network.

Seven & I Holdings buys Speedway gas stations from Marathon Petroleum for $21 billion

On August 3, **Seven & I Holdings** announced that it was buying Speedway gas stations from **Marathon Petroleum** for $21 billion. This will provide Seven & I Holdings, the owner of 7-Eleven, with valuable structural capital as it will add 3,900 convenience stores, bringing its retail footprint in the U.S. and Canada to 14,000 stores, ahead of **Alimentation Couche-Tard**'s portfolio of 10,000 stores. Under the deal, Marathon will supply 7-Eleven with 7.7 billion gallons of fuel per year for 15 years (wsj.com). We note that Seven & I Holdings was close to a deal for Speedway back in the fall but talks fell through with the pandemic in March.

Pandemic leads to scarcity in used vehicles

According to Cox Automotive, used car inventory fell under 2.2 million vehicles in July, down 20% year-over-year (wsj.com). As this means there are 370,000 fewer used vehicles in stock compared to a year ago, this implies that **Hertz** shouldn't have any problem reaching its requirement to sell 182,521 leased vehicles from its fleet by the end of this year. It appears that the pandemic has led to a scarcity of used vehicles. On the supply side, fewer people have traded in their vehicles or returned leased vehicles, while on the demand side we are seeing new demand for cars from those seeking a safer option than mass transit as they return to the workplace.

Amazon will invest $10 billion in Kuiper satellite internet system

On July 30, **Amazon** announced it will be investing over $10 billion in Project Kuiper after receiving authorization from the Federal Communications Commission for its satellite internet system that it first announced last April. Amazon plans to launch a constellation of 3,236 low Earth orbit satellites to *"provide low-latency, high-speed broadband connectivity to unserved and underserved communities around the world"*. Amazon plans to deploy Kuiper in five stages and start broadband services once it has 578 satellites in orbit (cnbc.com). We note a month ago, Amazon's AWS established a new space unit called Aerospace and Satellite Solutions to provide services for nearly every space sub-sector and last April, it said that AWS Ground Station was the vital link for transmitting data to and from satellites in orbit. SpaceX is also in this space race as just over a month ago, it applied to the CRTC for a Basic International Telecommunications Services license so it can beam high-speed internet via SpaceX's Starlink satellites to offer high-speed internet to Canadians living in remote areas. Both Amazon's Kuiper and SpaceX's Starlink could be timely given the rising work-from-home movement is starting to make people re-think where they live and could start to spur an exodus from cities to more remote areas.

Walmart rolls out voice assistant to all store employees as Flipkart launches hyperlocal goods delivery

On July 29, **Walmart** announced it is rolling out its voice assistant, which it developed last year for use by Sam's Club employees, to all its store associates. "Ask Sam" will enable its employees to use their voice to look up prices, access store maps, find products, view sales info and even access COVID info (techcrunch.com). We believe this could foreshadow Walmart moving into v-commerce, especially since Flipkart has moved into v-commerce with the launch of its own assistant in June. Speaking of Flipkart, it just launched Flipkart Quick, a hyperlocal goods delivery service. Flipkart is leveraging its structural capital (supply chain infrastructure and new location mapping technology) to offer 90-minute delivery of over 2,000 products from local neighbourhood stores, warehouses and retail chains (techcrunch.com).

One-third of business travel could go away, air travel is forecast to remain below pre-COVID levels until 2024

On July 28, the International Air Transport Association warned that air travel will not return to pre-COVID levels until 2024, a year later than it previously forecast back in May. But there will be a bifurcation in demand — although leisure travel is forecast to fully rebound, business travel is not. In fact, Robert Crandall, the former CEO of **American Airlines**, expects that one-third of business travel will go away as a result of the rapid adoption of videoconferencing technology like **Zoom** (wsj.com). As a result of this permanent reduction in higher-margin business travel, companies in the hospitality industry will need to significantly change their business models and strategies. Like with the structural shift to working from home, we expect the structural shift away from business travel will lead to disruption across a wide number of sectors. For example, on July 28, the Consumer Technology Association announced that its annual Consumer Electronics Show (CES) in January will be online only (financialpost.com). It's interesting as this is a complete reversal from the defiant stance it took on June 3 when it announced that it would be going ahead with its in-person CES event in Las Vegas. This will have a negative impact on the hospitality sector in Las Vegas as the CES is one of the largest events in the city, attracting 175,000 attendees.

Snap and Facebook enter into licensing agreements with major music labels

Only a few weeks after Spotify signed a new global, multi-year licensing agreement with Universal Music Group (**Vivendi SA**), we are starting to see social networks such as Snap and Facebook enter into licensing agreements with Universal and other major music labels. For example, **Snap** is introducing a new feature that will let Snapchat users creatively express themselves through adding licensed music tracks to their videos. Snap has signed licensing deals with music labels such as **Warner Music Group**, Universal Music Group, National Music Publishers Association and Merlin (variety.com). And **Facebook** is rolling out access to licensed music videos on its platform in the U.S. Facebook has entered into partnerships with top music labels like **Sony** Music, Universal Music Group, Warner Music Group and BMG to let its users discover, watch and share music videos. For example, Facebook users will be able to follow their favourite artist and receive their latest music video releases in their news feed. This is a direct competitive threat to YouTube, which is the largest global music video-streaming platform outside of China (techcrunch.com).

California Pizza Kitchen, Lord & Taylor and Tailored Brands declare bankruptcy

The retail and restaurant apocalypse continues. On July 30, California Pizza Kitchen, which operates over 200 casual dining restaurants in the U.S. and abroad, filed for Chapter 11 bankruptcy (finance.yahoo.com). We note just over a month ago, on June 25, the parent of Chuck E. Cheese filed for bankruptcy. On August 2, Lord & Taylor, the oldest department store in the U.S. with 38 locations, filed for bankruptcy along with its venture-backed owner Le Tote (wsj.com). It's ironic as it was only a year ago that Le Tote, a seven-year-old online fashion subscription rental service, bought the iconic nearly 200-year-old luxury department store brand from Hudson's Bay Company for $100 million. But this will still negatively impact Hudson's Bay Company as part of the payment was in the form of a $25 million secured two-year promissory note, and as Hudson's Bay Company kept ownership of some of the real estate assets, it is still responsible for the rent payments, which amount to tens of millions a year. On August 2, **Tailored Brands**, the leading menswear retailer, also filed for bankruptcy (wsj.com). Tailored Brands operates over 1,400 stores across the U.S. and Canada, including 700 Men's Wearhouse stores, 490 Joseph A Bank stores, as well as Moore's in Canada and family retailer K&G Fashion Superstore.

The retail apocalypse is leading to a collapse in rents as according to CBRE, average asking rents across the 16 retail corridors in Manhattan in Q2 declined 11% to $688 per square foot, dropping below $700 per square foot for the first time since 2011. In addition, the number of available ground leases reached 235, above the record of 230 set in 2013. Asking rents declined 38% to $437 per square foot on Prince Street in Soho, 15% to $882 per square foot on the luxury row of Upper Madison

Avenue and 5% to $3,000 per square foot on Upper Fifth Avenue (cnbc.com).

High operating leverage will create fragility for office REITs as tenants start to vacate

Although the longer duration of office real estate leases provides office REITs with a degree of immunity to the coronavirus, once tenants do start to vacate they will be in trouble as they have a high level of operating leverage given the fixed costs of heat, electricity and building staff (wsj.com). WeWork's revenue model is even more fragile as it rents real estate space by the number of desks, not square feet, and in the new age of physical distancing it will need to de-densify and allocate more square feet per desk (wsj.com).

Home Depot opening three distribution centres to capitalize on home improvement spending boom

On August 4, **Home Depot** announced that it will open three distribution centres in Atlanta over the next 18 months to speed up deliveries (cnbc.com). We note that even though Home Depot's e-commerce sales grew 79% in Q1 it only represents under 15% of its total sales. As we stated in our May 12 research note, *Home Sweet Home*, we expect the pandemic will create a multi-year tailwind for home improvement spending as the home has emerged as the centre of society.

Google makes $450 million strategic investment in ADT as it announces a new undersea cable

On August 3, Google (**Alphabet**) announced that it is buying a 6.6% non-voting stake in **ADT** for $450 million. This investment is highly strategic as Google is entering into an exclusive hardware deal with the home security company which will combine the structural capital of ADT's installation, service and professional monitoring network with the supplier capital of Nest's products like alarm systems, cameras, doorbells and thermostats. The deal will help ADT compete better in the smart home market as ADT will offer Nest products to its customers this year and the two companies will debut a jointly developed product next year. In addition, each company will commit $150 million for co-marketing, product development, technology and employee training (wsj.com). On the infrastructure side, Google is building a massive undersea fibre optic cable to connect the U.S. to the U.K. and Spain, its first since 2003. The Grace Hopper Cable System, named after the pioneer American computer programmer, will provide "*better resilience for the network that underpins Google's consumer and enterprise products*" like Google Cloud, Gmail and Meet (cnbc.com).

Over 10,000 Tyson employees have tested positive for coronavirus since start of pandemic

According to a new study by the Food & Environment Reporting Network, over 10,000 **Tyson Foods**' meat processing plant employees have tested positive for coronavirus in the U.S. since the start of the pandemic, representing 10% of its base of 100,000 employees. In fact, Tyson accounts for 20% of the nearly 50,000 food processing and farmworkers that have tested positive for coronavirus (forbes.com).

Costco launches same-day grocery delivery in Canada; Amazon launches Amazon Fresh in U.K.

In Canada, **Costco** just launched same-day online grocery delivery through Instacart. This is great as for the first time Canadians will be able to have fresh grocery products (produce, meat, seafood, deli) from Costco delivered to their door (ctvnews.ca). But as I discovered on the weekend, it's not available everywhere yet as I was not able to get delivery to my home in West Vancouver. Big developments for Amazon in the U.K. On July 28, Amazon launched Amazon Fresh, its new free two-hour grocery delivery service for Prime members in London and Southeast England. Amazon plans to roll out Amazon Fresh, which offers over 10,000 grocery items, across the U.K. to reach almost 40% of households by the end of this year (cityam.com). And on August 4, the U.K. Competition and Markets Authority (CMA) gave Amazon approval to buy the 16% minority stake in Deliveroo it announced last May (cnbc.com). We note that last July the U.K. issued an enforcement order to pause any integration efforts between Amazon and Deliveroo. The CMA stated it had "reasonable grounds for suspecting" that Amazon and Deliveroo "ceased to be distinct" or were planning to merge following Amazon leading Deliveroo's $575 million Series G round in May. Adding further to the intrigue, Amazon retreated from the U.K. in November 2018 as it quietly closed Amazon Restaurants U.K. after finding it too difficult to compete with Deliveroo, **Uber** Eats and Just Eat (**Just Eat Takeaway.com**).

NBA partners with Twitter to create fan engagement during ghost games

The NBA is partnering with **Twitter** to virtually re-create the "roar of the crowd" at its ghost games through its new "tap to cheer" function. The voting results will be displayed on interactive video boards in the basketball arena which will also broadcast tweets curated by NBA and Twitter. Twitter is looking to attract marketers and sponsors wanting to be part of the conversation (forbes.com). The NBA will also be filling its virtual stands with over 300 cheering fans through **Microsoft**'s new "Together Mode" on its Microsoft Teams videoconferencing platform.

Burberry opens its first "social retail" store in partnership with Tencent in China

Burberry Group opened its first "social retail" in Shenzhen in partnership with **Tencent Holdings**. The "social retail" store leverages Tencent's technology to create digital and physical spaces that blend retail and social media. For example, all clothes are labelled with QR codes and shoppers can unlock exclusive content and personalized experiences with WeChat and then share them on its Weibo social media platform. Burberry plans to roll out the concept across Burberry's network of 61 stores in China (bbcnews.com).

Roblox kids' gaming app sees 30% increase in user base to 150M

during pandemic

Roblox, the most popular gaming app for kids, saw its user community increase 30% during the pandemic, from 115 million to 150 million. In addition, its community of 345,000 developers is on track to earn over $250 million in 2020, over double their earnings of $110 million last year (techcrunch.com). Kids have been flocking to gaming platforms to escape reality while they're stuck at home. According to a study in May by Qustodio, a digital safety app maker, the time spent playing games rose 23% since the lockdown, from 66 to 81 minutes, with the most popular gaming app being Roblox with a 54% share, ahead of Minecraft's (Microsoft) 31% share.

UPS and FedEx raise prices as much as double-digits to offset higher costs owing to shift to B2C

To help offset the increased cost as a result of the surge in volume of B2C shipments, which are three times more costly than B2B deliveries, **UPS** and **FedEx** are raising prices on some large shippers by as much as double-digits. The pandemic has led to a quantum shift to online shopping, with residential shipments now accounting for over 70% of UPS and FedEx total shipments, up from just over half prior to the pandemic (wsj.com). We note that on June 3, UPS and FedEx announced they will be adding delivery surcharges to some residential shipments in the U.S.

Eargo raises $71 million to meet accelerated demand for its DTC hearing loss solution

Eargo, a DTC hearing aid company, just raised a $71 million Series E round to expand commercialization to meet accelerated demand for its DTC hearing loss solution. As a result of the pandemic, Eargo's online hearing screens and virtual support offer not just more convenience, but a safer option for people shopping for hearing aids (venturebeat.com). We note Eargo was founded in Mountain View in 2013 to advance its accessibility-driven mission *"to empower the world to hear life to the fullest"*. In April 2019, Eargo raised a $52 million Series D round and launched Neo, a small and virtually invisible hearing aid with Bluetooth connectivity that comes in an AirPods-style chargeable case, for a cost of $2,550.

Tempo raises $60 million for its interactive AI-powered home fitness platform

Tempo, an interactive AI-powered home fitness platform, just raised a $60 million Series B round. Tempo seems a bit like **lululemon**'s newly acquired Mirror as it features a 42" tall screen offering on-screen fitness trainers and a bit like **Peloton** as it comes with hardware equipment (weights) and creates a sense of competition and community through its digital class leaderboard. The cost for Tempo is an upfront $2,000 for the hardware (mirror and weights) and a $39 monthly membership fee (techcrunch.com). We note that Tempo was founded in San Francisco in 2015.

Spotify's monthly users rise 29% in Q2 as it rolls out Group Session for Premium members

We gained the following new insights from Spotify's Q220 conference call on July 29 on how it is positioning itself to thrive during and after the pandemic:

- **Increasing User Base**: Monthly active users reached 299 million, up 29% year-over-year, with Premium subscribers representing 46% of the total.
- **Increasing Podcast Listening**: Podcast consumption is up over 100% and the percentage of users listening to podcasts reached 21%, up from 19% a year ago.
- **Growing Podcast Inventory**: Podcast catalogue has reached over 1.5 million shows, with half being launched this year.
- **Recovering Advertising Revenue**: Advertising revenue rebounded from being down 25% in April and May to down only 10%

in June.

- **Attracting Advertisers Through Podcasts**: *"we are seeing advertisers really wanting to invest in podcasting as a media...deal we struck with **Omnicom** at the last couple weeks, which is a $20 million deal to invest in podcast advertising moving forward."*
- **Lowering Customer Acquisition Costs for Artists**: *"used to be that distribution was the single largest cost of a label. Today, the single largest cost of a label is promotion and marketing. And what's so exciting to me is that Spotify is the platform where most people are consuming and discovering contents."*

Spotify continues to innovate as it is rolling out a new "Group Session" co-listening feature for Spotify Premium. "Group Session" enables up to five Spotify Premium members to listen to a playlist of streamed music or podcasts together at the same time. The playlist is controlled by everybody and synched to their accounts so everyone can listen simultaneously. It's interesting as "Group Session" actually debuted in May for in-person parties but Spotify quickly modified it for the age of physical distancing (techcrunch.com). The pandemic is spurring innovation for media platforms to enable people to socialize together. A few weeks ago Amazon Prime Video launched a new "Watch Party" co-viewing feature for U.S. Prime members that enables up to 100 Amazon Prime members to watch video content together at the same time and socialize through the built-in chat feature which supports text and emojis.

Starbucks looks to meet new safety needs — improves drive-thrus, adds curbside pick-up & accelerates rollout of pick-ups

Although Starbucks will face headwinds as people continue to work from home, Starbucks' Q3 2020 conference call provided us with new insights into how it is adapting its structural assets to meet the new consumer needs for safety and convenience:

- **Growing Membership Base**: As the safest way to order during the pandemic is through the app, Starbucks is saw a dramatic increase in new Starbucks Rewards members during the quarter. Starbucks added 3 million new members in the U.S., up 17% year-over-year, and there were 2 million more 90-day active members in China, up 9% year-over-year. Starbucks Rewards as a percentage of tender reached 46%, up from 42% a year ago.
- **Improving Drive-Thru:** *"we can now have a Starbucks partner out there taking orders walking through that line of cars, which is going to dramatically increase the throughput at drive-thru."*
- **Introducing Curbside Pickup**: *"introducing a new curbside pickup experience that will be available in 700–1,000 locations by the end of this quarter."*
- **Accelerating Rollout of Pick-up Stores**: *"plan to accelerate the development of over 50 of these stores over the next 12 months to 18 months with a view to have several hundred in the U.S. over the next three years to five years."*

Looking forward, Starbucks is also positioned to capitalize on its strength as a strong tenant to lobby to renegotiate its leases or defer rent payments, as evidenced by this statement: *"we also expect margin benefits from ongoing efforts to renegotiate operating leases."*

Google's advertising revenue declines 8% in Q2 — its first drop ever

Google's advertising revenue in Q2 dropped 8% to $29.9 billion, the first drop in the company's history. On the positive side, Google Cloud's revenue increased 43% to $3.0 billion, but this only accounted for 8% of its total revenue, which declined 2% to $38.8 billion. However, looking forward, Google's ad revenue gradually improved in the quarter in Search, YouTube and Network, with Search revenue essentially flat to last year by the end of June. Google is also gaining traction with Google Meet, with saw a peak of more than 600 million participants in a single week. And it is looking to build equity with families as it has launched Camp YouTube, a virtual summer camp for kids, and a special kids tab with only teacher-approved apps.

Facebook's EPS nearly doubles as its revenue increases 11% in Q2

Facebook proved its antifragility during the pandemic with its revenue increasing in Q2 2020 by 11% to $18.7 billion and EPS nearly doubling to $1.80. The global lockdowns led to increased user engagement, with daily and monthly active users increasing 12% to 1.8 billion and 2.7 billion, respectively. Facebook has become a lifeline for small businesses during the pandemic with the number of small businesses increasing during the quarter by 29%, from 140 million to 180 million, and the number of active advertisers increasing 13%, from 8 million to 9 million. So, although the average price per ad declined 12%, this was offset by a 40% increase in the volume of ad impressions, resulting in Facebook's advertising revenue rising 10% to $18.3 billion. The big insight we gained into the work-from-home movement was that the biggest benefit for companies could be access to talent, not just cost savings, as evidenced by Mark Zuckerberg's statement: *"the reason why we're shifting to more remote work is that we think that culturally it will allow us to attract more talented people. We're not doing this primarily as a cost saving measure"* (seekingalpha.com). However, Facebook also just leased 730,000 square feet of office space at the redeveloped James. A Farley Post Office building in NYC from **Vornado Realty Trust**. The grandiose building, which was built in 1912, occupies an entire city block and is located just a block south of Penn Station (techcrunch.com). We note that Facebook was in talks to lease this space back in September, before the pandemic.

Amazon's EPS nearly doubles as its net sales skyrocket 40% in Q2

Amazon's net sales skyrocketed 40% in Q2 2020 to $88.9 billion and EPS nearly doubled to $10.30 (iraboutamazon.com). This is impressive, especially given Amazon invested over $4 billion on COVID-related expenses in the quarter to keep its employees safe and get products to customers. Increased demand from Amazon Prime members, who shopped more often with larger basket sizes, led to a 48% increase in online store sales to $45.9 billion, double its 24% growth rate in Q1. The other big driver was online grocery sales, which tripled year-over-year. Amazon Prime Video also saw its worldwide streaming video hours double year-over-year. Amazon's profit driver continues to be its high-margin AWS division, where net sales rose 29% to $10.8 billion and its operating margin rose 580 bp to 31.1%. AWS is now at a $43 billion run-rate, up from $41 billion in Q1.

Amazon reported sales growth of 43% in its North American division and 38% in International, up significantly from sales growth of 29% and 18%, respectively, in Q1. For the first time ever, Amazon generated positive operating income in International, with its margin improving 520 bp to 1.5% which more than offset the slight 10 bp decline in North America to 3.9%, resulting in its overall operating margin rising by 170 bp to 6.6%. Amazon's "Other" revenue, which is mainly advertising revenue, rose 41% to $4.2 billion. Its negative shipping delta widened by $4.2 billion in Q2 to $7.6 billion as the 68% increase in its shipping costs to $13.7 billion more than offset the 29% increase in its subscription services revenue to $6.0 billion.

We gained the following new insights from Amazon's Q2 2020 conference call on July 30:

- **Investing to Keep Employees Safe**: Amazon plans to incur an additional $2 billion in COVID-related expenses in Q3.
- **Building Customer Equity**: Amazon recently partnered with the Boys & Girls Club of America to launch Camp Prime, a virtual summer camp, similar to Camp by Walmart.
- **Expanding Online SNAP**: Amazon's online SNAP benefits are now

available in 39 states, reaching 90% of American SNAP households.

- **Expanding Warehouse Capacity:** Amazon expects to increase its network square footage by 50% this year, with the majority of capacity expected to come online in H2. This is up significantly from 15% growth last year.

Shopify's revenue nearly doubles in Q2 owing to quantum shift to online shopping

"the COVID-19 pandemic fundamentally shifted the way businesses and consumers interact. It has catalyzed e-commerce, introducing major changes in buyer behavior and pulling forward what retail would look like in 2030 into 2020." As evidenced by these comments by Tobi Lutke, CEO of **Shopify**, the pandemic has led to a quantum leap in the shift to online shopping. This has directly benefitted Shopify, which saw its revenue reach $714 million in Q2, up 97% from a year ago. Shopify's Q2 2020 conference call on July 29 provided us with the following new insights into how Shopify is currently thriving from the pandemic:

- **Demand Side — Consumers Shifting Online**: *"GMV growth overall was really driven by the sudden shift to consumer spend from offline to online driven by COVID...Stores selling on Shopify sold 1.5 times what they did in Q4 of last year, the seasonally strongest quarter of the year..."*
- **Supply Side — Retailers Shifting Online**: *"In Q2, we enrolled more merchants and increased fulfillment volumes by 2.5 times over Q1, as existing merchants fulfilled more orders and new merchants brought on new volume."*

More importantly, Shopify is positioned to thrive during and after the pandemic as it expands its total addressable market to companies that are discovering the value in this new layer of digital resiliency:

- **Retailers Offering Curbside Pick-up**: *"39% of brick-and-mortar merchants in our English-speaking geographies adopted some form of local in-store curbside pick-up delivery sources in Q2. That is up from 26% in early May...That's compared to like 2% at the end of February."*
- **Established Retailers Going Online**: *"we know that a higher percentage than normal were established businesses rushing online. Shopify Plus had a record quarter of net adds."*
- **CPGs Going DTC**: *"large CPGs that are rushing to go direct-to-consumer. So that's the reason why seeing brands like Hurley and Schwinn and Snickers and Molson-Coors and the Chipotle farmers market, all use Shopify."*

Chapter 26: Blowin' in the Wind

August 11, 2020

As the U.S. reached the grim milestone this Sunday of 5 million coronavirus cases and over 160,000 deaths (implying 1 in every 2,000 Americans has now died from coronavirus), my mind drifted to the last stanza in Bob Dylan's famous 1962 protest song, "Blowin' in the Wind":

> *Yes, 'n' how many times must a man look up*
> *Before he can see the sky?*
> *Yes, 'n' how many ears must one man have*
> *Before he can hear people cry?*
> *Yes, 'n' how many deaths will it take 'til he knows*
> *That too many people have died?*
> *The answer, my friend, is blowin' in the wind*
> *The answer is blowin' in the wind*

While the answer to how much longer the coronavirus pandemic will last is still blowin' in the wind, we are starting to gain insights into the powerful new headwinds and tailwinds being created by coronavirus. As SPG now faces headwinds in leasing its vacating department store space to experiential tenants like restaurants, theme parks and gyms, it is considering turning this space into mini-warehouses for Amazon, which will accelerate Amazon's same-day delivery tailwind. Just like we are seeing the future of dystopian ghost malls, we are also seeing the future of ghost movie theatres as Disney is going direct to Disney+ with its new Mulan blockbuster movie. The headwind for cruise lines is relentless as the suspension of U.S. cruise lines has been extended until at least October 31. And while Uber is facing headwinds for Mobility as bookings fell 73% in Q2, it is enjoying tailwinds for Delivery as bookings skyrocketed 113%. The work from home movement (WFH) is gaining momentum as Uber and Facebook just extended their WFH policy to next summer and this is creating a powerful new tailwind for real estate which Rich Barton of Zillow refers to as the "great reshuffling".

SPG is looking to turn its vacating department stores into Amazon warehouses

The future of dystopian ghost malls is here. **Simon Property Group** (SPG) is exploring the idea with **Amazon** of turning its vacating department stores into Amazon warehouses. JC Penney, which filed for bankruptcy on May 15 and plans to close at least 30% of its locations, is a core anchor tenant for SPG with 65 department stores in its malls. In addition, SPG still has exposure to Sears Holdings, which filed for bankruptcy back in October 2018, with 11 department stores in its malls (wsj.com). Prior to the pandemic, SPG was confident it could lease out this space to experiential tenants like restaurants, theme parks and gyms, but this is no longer a viable option. The risk for SPG is that bringing in Amazon as an anchor tenant would not bring any foot traffic to the mall and trigger a co-tenancy clause, which would allow the remaining mall tenants to exercise their right to terminate their lease or renegotiate terms with lower rents. In addition, SPG would be empowering its enemy as this would enable Amazon to accelerate its strategy to open 100,000-square-foot mini-fulfillment centres, which it first launched in March, to bring faster same-day delivery to

Prime members.

Zillow is positioned to thrive from the convergence of new real estate and technology tailwinds

Zillow is proving to be antifragile as its revenue rose 28% in Q2 to $768 million, its traffic rose 12% to a record high of 218 million MAU, and it ended the quarter with $3.5 billion in cash and investments. Although Zillow's Premier Agent revenue declined 17%, this was more than offset by the 82% increase in its Zillow Offers revenue to $454 million, as it sold 1,437 homes and bought 86, ending the quarter with 440 homes. On Zillow's Q2 2020 conference call on August 6, we gained further insights into how Zillow is positioned to thrive from the convergence of the following two powerful new tailwinds:

- **Real Estate Tailwind (new needs and desires for a home)**: *"Great reshuffling is driving unusually high interest in home shopping...People in all sorts of situations are rethinking their living space, and they're coming to Zillow for help to rent, buy, sell, finance and to close. Zoom meetings are changing the way families think about space and privacy. Home offices are in high demand. Backyards are more desirable than parks and gyms. Work-from-home policies are eliminating the commute for many. There's an endless list of considerations. Millions of people are currently considering upsizing, downsizing, getting closer to family, further from the office. We're not going to just go back to the way things were. This is a tectonic shift that we expect to play out for years to come."*
- **Technology Tailwind (rapid adoption of virtual tools)**: *"Three out of four U.S. adults said they want to use video or virtual 3D tour technology to shop for a home right now. Sellers are creating three times as many Zillow 3D home tours as they were in March. Real estate 2.0 will be an integrated transaction with virtual shopping, digital document routing, and one day, a trade-in button for your house."*

Teladoc Health's $18.5 billion acquisition of Livongo Health will create a global leader in consumer-centred virtual care

On August 5, **Teladoc Health** announced it was buying **Livongo Health** in a cash/share deal worth $18.5 billion. The two state the merger will create *"a global leader in consumer-centered virtual care"* by bringing together the complementary businesses of Teladoc's virtual healthcare platform with Livongo's virtual coaching platform for diabetes and other chronic conditions. Teladoc is exchanging 0.592 shares plus $11.33 in cash for each share of Livongo, and after the deal Teladoc will own 58% and Livongo will own 42% of the combined company, which will have $1.3 billion in combined revenue (wsj.com).

Twilio's revenue rises 46% in Q2 as it benefits from digital transformation tailwind

"We are just scratching the surface of this huge opportunity as companies around the world re-imagine their customer engagement for the digital world." This statement from Jeff Lawson, CEO of **Twilio**, illustrates how the pandemic is acting as a positive growth catalyst for Twilio who saw its revenue rise 46% in Q2 to $401 million as its base of active customer accounts grew 24% to over 200,000. It's fascinating as during Twilio's Q2 2020 conference call on August 4, the company shared how its recent global survey revealed that 97% of companies have accelerated their digital transformation efforts, with their digital communication strategies accelerated by an average of six years.

DoorDash opens ghost convenience stores as Amazon brings Amazon Go to U.K.

DoorDash is launching DashMat, a micro-fulfillment centre that stocks 2,000 convenience-store items. DoorDash is opening DashMats in eight cities across the U.S. (techcrunch.com). This move to vertically integrate backward into what we call "ghost convenience stores" is interesting as it was only on April 1 that DoorDash expanded beyond food delivery when it partnered with 7-Eleven (**Seven & I Holdings**),

Wawa, Circle K (**Alimentation Couche-Tard**) and **Casey's General Stores** to offer delivery from 1,800 convenience store locations across the U.S. In the U.K., Amazon is launching 10 Amazon Go stores with the potential to follow with 20 more stores (thescotsman.com).

Disney's new *Mulan* movie will go direct to Disney+

On August 4, **Disney** announced that its new blockbuster movie, *Mulan*, will be skipping the movie theatre and going direct to its new Disney+ streaming platform on September 4 for $29.99 (cnbc.com). The theatrical debut of Mulan had already been pushed back from July 24 to August 21 to being delayed indefinitely. This is precedent setting as although Disney already went direct to Disney+ with Hamilton on July 3, this is the first time Disney will try to sell its content on Disney+ above the subscription cost. As Disney owns the digital distribution channel, it is much more attractive for Disney from a revenue cut perspective, as it will get to keep 100% of digital rentals versus only 50% of box-office sales. In addition, Disney can use *Mulan* to attract new customers to Disney+, which added 6 million subscribers in the past three months, increasing its base 11% to 60.5 million subscribers. Combined with Disney's full portfolio of DTC businesses, including Hulu and ESPN+, Disney's total global reach now exceeds 100 million paid subscribers.

Zoom continues to innovate to improve videoconferencing experience

Zoom is improving the experience for business meetings by adding features which enable you to touch up your appearance, suppress background noise, and move and resize your video presentations. It has also added playful features such as virtual filters and emojis to make chatting with friends and family more fun (blog.zoom.us).

Uber and Facebook extend WFH policy to next summer

On August 4, **Uber** announced its employees have the option to continue working from home through June 2021 (cnbc.com). On

August 7, **Facebook** followed Google and Uber's lead and announced it is extending its work-from-home policy for employees until July 2021. In addition, it will provide employees with an additional $1,000 to spend on home office needs (techcrunch.com).

Virgin Atlantic Airways files for bankruptcy in U.S. as U.S. cruise line suspension is extended to October 31

On August 4, Virgin Atlantic Airways, part of Richard Branson's Virgin Group, filed for bankruptcy protection in the U.S. (theverge.com). Cruise line companies are also looking fragile as on August 5 the Cruise Lines International Association announced the cruise lines have agreed to extend the voluntary suspension of all U.S. cruises until at least October 31 (cruiseindustrynews.com). We note that on July 16 the CDC extended the no-sail order for all cruise ships from July 24 to the end of September.

Google adds homeschooling features to Assistant as it rolls out digital learning to 190,000 schools in India

With the prospect of many kids not returning to school classrooms in September, Google (**Alphabet**) has timely added new homeschooling features to Google Assistant. One of these is Family Bell, an alarm-like reminder to act like a school bell. The other is a new "animal of the day" feature which will teach kids facts, sounds, and give them a creative task for a different animal each day (theverge.com). In India, Google is rolling out its digital learning platform to 23 million students and teachers at 190,000 schools in the state of Maharashta, the worst hit state in India with over 460,000 coronavirus cases. Google will be providing them with free access to digital tools such as G Suite for Education, Google Classroom, Google Forms for tests and Google Meet for videoconferencing (techcrunch.com). Google is moving quickly on its education initiative as it was only last month that it partnered with CBSE, the Indian government body overseeing education, to deliver a "blended learning experience" across 22,000 schools by the end of this year.

Trump issues Executive Order to ban TikTok & WeChat as Facebook launches a TikTok competitor

On August 6, President Trump issued a pair of executive orders that will ban U.S. firms to stop doing business with TikTok and WeChat (**Tencent Holdings**) starting September 15 (wsj.com). Although Trump is trying to broker a deal to sell TikTok to **Microsoft**, TikTok seems to be seeking other suitors as **Twitter** has held preliminary talks about a possible combination with TikTok (cnet.com). And TikTok itself plans to sue the Trump administration as early as Tuesday, arguing that Trump's action to ban TikTok is unconstitutional and that his justification of TikTok being a threat to U.S. national security is baseless (theverge.com). Facebook is positioned to capitalize on the uncertainty over the future of TikTok as on August 5 it launched a TikTok competitor on Instagram. Reels enables you to create a 15-second clip on Instagram which you can overlay audio or add selected augmented reality effects and then share it publicly or with friends on Instagram (cnbc.com).

Uber acquires U.K. taxi software company

On August 5, Uber acquired Autocab, a U.K. taxi software company. Autocab was founded in Manchester in 1989 to provide private hire and taxi operators with technology to run their businesses. Ironically, Uber will also be acquiring the IGo marketplace that Autocab launched in 2017 to help taxi companies compete against Uber (cnbc.com).

Uber's Q2 bookings drop 35% as 73% decline in Mobility offsets 113% rise in Delivery

Uber's gross bookings in Q2 dropped 35% to $10.2 billion; although bookings from Delivery (formerly Uber Eats) skyrocketed 113%, this was more than offset by the 73% decline in Mobility (formerly Ridesharing). On a customer basis, this was driven by a 44% decline to 55 million monthly active users, which, combined with the 21%

decrease to 13.4 trips per user, led to a 56% decline in the number of trips to 737 million. This was partly offset by a 48% increase in the average booking cost per trip to $13.87.

We gained the following new insights from Uber's Q2 2020 conference call:

- **Multi-Platform Model Provides a Valuable Hedge**: *"we have a hugely valuable hedge across our two core segments"*. Delivery accounted for 77% of total gross bookings in Q2 versus 29% a year ago.
- **Sharing Economy Model Provides Operating Cushion:** As more than two-thirds of Uber's cost of revenue and operating expenses are variable, its mobility segment was able to generate $50 million in EBITDA profit despite a 73% drop in gross bookings.
- **Mobility Is Recovering:** In the month of July, Mobility was down 53% year-over-year, an improvement from the 73% average decline in Q2. *"Gross bookings of Hong Kong and New Zealand at times exceed pre-COVID highs. European trends have also been encouraging. France, Spain and Germany, amongst others, have improved to being down 35% or less year-over-year recently. The U.S. is lagging. The GV is down around 50% to 85% in our top markets."*
- **Delivery Is Skyrocketing:** *"New eaters in the second quarter were up over 50%. We're seeing double-digit increases in basket size."* Delivery bookings reached a $30 billion run-rate at the end of Q2 and Delivery was up 134% year-over-year in July, an improvement from the 113% average gain in Q2.
- **Leveraging Eats to Move into Delivery**: *"Using our existing network, we're moving quickly into new delivery as a service offering... we're ramping up our subscription efforts, including nationwide allotments of Eats Pass, which combines free food and grocery delivery."*

About the Author

Barbara Gray is a former top-ranked sell-side Equity Analyst and the founder of Brady Capital Research Inc., a leading-edge investment research firm focused on structural disruption. Her two decades of sell-side equity research experience, combined with her creative ability to piece together emerging structural disruption trends, enables Barbara to come up with unique insights for her institutional investment and corporate clients.

Barbara is a Chartered Financial Analyst (CFA) and graduated from the University of British Columbia with a Bachelor of Commerce in Finance. She is also the author of *The New Cyber Decade* (2020), *Secrets of the Amazon III* (2019), *Secrets of the Amazon 2.0* (2018), *Secrets of the Amazon* (2017) and *Ubernomics* (2016).

Barbara lives in Vancouver, Canada with her husband and two sons. You can follow her on Twitter at @barbcfa, reach her on LinkedIn or email her at barb@bradycap.com.

Disclosure

I, Barbara Gray, certify that the views expressed in this book accurately reflect my personal views about the subject company (ies). I am confident in my investment analysis skills, and I may buy or already own shares in those companies under discussion. I also certify that I have not and will not be receiving direct or indirect compensation from the subject company(ies) in exchange for publishing this commentary.

The author holds a long position in Alphabet (GOOG-NASDAQ), Amazon (AMZN-NASDAQ), Facebook (FB-NASDAQ), Farfetch (FTCH-NYSE), lululemon athletica (LULU-NASDAQ), Nike (NKE-NYSE), Spotify Technology (SPOT-NYSE), Stitch Fix (SFIX-NASDAQ), Tesla (TSLA-NASDAQ), Twilio Inc. (TWLO-NYSE), Twitter (TWTR-NYSE), Uber Technologies (UBER-NYSE), Walmart Inc. (WMT-NYSE), Zillow Group (Z-NASDAQ) and Zoom Video Communications (ZM-NASDAQ) and a short position in Lyft (LYFT-NASDAQ).

This investment analysis excludes any target price, and is not a recommendation to buy or sell a stock. It is intended to provide a means for the author to share his experience and perspective exclusively for the benefit of the clients of Brady Capital Research Inc. The book may contain statements and projections that are forward-looking in nature, and therefore subject to numerous risks, uncertainties, and assumptions. The author does not assume any liability whatsoever for any direct or consequential loss arising from or relating to any use of the information contained in this note.

This information contained in this commentary has been compiled from sources believed to be reliable but no representation or warranty, express or implied, is made by the author or any other person as to its fairness, accuracy, completeness or correctness.

This book does not constitute an offer or solicitation in any jurisdiction.

* 9 7 8 1 9 9 9 4 8 8 4 8 2 *